A HANDBOOK OF MEDICAL HYPNOSIS

A Handbook of Medical Hypnosis

Fourth Edition

GORDON AMBROSE, LMSSA, FRPSL

Immediate Past President of the National Division of the British Society of Medical and Dental Hypnosis; Member of the British Council of Representatives and the Ethical Committee of the International Society of Hypnosis (USA); formerly Assistant Psychiatrist and Senior Registrar, Prince of Wales's Hospital, Tottenham

GEORGE NEWBOLD, MB, BS, MRCS, LRCP, MMSA, DObstRCOG, DCH

Senior Medical Officer, South Glamorgan Institute of Higher Education and the Welsh College of Music and Drama; formerly Obstetrician and Gynaecologist, Orsett Hospital, Essex; Member of the Medico-Legal Society

BAILLIÈRE TINDALL · LONDON

A BAILLIÈRE TINDALL book published by
Cassell Ltd.
35 Red Lion Square, London WC1R 4SG

and at Sydney, Auckland, Toronto, Johannesburg

an affiliate of
Macmillan Publishing Co. Inc.
New York

© 1980 Baillière Tindall
a division of Cassell Ltd.

All rights reserved. No part of this publication may be reproduced, stored in a retrieval system or transmitted, in any form or by any means, electronic, mechanical, photocopying or otherwise, without the prior permission of Baillière Tindall, 35 Red Lion Square, London WC1R 4SG

First published 1956
Third edition   1968
Fourth edition   1980

ISBN 0 7020 0823 0

Set by Academic Typesetters, Gerrards Cross
Reproduced from copy supplied
printed and bound in Great Britain
by Billing & Sons Limited
Guildford, London, Oxford, Worcester

British Library Cataloguing in Publication Data
Ambrose, Gordon
　A handbook of medical hypnosis. — 4th ed.
　1. Hypnotism — Therapeutic use
　I. Title　II. Newbold, George
　615′.8512　　RC495

ISBN 0-7020-0823-0

CONTENTS

Preface	vii
1. History of Medical Hypnotism	1
2. The Medical Hypnotist and the Law	11
3. The Hypnotic State and its Phenomena	22
4. The Induction of Hypnosis	41
5. Hypnosis in General Medicine	59
6. Hypnosis in the Neuroses	96
7. Hypnoanalysis and Hypnosynthesis	122
8. Hypnosis in Anaesthesia	136
9. Hypnosis in Paediatrics	143
10. Hypnosis in Gynaecology	154
11. Psychodynamics of Pregnancy and Labour	171
12. Hypnosis in Dermatology	197
Index	207

PREFACE

Few people would now dispute that psychological and emotional factors may play as decisive a part in illness as they do in the rest of human life. The unity of mind and body, psyche and soma, has been recognized in the past and is now once again being acknowledged by a medical profession confronted with a variety of psychological and psychosomatic disorders that our modern technological society has done little to relieve. The 'high technology' approach to these problems has been the development of the drug treatments that are now in general use. By contrast, hypnosis is a comparatively harmless non-invasive therapeutic technique which offers the medical practitioner the opportunity of getting to the root of stress-related conditions and effecting fundamental improvements rather than merely relieving symptoms.

In this book our main objective has been to describe methods of treatment that work. We have not provided any far-reaching theories as a basis for the techniques described, for such theories can only be speculative. It has also been our aim to bring to the attention of our medical colleagues the wide applicability and the diversity of applications of hypnosis in medicine. In the twelve years since the last edition appeared, interest in hypnosis as an object of research and in the use of hypnosis for medical purposes has continued to increase throughout the world, but the true extent of the benefits obtainable by the medical use of this powerful technique is still not generally recognized.

This book has been written to provide the general practitioner and student with an introduction to a technique of potentially enormous value and perhaps also to suggest to specialists and consultants that there may be useful applications of hypnosis in their own fields which have not yet been fully developed. In anaesthesia, for instance, it has been found that chemical anaesthetics and muscle relaxants can sometimes be dispensed with entirely in cases of minor surgery and that when drugs are necessary the dose required to produce satisfactory analgesia can often be greatly reduced. Hypnosis also has easily-identified applications in obstetrics, since one of its principal benefits is the state of deep physical and mental relaxation that the subject can achieve. Many ante-natal exercises aim at producing a condition of relaxation which is totally familiar to practising medical hypnotists: training expectant mothers in autohypnosis has been shown to permit comparatively comfortable and trouble-free childbirth. More generally, illness is always accompanied by some degree of anxiety, the relief of which may by itself be enough to allow the natural healing processes to go ahead unimpeded by psychological factors. However, it is in the treatment of psychosomatic conditions that hypnosis would seem to be of greatest value.

It is the experience of the authors and indeed of most practising medical hypnotists that many cases previously thought to be organic in origin are fundamentally psychosomatic. Examples of such cases are to be found throughout dermatology and gynaecology and, above all, in the treatment of allergies. They also include many of the 'medical' problems of childhood. Detailed case histories are to be found in the pages that follow. Such conditions are often susceptible to treatment by hypnosis. Hypnosis offers straightforward relief of stress by deep relaxation and makes the way much easier for the psychotherapy that may be necessary to uncover the psychological roots of the problem. Recall of buried memories is facilitated and it is possible to regress certain subjects to an earlier phase of their lives. Previously repressed natural emotional responses become more readily available and sometimes the patient is able to 'abreact' (i.e. 're-live') traumatic episodes, allowing them their full emotional impact for the first time. As we might expect, hypnosis is also an appropriate form of treatment for some behavioural disorders, particularly in children, and for some forms of psychological disturbance that may have no physical manifestation at all. Where it is applicable, hypnosis is not only safer than some accepted psychiatric methods but appears to produce a quicker response to therapy. The use of hypnosis in analysis is covered in the very important chapter on hypnoanalysis, which has in this edition been extended and revised to include hypnosynthesis, since suggestion is one of the principal tools of the hypnotherapist. Often the suggestions involved are of an ego-strengthening nature, coupled with requests for increased psychodynamic insight, but suggestion can also be used directly for symptom removal in carefully selected cases, particularly in general practice.

Preface

The book has been revised throughout and major changes since the last edition include the complete rewriting of the chapters on paediatrics, the neuroses and hypnosis in general medicine and the updating of the chapter on medical hypnotism and the law. The chapter entitled 'The psychodynamics of pregnancy and labour' replaces the chapter in the last edition on 'Hypnosis and suggestion in obstetrics'.

We would like to express particular thanks to the editor of the *Journal of the Royal College of Psychiatrists* who, when we were embarking on the revision of this book, enabled us to get in touch through the columns of the *Journal* with colleagues who were currently engaged in the clinical practice of hypnotherapy or in research, or in both. We are appreciative of the action of the Council of the Royal Society of Medicine of London who have, since the last edition of this book, provided a forum for the discussion of matters relating to the role of hypnosis in modern medicine by the formation of a section of Medical and Dental Hypnosis — a fitting memorial to the pioneering work of men such as William Moodie, J.A. Hadfield, Alexander Kennedy, Ferguson Rodger and E. A. Bennet. We are also grateful to all those who have given us the benefit of their own experience in the field of medical hypnosis and have sent us papers embodying the results of their work. Where applicable these have been acknowledged in the text or in the bibliography at the end of each chapter. Thanks are due also to Lis Warren for being 'on call' at all times and for helping in many ways, and to our publishers for their friendship and help in making this book an objective and true rendering of our view of hypnosis and its place in modern medicine

June 1980   GORDON AMBROSE

GEORGE NEWBOLD

CHAPTER 1

HISTORY OF MEDICAL HYPNOTISM

Hypnotism and its medical application, hypnotherapy, are as old as recorded history, perhaps older. Many of the world's most ancient civilisations were familiar with hypnotic phenomena, although their manifestation was then usually linked to a belief in magic or to the rituals of religion. The healing properties of hypnosis were recognized and made use of by the priest-physicians of ancient Egypt, and in the 'sleep temples' of classical Greece. In the British Isles, hypnotism was practised among the early Celtic inhabitants and was then known as 'Druidic sleep', for the priestly sect of the Druids, the physicians of the time, would often place a sick person in a condition of artificial slumber identical with hypnosis in order to cure him of his complaint. There is also evidence that across the Atlantic, in the pre-Columbian New World, the hypnotic state was commonly used by native medicine-men in their attempts to heal many of the illnesses prevalent in their society. The desired effect was usually achieved by means of incantations, sometimes combined with the use of certain hallucinogenic drugs such as the 'aya huasca' vine found in the regions of the Upper Amazon.

This close association of hypnotism with the practice of various religious rites was almost universal in its extent in ancient times. In this respect it differed little, if at all, from any other branch of medicine. Similarly, it was frequently influenced by the prevailing superstitions of the time, and it is only comparatively recently that the whole subject has been studied in anything like a true scientific spirit. The scientific history of hypnotism is often considered as commencing with Mesmer but in fact the relationship of hypnosis to mesmerism more closely resembles that of chemistry to alchemy or astronomy to astrology. However, since mesmerism is inseparable from any historical account of the subject, a short account of the movement and its founder follows.

Franz Anton Mesmer (1734-1815) was born on 23 May 1734 at Iznang on Lake Constance, where his father was a gamekeeper. As a young man he had shown evidence of a versatile turn of mind and before obtaining his medical degree had studied philosophy, theology and law at Dillingen and Ingolstadt. He was also greatly interested in music and astrology, the second of these two interests being later largely responsible for the theory which he held concerning the nature of hypnotic phenomena. In 1774 he was introduced to the properties of the magnet by Father Maximilien Hell, a Jesuit priest, and became fascinated by the supposed power of this object to cure disease. Mesmer believed, at this time, that perfect health depended upon the individual maintaining a correct relationship with the heavenly bodies, and that the magnet was able to restore this relationship when it had become disturbed, causing disease. The magnet, or magnetized object, was supposed to produce the cure by means of a subtle, mysterious fluid which entered the body of the sufferer, and thus healed him of his complaint. This fluid Mesmer called 'animal magnetism'. His thesis, which he wrote in 1766 for his doctorate and which was entitled *De Planetarum influxu* ('On the influence of the planets'), gives us an early indication of the way in which not only he but many of his contemporaries regarded medical science in the eighteenth century.

In 1768, soon after Mesmer began the practice of medicine in Vienna, he married Anna von Bosch, the wealthy widow of Privy Councillor von Bosch who had been a high-ranking officer in the Austrian Imperial Army. He moved in exalted and artistic circles and lived in a fashionable part of the city. After his adoption of the magnet as an instrument of healing, his house at 261, Landstrasse, became the centre of attraction for thousands of patients. His reputation soon spread throughout Austria and across the frontiers to other parts of Europe. The Bavarian Academy of Sciences made him a member and other honours came to him.

Unfortunately for Mesmer, however, it appears that his continued success aroused feelings of jealousy among certain of his professional colleagues, and later a rift opened between him and the Medical Faculty. The exciting cause of this dispute was his treatment of what we now know to have been a case of hysterical blindness in a young pianist named Maria Theresa Paradis. This young woman was a protegée of the Empress Maria Theresa who had bestowed a pension upon her because of her blindness. Mesmer undertook to cure her of this disability and for a while vision was apparently restored. Later a relapse occurred — probably because of a fear that if she regained her sight the royal pension would cease — and the patient was removed from Mesmer's care. The latter, as a result, left Vienna for Paris in 1778.

In the French capital Mesmer was successful in obtaining access to Marie Antoinette through the influence of Dr Charles d'Eslon, who was physician to the Comte d'Artois, the King's younger brother. D'Eslon and Mesmer between them founded a clinic in the Rue Montmartre and scenes reminiscent of those in Vienna became the order of the day. Animal magnetism became the rage and for five hectic years all and sundry were treated at the clinic. Soon it became impossible to treat each patient separately, so Mesmer devised his famous *baquets*, which were large tubs filled with water containing bottles and iron filings, and from which projected numerous iron rods. These rods were then grasped by the patients so that they could receive the healing virtue of the magnetic fluid in the tubs. From this period comes the amazing story of crowds of people surrounding a 'magnetized' oak tree in the Bois de Boulogne in the fervent expectation of being cured of their complaints.

In 1784 the French government under Louis XVI set up a body of Commissioners under the Presidency of Benjamin Franklin to enquire into and to report upon the truth, or otherwise, of animal magnetism. Other members of the commission were Dr Guillotin, who gave his name to the instrument of capital punishment, Jussieu the botanist and Lavoisier the chemist. When their report was published and it became known that they attributed the phenomena to the effects of the imagination, rather than to the activities of a mysterious magnetic fluid, there was a reaction against Mesmer and his associates and their popularity waned. Mesmer then left France, just before the outbreak of the French Revolution. He is reported to have returned once again to Paris for a short while in 1801 when, following negotiations with the Directory, he was awarded a small pension as compensation for his loss of property during the years of the Terror. He later retired, almost forgotten, to Frauenfeld in Switzerland, on the shores of that Lake Constance which he had known so well as a boy. During this last period of his life it is said he lived very simply and spent his days largely in treating the impoverished peasants of the surrounding neighbourhood. In 1812 Mesmer received an invitation from the Prussian Academy to demonstrate once more his method in Berlin, but he refused. Three years later he died at Meersburg on 5 March 1815, the year of Waterloo.

Although 'animal magnetism' is now discredited as a satisfactory explanation of hypnotic phenomena, Mesmer's role in the history of hypnotism is an important one, for it was he who initiated the movement which was afterwards taken up and modified by others. During his lifetime one of his pupils, the Marquis de Puységur, stumbled upon the phenomenon of somnambulism, which excited considerable interest and led to a renewed enthusiasm for mesmerism especially in Germany. A few years after Mesmer's death the Abbé Faria of Portugal published a book called *De la cause de sommeil lucide ou étude sur la nature de l'homme* in which he stated his opinion that mesmeric phenomena depended upon the disposition of the subject and the state of his mind. This view, which stressed the subjective nature of the phenomena, unfortunately met with little response at the time, so that the development of a really satisfactory method of hypnotherapy was further delayed.

A case of somnambulism is recalled in the *Memoirs* of the Baroness Henriette Louise d'Oberkirch a friend of Goethe. She relates how one of the Marquis de Puységur's subjects, a young girl from the Black Forest region of Bavaria, predicted the horrors of the French Revolution while she was in a somnambulistic trance. Another classic description of somnambulism can be found in Act V, Scene I, of Shakespeare's *Macbeth*, in which the doctor and a waiting gentlewoman observe the antics of the sleep-walking Lady Macbeth. 'This disease', remarks the physician, 'is beyond my practice: yet I have known those which have walked in their sleep who have died holily in their beds.'

In the first quarter of the nineteenth century, therefore, interest in hypnosis was largely spasmodic because of the lack of an adequate theory to explain its nature. The mesmerists continued to be active here and there on the continent of Europe until some time towards the end of the eighteen-forties, when the rise of a mechanistic philosophy (mainly in Germany) caused their influence to wane considerably.

The next stage in the history of medical hypnotism may be said to begin with the work of *John Elliotson* (1791-1868), who was the first occupant of the Chair of Medicine at the newly founded medical school attached to University College Hospital in London. Elliotson, who was a man of outstanding energy and ability, believed that the progress of medical science should not be hampered by a slavish adherence to outworn doctrines, and it was this belief which led him to introduce Laennec's 'new-fangled' stethoscope into this country. Other evidence of his vigorous mind was his experimentation in his own practice with a wide variety of drugs, some of which he dispensed in such large doses that it caused a certain amount of consternation among his colleagues. However, he established the importance of potassium iodide in medicine and also the value of prussic acid in the treatment of vomiting.

Following a visit by the Frenchman Dupotet to this country, Elliotson became greatly interested in the subject of mesmerism and took up the cause with enthusiasm. He was soon giving public demonstrations in the wards of the hospital and for his subjects he used some of the patients. These demonstrations attracted large and often distinguished audiences, but they also led to friction between Elliotson and the hospital authorities. In 1838 Thomas Wakley, the first editor and the founder of the *Lancet*, undertook a test of Elliotson's claims that mesmeric phenomena depended upon the transmission of a physical force such as the 'animal magnetism' of the early mesmerists. Closely linked with this theory was the belief that certain metals had greater 'magnetizing' properties than others; gold was supposed to be more powerful than nickel which, in its turn, was superior to lead. When Wakley conclusively proved that there was no difference at all between the effects produced by a disc made of nickel and one of lead, many people began to look upon Elliotson as an impostor. The governors of the hospital declared that demonstrations of mesmerism within the hospital precincts should cease and as Elliotson was not prepared to abandon his work he immediately resigned his posts as Physician and Professor at the medical school.

With the help of some supporters Elliotson established a mesmeric hospital in Fitzroy Square, and also started a journal called the *Zoist* for the express purpose of propagating the theory of animal magnetism. In this journal, which numbered among its contributors eminent writers like Herbert Spencer, many case histories of mesmeric cures ranging from surgical operations to various types of medical disorders were reported. Phrenology and clairvoyance were also discussed in its pages. Elliotson died on 29 July 1868 in Davies Street, Berkeley Square, maintaining to the last his convictions as a mesmerist. There is no doubt that his work, by emphasizing the importance of his method in the cure of disease, prevented the subject from falling into complete obscurity as it might otherwise have done. He focused attention particularly on the treatment of the psychoneuroses and functional disorders which were little affected by more orthodox methods of treatment through drugs. It is somewhat strange that he did not seem to anticipate modern theories concerning the subjective nature of hypnosis, for in many other respects his ideas have a curiously modern flavour about them. His views on the upbringing and treatment of children, for instance, are completely in accord with those which are universally accepted today, and must have appeared revolutionary to his contemporaries.

Towards the middle of the nineteenth-century interest in mesmerism had grown considerably in the USA and national figures like Elizabeth Blackwell, the first woman ever to qualify in medicine, and Edgar Allan Poe refer to it in their writings. Mary Baker Eddy was introduced to it by a mesmerist named Phineas Quimby, who was the anaesthetist at the first surgical operation performed under hypnosis in the United States. Henry James refers to mesmeric activities in one of his novels.

In India also, the analgesic and anaesthetic properties of the hypnotic state were being demonstrated in dramatic fashion by *James Esdaile* (1808-59), a native of Perth in Scotland. In the course of seven years' work in Calcutta he performed about three hundred major operations and thousands of minor ones quite painlessly with the aid of mesmerism. The majority of his major cases were the removal of huge scrotal tumours although nineteen amputations are recorded as well. Esdaile's work received the official sanction of the Government of Bengal, which established a special mesmeric hospital in Calcutta where he could work (Esdaile 1847). One noteworthy feature of his cases was the low operative mortality and the rapid healing which ensued.

Many of Esdaile's operations were described in detail in the columns of the *Zoist*, but most of the professional journals of the time seem to have been closed to him – in spite of the fact that Sir J. Y. Simpson of Edinburgh had urged that they be made widely known. This reluctance on the part of official medical science to embrace the cause of mesmerism, as hypnosis was still called, may be largely explained by the continued absence of any theory of hypnotism acceptable to the scientific mind. So long as the concept of some physical agent as the cause of mesmeric phenomena was held by its practitioners, many worthy men like Elliotson and Esdaile would continue to be branded as impostors and charlatans. Moreover, as the opportunities for observing hypnotic phenomena increased, it was becoming realized more and more that such an explanation was an inadequate one.

It was at this point that mesmerism was rescued from the morass into which it was sinking by the efforts of an Edinburgh surgeon, *James Braid* (1795-1860). After practising in his native Scotland for some years, Braid removed to Manchester where he continued to live for the rest of his life. On 13 November 1841, he witnessed a demonstration of mesmerism given by Lafontaine, a relative of the famous French poet and writer of fables. Although his views at this time were largely sceptical ones, Braid was convinced of the genuineness of the phenomena he observed on this occasion, and he thereupon determined that he would do his utmost to establish the subject upon a proper scientific foundation. He first made a series of experiments upon his friends and relatives, and before long he came to the conclusion that the phenomena of mesmerism were wholly subjective in character and were not dependent upon any magical powers possessed by the operator. In 1842 he approached the Medical Section of the British Association in Manchester with an offer to read a paper on hypnotism. This was refused, but Braid later gave a private lecture-demonstration to many members of the same Association at a *conversazione* (Braid 1844). In 1843 he had published his *Neurohypnology, or The Rationale of Nervous Sleep*, and in this work he proposed that the phenomena should be termed 'hypnotic' rather than 'mesmeric' – and thereby coined a new work in the English language. At first the word 'neurohypnotism' was used, to denote 'a condition of nervous sleep', but soon afterwards Braid shortened it to the familiar 'hypnotism' we know today.

There is ample evidence that Braid was a careful and competent observer and possessed of a true scientific spirit of enquiry. During his lifetime his own views concerning the manner in which hypnotic changes occurred became considerably modified. At first, he thought that although the phenomena were subjective and were brought about by an alteration in the subject's own mind, the exciting cause was a physical one, such as fixed gazing at a bright object. This particular method of induction, which he used in his early experiments, is often referred to as 'Braidism'. Later on he came to believe that a condition of 'monoideism' produced by concentrating the attention provided the best explanation. Towards the end of his life, however, Braid had come to realize that the condition was, in essence, a conscious one (in spite of the name 'hypnotism', from the Greek word meaning 'sleep') and that several ideas could be planted in the subject's mind at the same time. He was also aware of the influence of suggestion in exciting the phenomena but did not consider this a completely adequate theory for explaining them.

Although Braid encountered a good deal of opposition to his work during his lifetime there is no doubt that he was much more successful, so far as the medical profession was concerned, than most of his predecessors. Numerous copies of his published works were sold and he was to a large extent responsible for the revival of interest in hypnotism in France, which occurred mainly through the efforts of Dr Azam of Bordeaux who had become acquainted with Braid's work in 1859. Broca, the celebrated neurologist, subsequently read a paper describing Braid's methods to the French Académie des Sciences.

Following Braid's death from cardiovascular disease on 25 March 1860, the next chapter in the story of hypno-therapy was written in France by *Dr. A. A. Liébeault*, a country general practitioner of Nancy. Liébeault took up the serious study of hypnotism in the year that Braid died, and at about the same time that Azam and Velpeau were making known the work of the Manchester surgeon. This hard-working country doctor is said to have treated all his patients free so long as they allowed him to use hypnotic methods. As a result of this offer to the French peasants of gratuitous service, Liébeault was soon overwhelmed with patients seeking his help. In spite of pressure on his time, he took the opportunity to write a book entitled *Du sommeil et des états analogues, considérés surtout au point de vue de l'action de la morale sur le physique* in which he described many of his cases. Although an immense amount of care and meticulous attention to detail went into the preparation of this work, it excited little attention and most of Liébeault's colleagues regarded him as a fool. Undeterred by the neglect and ridicule of the French medical profession, Liébeault continued for many years in his self-appointed task of curing the poor of Nancy and the surrounding neighbourhood. In 1882, however, his fortunes were destined to undergo a dramatic change for, in that year, he cured a severe case of sciatica which *Professor Bernheim* of Strasbourg had treated in vain for about six months. As a result, Bernheim visited Liébeault at his clinic and was so impressed by what he saw and heard there that he became an ardent admirer and supporter of 'the good Father Liébeault' (as he was known throughout the adjoining countryside).

In 1884 Bernheim himself published a book called *De la suggestion*, and the reception which this volume had was vastly different from that accorded *Du sommeil*. Liébeault's name became world-famous almost overnight and medical men from all countries converged on Nancy in order to study his methods. Between them, Bernheim and Liébeault founded what came to be known as the 'Nancy school of hypnotism', although this description is not a particularly apt one when applied to a number of physicians who were only loosely associated and whose opinions were by no means always held in common.

The distinguishing features of the Nancy school were mainly beliefs that hypnotic phenomena were caused by suggestion acting on and through the subject's own mind, and that the hypnotic state was essentially a normal one. This latter was the very opposite of the view held by *Jean Marie Charcot*, the somewhat pugnacious and redoubtable French neurologist, who held that the condition was a pathological one and was closely related to hysteria. Charcot and his followers are sometimes referred to as the 'Salpêtrière School' and for a while their opinions carried some weight, largely owing to the international reputation of their leader. There was very little foundation in fact for Charcot's assertions since he experimented with very few subjects, most of whom were already under treatment in hospital for symptoms of hysteria or neurotic disorder. Conclusions drawn from observations made on such clinical material were bound to be erroneous.

In spite of Charcot's standing in European medicine the theories of Liébeault and Bernheim became more and more generally accepted and were officially endorsed at the International Congress of Hypnotism held in Paris in 1900. Since then interest in hypnosis has in most countries been intermittent, but has never ceased entirely.

During one of the revivals of interest in hypnotherapy at the close of the nineteenth century, *Sigmund Freud* began to use it in the treatment of some of his own patients. It was then that he made his momentous discovery that there existed in the minds of some hypnotized patients events which they had completely forgotten but which, nevertheless, were capable of producing psychoneurotic symptoms. Later, when he found that he could not deeply hypnotize all his patients he abandoned hypnosis and elaborated his method of psychoanalysis.

At about the same time *J. Milne Bramwell*, who did much to raise the status of hypnotherapy in the eyes of the medical profession, was practising with great success as a medical hypnotist in London. Other prominent workers of this period were *Boris Sidis* of the United States, *August Forel* of Switzerland, and *Pierre Janet* in France. In 1891 the British Medical Association appointed a committee to enquire into the nature and value of hypnotism, and in the following year the committee presented its report. This declared, *inter alia*, that the members were satisfied that hypnotic phenomena were genuine and hypnotism was valuable as a therapeutic agent. They were also of the opinion that it should be employed only by qualified medical practitioners and should not be used for purposes of public exhibition or entertainment. Another professional body which investigated the subject at this time was the Society for Psychical Research, under its president, Sir Oliver Lodge, F.R.S. This Society published reports and articles on hypnotism from time to time in its

Proceedings, and was largely instrumental in making known the important contributions of Gurney and Myers to the theoretical aspects of the subject. During the twentieth century two World Wars placed hypnotherapy firmly among the most successful techniques for the treatment of shell-shock and battle neurosis. To a large extent the credit for this is due to the pioneering work of William Brown and J. A. Hadfield. The experience gained in treating casualties of war has been reflected in the present world-wide increase of interest in the use of hypnosis for medical purposes as a method of treating casualties of stress and anxiety in civilian life. Many branches of medicine and surgery have benefitted as a result, and the psychological and physiological phenomena of hypnosis have now emerged as serious subjects for scientific study and research. In the United Kingdom S. J. Van Pelt was one of the first to popularize the use of hypnotherapy after World War Two and since then recognition of the importance of psychosomatic factors in medicine has gained increasing support in many directions. This widespread renewal of interest appears to have every prospect of being self-sustaining, and numerous scientific and medical articles bear witness to this emergence from comparative obscurity.

BIBLIOGRAPHY

BRAID, J. (1844) Conversazione on hypnotism. *Med. Times*, *10*, 137.
BRAMWELL, J. M. (1930) *Hypnotism, its History, Practice and Theory*, 3rd ed. London: Rider.
D'ESLON, Charles (1780) *Observations sur le Magnétisme Animal.*
ELLIOTSON, John (1843) *Numerous Cases of Surgical Operations without Pain in the Mesmeric State.* London.
ESDAILE, J. E. (1847) *A Record of Cases Treated in the Mesmeric Hospital from November 1846 to December 1847 with Reports of the Official Visitors.* Printed by order of the Government, Calcutta.
MESMER, Franz Anton (1775) *Schreiben über die Magnetkur an einen auswärtigen Arzt.* Vienna.
NEWBOLD, G. (1949–52) Famous names in hypnotism. *Br. J. med. Hypnot.*, *1.2*, 3–8; *1.3*, 2–7; *1.4*, 3–7; *3.3*, 2–7.
ROSEN, G. (1946). Mesmerism and surgery, a strange chapter in the history of anaesthesia. *J. Hist. Med.*, *1*, 527.
WESLEY, J. (1903) *The Journal of the Rev. John Wesley.* London.

CHAPTER 2

THE MEDICAL HYPNOTIST AND THE LAW

It has long been recognized that all registered medical practitioners stand in a special relationship with regard to the law. They are granted privileges denied to those not on the Medical Register and they are obliged to fulfil certain statutory requirements which do not affect the lay citizen. Furthermore, they have to consider not only their duty towards the state but also the needs of their patients, and the two may not be in harmony. If any conflict arises, traditional ideas concerning the nature of the doctor-patient relationship require the doctor to put the interests of his patient first unless there are very exceptional circumstances.

One of the cardinal tenets in any code of medical ethics has always been that anything which the patient may disclose to his doctor, or anything which the latter may discover during the course of his examination, should be strictly confidential and should not be disclosed to any third party without the patient's consent. It is essential for the proper practice of medicine that the patient should be able to feel that he can trust his physician. During the course of the usual kind of examination and treatment, it would be fairly safe to assume that whatever the patient might reveal to his doctor, it was done freely and with full conscious knowledge of its import. If there was anything which the patient wished to keep secret even from his doctor he would probably do so, although some patients might feel impelled to reveal information they would rather withhold if questioned in a manner reminiscent of cross-examination in court.

When, on the other hand, we come to consider the history derived from an individual in a condition of deep hypnosis, doubts may arise concerning the entirely voluntary nature of all the disclosures made. Can we be certain that if he were in the normal waking state he would have willingly volunteered such information, if he had been aware of it? Sometimes during the hypnoanalysis of a somnambule material is uncovered which the patient has completely forgotten. Should this material be treated any differently on a legal-ethical level from that which is consciously obtained? In the writer's opinion such information should be protected by law, so that not even a judge of the High Court can compel its disclosure in evidence given by a medical practitioner without the willing consent of the patient concerned. Moreover, such consent should only be obtained after all the circumstances have been explained to the patient and all the relevant facts placed before him. If the information contains certain knowledge which he wishes to conceal because he thinks it might prejudice his own case, this refusal to permit disclosure to the court would then of itself be prima facie evidence against him, and judge and jury would be free to draw their own conclusions from his silence. The author's views (Newbold 1953) are, of course, not necessarily accepted by all who practise hypnotherapy. The primary object of any court must be to see that justice is done and in the attainment of this goal many factors have to be taken into consideration.

The medical hypnotist, like any other doctor, may also be concerned with the legal question of negligence. This can be a matter of some importance for, since the inception of the National Health Service in the United Kingdom, there has been a decided increase in the number of actions for negligence which have been brought against medical practitioners. The National Health Service Act abolished the old principle of voluntary hospitals and placed their control under the Ministry of Health and aggrieved patients felt less compunction about suing a government department. The granting by the State of financial assistance to litigants may also have contributed to the increase in the number of actions that have been brought. The law, it is important to note, has not been changed in respect to professional negligence, for it has always insisted that a qualified medical practitioner must exercise a reasonable degree of care, commensurate with his status, when treating his patients. Not only should a doctor take care with the examination of his patient and in the carrying out of any technical measures he may employ, but he should also pay attention to what he says. The vast majority of persons are influenced at some time or other by the words of their physician and may be made to feel happy or depressed in consequence. If such an effect can be produced during the normal conscious state, how much more meticulous should the medical hypnotist be in his speech when undertaking the treatment of those who are in a particularly susceptible frame of mind! The hypnotherapist should, therefore, strive to make the meaning of his words clear, to avoid ambiguity, and to do nothing which would leave his patient in a disturbed mental condition. It is possible that, just as in the performance of an appendicectomy a greater degree of skill would be expected from a surgeon than from a general practitioner, so a medical hypnotist might be required to be more particular with his suggestions than would a physician who did not use the hypnotic state at all. This extreme degree of care makes it all the more necessary that anyone who practises hypnotherapy should be a properly qualified medical practitioner with a good all-round knowledge of general medicine and a practical knowledge of psychological mechanisms. The practice of hypnosis should therefore be restricted to registered medical practitioners, except in dentistry, where hypnosis is employed only for a limited purpose, and in hypnotherapy by qualified psychologists in carefully selected cases. The treatment of patients wishing to be delivered from compulsive habits such as smoking would thus fall within the scope of psychotherapists or psychologists without medical qualifications. This aspect of hypnotherapy has, so far, not been dealt with by legislation, for the Hypnotism Act, 1952, still allows any unskilled person to treat 'mental or physical disease' by this method.

One problem which cannot be omitted from any discussion of the medico-legal aspects of hypnosis is the possibility of using it in order to facilitate or to cover up the committing of a crime. In the first place, a doctor using hypnosis may himself be accused of a criminal offence against a patient whom he has hypnotized. Usually such an accusation takes the form of a charge of rape or indecent assault, and may cause the practitioner considerable difficulties. He may shrink from the threat of publicity attendant upon a criminal trial and, as a result, find himself the victim of some unscrupulous blackmailer. Even if the allegation is completely unfounded the persistence of rumours or whispers of misconduct may be quite sufficient to wreck his professional reputation. Fortunately, however, the law requires corroborative evidence in charges of a sexual nature, and most accusations of this kind which are alleged to have occurred during hypnosis are very similar to those which are sometimes made by patients who have received nitrous oxide anaesthesia. It is now well recognized that in certain circumstances some persons may experience sexual fantasies which, at the time, have all the appearance of reality. Moreover, these may be accompanied by other signs and symptoms of definite hysterical reactions in such individuals.

The hypnotherapist would be wise to take every precaution against the possibility of any such accusation being made or believed. First of all he should have the highest regard for the ethics of his profession and should maintain a high standard of personal integrity so that charges of impropriety become less credible. Secondly, it is as well to have an independent witness of any proceedings conducted under hypnosis. This more especially applies to the treatment of female patients by a male physician, but even if doctor and patient are of the same sex there would be no harm in taking such a precaution in case of a possible accusation of homosexual assault. Ideally, hypnotherapy should be practised in a specially constructed clinic where a witness, preferably a nurse, can see and hear without herself being seen. In the Report published by the British Medical Association Committee on Hypnotism as long ago as 1892, it was stated that 'under no circumstances should female patients be hypnotized except in the presence of a relative or a person of their own sex'. It is best in all cases to ascertain beforehand what the patient's own wishes are regarding the presence of a third person in the room during the course of treatment, and to respect these wishes as much as possible. Most patients seem to prefer not to have anyone other than the doctor in close proximity to them, but sometimes it is found that they will more readily enter the hypnotic state if they can have a trusted friend or relative near at hand.

There is a third possible safeguard for the medical hypnotist. This is the use of a tape-recorder so that all that is said during the course of treatment is automatically recorded. On a few occasions recently this type of evidence has been accepted in certain of our courts and it has been suggested that the police should use it as a routine measure when taking statements from suspects, instead of relying upon the traditional method of writing.

Until the suggestion that there is something sinister about the use of hypnotism is finally dispelled from the public mind, it would seem reasonable for the practitioner in this field of medicine to give thought to ways of keeping his reputation unsullied. Unfortunately even today far too many people still associate hypnotism with the 'compelling hypnotic powers' of an individual like the fictional Svengali who forced the submission of others to his will.

Another way in which it is sometimes feared that hypnosis may lend itself to crime or anti-social activity is that an unscrupulous hypnotist may so influence his subject that the latter will be prepared to commit an offence at the instigation of the former. One celebrated case in which this was put forward as a defence to a charge of murder occurred in Paris in the year 1888. A woman named Bompard was jointly accused with a man called Eyraud of killing her lover. In her defence the woman stated that at the time of the crime she was under the hypnotic influence of Eyraud and, therefore, her counsel suggested, she could not be held personally responsible for her part in the murder. Apart from the question of hypnotism, this case is also memorable in medico-legal circles because of the method used by the accused in dispatching their victim. While the lover Gouffé, was engaged in the usually pleasant pastime of making love to Bompard, Eyraud slipped a noose over his head, hanging him (Lacassagne 1890).

In addition to fears over the possibility of such malign influence as that just described, some medico-legal authorities — probably the majority — are concerned with the possibility of diminished personal responsibility resulting from the use of hypnosis. For example, Dr Letitia Fairfield (1952) has pointed out that 'The practice of hypnotism is apt to be associated with such sensational — or even serio-comic — circumstances that it is easy enough to lose sight of the fact that it involves serious problems, both medical and legal.' After raising the question of whether or not hypnosis can influence a person's moral judgment so that the commission of a criminal act becomes more likely, she goes on to state ' . . . Instigation to crime is, however, one of the least likely dangers of hypnotism. A more practical consideration is that a condition of subservience to another person might be produced, inconsistent with the degree of personal responsibility which medicine and the law regard as normal. . . . Another unpleasant possibility is that of leaving the subject's mind clouded by depressing disturbing suggestions at the end of the séance. The trained medical hypnotist knows how to avoid this danger; with the untrained practitioner one cannot have the same confidence and the chance of some long-standing mental damage being inflicted in this way is not negligible.'

During the past hundred years or so a good deal has been written about the possibility of inducing a somnambulist to commit a crime by giving him suitable hypnotic and post-hypnotic suggestions. Experiments have been carried out by workers in various countries in an effort to determine whether or not this would be possible. Although the conclusions drawn are not unanimous, it is safe to say that the weight of authoritative opinions is now against the likelihood of such an event occurring. Most of the available evidence seems to show that if an individual commits a criminal or anti-social act as the result of hypnotic suggestion, it is more than probable that he would have done so in any case. Hypnosis then becomes merely an excuse for such behaviour in an attempt to avoid legal responsibility for the act. On the other hand, it has sometimes been noticed that the hypnotic state may even result in a *strengthening* of the moral nature of an individual, and Bramwell (1930) gives some interesting cases where this has actually been demonstrated. For instance, female patients who have shown not the slightest hesitation, when normally conscious, in exposing their bodies for examination by a male physician have resolutely refused to undress when requested to do so while they were hypnotized. There are many other reports in the literature of somnambulists who have declared during hypnosis that certain suggestions which were given to them were 'wrong', and have firmly refused to carry them out. Others, when given suggestions which conflicted sharply with their normal convictions of right and wrong, have immediately 'awakened' from their hypnotic condition. Yet again, some subjects, when asked to perform a wrongful act, have merely pretended to do so and in this way have salved their conscience and found a way out of the dilemma.

Because of this apparent increase in the appreciation of moral values during the hypnotic state it has been suggested that the crime of false pretences might be facilitated by hypnosis. The view has been put forward that by appealing to the 'better nature' of a hypnotized subject it will be easier to induce him to sign a cheque or to part with money, supposedly in aid of some worthy or charitable cause. It does seem that this is probably the only type of crime for which hypnosis could be employed when dealing with an individual who, as well as being a good hypnotic subject, is at the same time a law-abiding citizen.

Another practical difficulty which confronts the potentially criminal hypnotist is that his victim who committed an offence while under 'hypnotic influence' would almost certainly render himself easily open to detection. This is because the hypnotized subject would only be likely to obey specific suggestions and instructions which were given him by the hypnotist. Therefore, unless all attendant circumstances had been foreseen by the latter and the appropriate measures taken to deal with them before they actually arose, the subject would not be able to cover up the evidence of his crime and discovery would inevitably follow.

Nevertheless, in spite of observations which seem to indicate that a deeply hypnotized person has an *increased* moral sense, rather than a diminished one, some people still feel that it is possible for hypnosis to be used for wrong purposes. It is thought that a skilful hypnotist, through repeated hypnosis, may be able to break down or circumvent the moral barriers of the subject's personality so that crime becomes possible. Before this argument is accepted at its face value, however, we must remember that constant and skilful suggestion may do as much in the non-hypnotic state. Until the precise nature of the hypnotic state is better understood there will doubtless continue to be some disquiet as to such undesirable results from the use of hypnosis, although most authorities today do not consider that the risk of an increase in the crime rate from this cause is a very real one. There is no doubt that some of the older writers, such as Forel and Bernheim, believed that hypnosis could be used for criminal purposes, but Moll, who had considerable experience in such matters, considered that this would occur only in exceptional cases.

Even in Mesmer's day some people had misgivings about the uses to which hypnotism could be put when it was employed by unscrupulous persons. When the French government set up their Commission of Enquiry into animal magnetism in 1784, this body issued a private report which discussed the possible abuse of the method in affording greater opportunities for sexual seduction. In its memorandum on the subject it stated that in its opinion 'such practices and assemblies may have an injurious effect upon morality'. Even today there is some evidence of the use of hypnosis by unqualified persons for their own personal gain. There is much to be said for restricting the practice of hypnotism to properly qualified individuals who belong to recognized professional organizations which insist upon a strict code of ethical behaviour from their members.

An interesting case reported by Reiter and illustrative of some of the medico-legal problems involved occurred a few years ago in Scandinavia. Two men, one of them the night watchman of a bank, were shot and fatally injured by a gunman who was trying to force an entry into the bank. After the shooting the criminal was easily apprehended by the police and charged with murder. From the forensic point of view this case is of interest for two reasons. In the first place, the defence pleaded diminished responsibility on the grounds that, at the time of the alleged offence, the prisoner was under the influence of a hypnotist who had, by skilful and painstaking hypnotic suggestion, so broken down the man's normal moral scruples that he became incapable of distinguishing between right and wrong. The defence therefore submitted that the real person who should have been charged was not the one who fired the shot but the hypnotist. Since there are still divergences of opinion as to how far hypnosis may affect one's moral judgment, it would seem that in this particular instance the fairest procedure would be to charge both men with the same crime. Secondly, this case illustrates the difficulty of ensuring that a person given hypnotic or post-hypnotic instructions to commit a criminal act will effectually carry them out. In this case, the appearance of the night watchman on the scene was unexpected and the details of the shooting and subsequent pattern of events were not foreseen by the hypnotist. Because of this, and the failure to prepare him adequately for his task, the robber became confused in his actions so that detection and arrest presented little difficulty.

Leaving the question of the *commission* of crime through the medium of hypnosis, let us now turn to the matter of its *detection* by the same method. The highly controversial topic of using a somnambulist for obtaining information by means of some form of 'extra sensory perception' is not discussed further since this chapter is concerned with the more practical medico-legal aspects. The possibility has already been raised of a deeply hypnotized person revealing matter which he would probably not otherwise have done. It has been suggested that use might be made of this technique in the interrogation of suspects by the police, but although hidden information may be obtained in this way in the course of hypnotic treatment for medical purposes *by a doctor*, it is more than possible that the same thing would not occur if hypnosis were used by the police. In the first place it has been shown that a hypnotized person may refuse to talk about certain things if he does not wish to do so. He may resolutely refuse to answer questions, or to make a statement, if the possibility exists that by so doing he is aiding his own conviction. On the other hand, such a method might be useful in establishing the truth if he is innocent: a guilty person, it would appear, is just as much likely to resist the truth under hypnosis as when he is in his normal state. A further disadvantage is that such a method could, at present, only be applied to a limited number of individuals because of the difficulty of securing a depth of hypnosis sufficient for this particular purpose. Lastly, it must be remembered that if interrogation under hypnosis is contemplated, it is necessary for the suspect or witness to give his consent and to co-operate freely in the procedure.

In spite of some of these more obvious difficulties, there are a number of authorities who advocate the use of hypnosis in suitable cases for the purpose of criminal investigation. Hypnotic techniques, if employed, should be used only for helping witnesses or complainants to recall certain incidents which have been buried in their memories and forgotten, either because of an accompanying trauma or because a fleeting or confused impression did not clearly register in their conscious minds. For example, Kleinhauz, Horowitz and Tobin, of the Scientific Interrogation Unit of the Israeli Police, published in 1977 an interesting account of this use of hypnosis during the interrogation of forty subjects who were involved as witnesses or victims of crimes such as rape, armed robbery and terrorism. They also set out safeguarding conditions which, in their view, should be adhered to when using such techniques. It is their opinion that hypnosis should not be employed for the questioning of suspects. The only exception to this rule should be if the suspect specifically requests hypnosis 'in order to help him to recall details which might provide him with an alibi'. Provided that the conditions listed by these authors are complied with there seems to be no ethical reason why hypnotic methods should not be used in the investigation of crime. Another writer, Haward (1977) suggests that hypnosis may also be used for interrogating an accused person when the purpose is to investigate the motive for an offence. In such cases hypnosis may be useful to the defence in providing 'facts in mitigation' which would otherwise be unavailable to the Court.

An interesting account of the use of hypnosis in interrogation is given by Richard Deacon in his book *The Israeli Secret Service*. Before the raid on the Entebbe airport in Uganda by Israeli paratroopers in an operation to secure the release of Jewish hostages following the hi-jacking of an airliner, some of the previously released hostages were successfully interviewed while under hypnosis. This was said to have been useful in assisting the Israeli military authorities to check on the lay-out and construction of the airport.

The authors are doubtful about the wisdom of advocating the general use of hypnosis by police officers themselves, with or without the concurrent employment of polygraph lie detectors. In the United Kingdom it would probably be much more acceptable to public opinion if the actual conduct of the hypnotic session was left to a professional medical hypnotist, with an experienced police investigator at hand to guide the questioning into channels relevant to the enquiry underway at the time.

One of the authors (G.A.) was once sent a patient by the police. This patient, referred to as A, had apparently left his car on a busy road while other cars were stationary at a red stop-light. He had then gone over to the driver of another car, B, and had violently attacked B through the open car window, punching him in the face. A was to be summoned for assault but he had complete amnesia of the event. He could agree only that his fist was bruised and painful the following day, but thought that he must have banged it against the head-rest of his bed. The police were doubtful about the incident, as nothing was known against the motorist A whereas B had a history of assault. As A was very willing to undergo hypnosis he was deeply hypnotised. His story unfolded over two hours. While driving along the motorway B had 'cut him up' and then made a rude gesture, shouting and swearing at him. He also called A a 'dirty b——' and this latter remark so incensed A that he left his car and hit B. A tape-recording was given to the police and no action was taken by them against either A or B. During the tape-recording A had demonstrated an obvious hypnotic abreaction, crying that he had never been aggressive before and that he could not imagine what had come over him. Clearly in this case hypnosis was helpful to all parties concerned: after hypnosis A eventually agreed to discuss his apparent lack of aggression and the subsequent amnesia.

Another aspect of hypnotherapy which warrants a brief notice in any consideration of medico-legal factors concerns its possible value in the treatment of homosexuality. The present trend in most countries is towards a relaxation of the legal restrictions on homosexual acts between consenting adults in private, but whatever the legal position may be a considerable degree of moral condemnation may be inflicted upon the participants and they may be open to blackmail. In this respect homosexuality differs from most other conditions in that the patient may seek help for non-medical reasons. Moreover, the treatment of homosexuality is still one of the most difficult problems in medicine, and there appear to be no measures which are universally applicable to all cases presenting such symptoms.

However, there is reason to believe that a considerable proportion of persons of both sexes who show homosexual tendencies may receive help from hypnotherapy. Such persons are those whose affliction is due to deeply rooted fears and anxieties concerning the opposite sex, or to a faulty psychosexual development during the early and most impressionable years of life. The case of true sexual inversion is not likely to be affected one way or the other by hypnotic methods of treatment, but cases have been reported of individuals previously driven to participating in sexual relations with members of their own sex because of an intense fear of approaching the opposite one who have been enabled to function in a natural heterosexual capacity. Under hypnosis their fears and tensions have been resolved, and their sexual urge has been directed into more usual channels.

Before concluding this chapter something should be said about the provisions of the Hypnotism Act, 1952, which, in spite of its shortcomings, is an important piece of legislation and a milestone in the story of hypnotism in this country. The Act makes it illegal for anyone to give exhibitions of hypnotism for public entertainment unless licensed to do so by the appropriate local authority and forbids the use of a subject under twenty-one years of age for this purpose. The use of hypnosis in the treatment of disease and for research is exempted from the provisions of the Act. Also excluded is the induction of self-hypnosis for whatever reason.

One of the main disadvantages of the Act, from the point of view of *medical* hypnotism, is that it does not restrict the practice of hypnotherapy to registered medical practitioners (or dentists). This being so, the question has been raised as to whether a hypnotist who is not a qualified doctor could be regarded as a medical auxiliary and so practise hypnotherapy under the supervision and direction of a registered medical practitioner. The main objection to this is that during treatment by hypnotic methods the entire procedure rests largely in the hands of the hypnotist himself. If the hypnotherapist had no proper medical training it is quite possible that his patient might develop signs or symptoms which called for a modification or even suspension of this particular method of treatment, and yet would pass unrecognized by the therapist. Hypnotherapy, it has often been stressed, is not merely the induction of the hypnotic state, but a system of treatment which demands a wide knowledge of medicine. The ability to hypnotize is only the beginning.

BIBLIOGRAPHY

BRAMWELL, J. M. (1930) *Hypnotism, its History, Practice and Theory*, 3rd ed., pp. 318-31. London: Rider.

CUDDON, E. (1955) *Hypnosis – Its Meaning and Practice*, pp. 89-100. London: Bell.

DEACON, Richard (1979) *The Israeli Secret Service*, p. 313. London: Sphere.

FAIRFIELD, Letitia (1952) Editorial, *Med.-leg. J., Lond., 20*, Part 2.

HAMMERSCHLAG, H. E. (1956) *Hypnotism and Crime*, Eng. ed. trans. J. Cohen. London: Rider.

HAWARD, L. R. C. (1977) Forensic hypnosis. *Hypnosis, 1*, 4-5.

HERON, W. T. (1952) Hypnosis as a factor in the production and detection of crime. *Br. J. med. Hypnot., 3.3*, 15-29.

KLEINHAUZ, M., HOROWITZ, I. & TOBIN, Y. (1977) The use of hypnosis in police investigation: a preliminary communication. *J. forens. Sci. Soc., 17*, 77.

LACASSAGNE, A. (1890) *Arch. Anthrop. crim.*

MOLL, A. (1909) *Hypnotism*, 4th German ed. trans. A. F. Hobkirk. New York: Scribner.

NEWBOLD, George (1953) Some medico-legal problems and the Hypnotism Act. *Br. J. med. Hypnot., 4.3*, 12-16.

REITER, Paul J. (1958) *Anti-social or Criminal Acts and Hypnosis. A Case Study*. Springfield, Ill.: Charles C. Thomas.

CHAPTER 3

THE HYPNOTIC STATE AND ITS PHENOMENA

THEORIES CONCERNING THE NATURE OF HYPNOSIS

Since the time of Mesmer there have been a number of theories put forward in an attempt to explain the changes which occur when a person passes from a normal waking condition into one of hypnosis. One of the difficulties encountered in any explanation is that so many of the phenomena found in a recognized hypnotic condition frequently occur sporadically among persons who seem to be in a normal state of mind. The absence of immediate pain from a kick whilst playing football is an example. It may therefore be more useful to do as Marcuse (1959) suggests; 'to define hypnosis by what it does rather than by what it is'.

Theories come and go and none of them is entirely satisfactory, but some of the most important are summarized below.

ANIMAL MAGNETISM

This was the theory supported by the mesmerists (Mesmer, Elliotson and others), and consists of the belief that a subtle, mysterious healing fluid ('animal magnetism') passes into the body of the hypnotized subject and then produces the phenomena observed. This view is mainly of historic importance but it is included since there are still some people who incline towards an explanation of this kind. This may be partly due to the revolution in physics which has transformed the nineteenth century ideas of a concrete materialistic science into something elusive and increasingly mysterious – one might almost say mystical.

MONOIDEISM

This theory originated with Braid. It supposes such mental concentration that a state of 'monoideism' is produced by a greatly narrowed field of consciousness. This theory is open to the objection that varied hypnotic phenomena can be evoked at the same time in the same subject.

PHYSIOLOGICAL THEORIES

These include those of Bennet, who thought that hypnosis was characterized by alteration in the function of certain nerve cells of the cerebral cortex, and of Pavlov, whose view was that it was but a manifestation of normal sleep. Today we know that the hypnotic state is much more like ordinary waking consciousness than sleep. For instance the electroencephalogram (EEG) of a hypnotized subject shows a wave-pattern identical with that of consciousness. The basal metabolic rate is also unchanged by hypnosis, whereas it is lowered by about 10% during sleep. Similarly, during hypnosis the tendon reflexes, like the knee jerk, are present and normal, whereas during sleep they are either abolished or else greatly decreased. Another authority who attributed the hypnotic state to a change in the activity of the central nervous system was Heidenhain; he was of the opinion that hypnotic phenomena depended upon inhibition of the ganglion cells of the cerebrum.

Pavlov's theory was modified by Völgyesi (1963) who believes that hypnosis is a special state between waking and sleeping. As a corollary to this idea he assumes that anyone who sleeps can be hypnotized. This brings in 'animal hypnosis', and in his book Völgyesi devotes a considerable section to hypnotic experiments with animals. Völgyesi's theory does not allow for the fact that it is virtually impossible to influence certain types of mental defectives, even though they have no difficulty whatever in sleeping.

One of the leading modern exponents of the physiological basis for the phenomena of hypnosis is B. D. Wyke of the Department of Applied Physiology of the Royal College of Surgeons in England. He regards hypnosis as 'a physiological state whose production involves the sequential operation of several specific neurological mechanisms'. Hernández-Péon and Donoso (1957) reported experiments on electrical potentials measured in the optic radiation beneath the occipital cortex when suggestions of varying light intensities were given. Wyke (1960) concluded that clear evidence exists that 'hypnotic suggestions directly modify the passage of sensory impulses from the periphery into the brain'. He further states that 'induction of hypnosis in fact involves in turn the phenomena of attention, habituation and conditioning, and we have been able to identify neurological mechanisms basically involved in each of these three aspects of behaviour, and therefore in hypnosis'.

PSYCHOLOGICAL THEORIES

Prominent among these are the theory of Pierre Janet that hypnosis is due to a condition of mental dissociation such as might occur in cases of 'multiple personality' and the idea of a subliminal consciousness which is associated with F. W. Myers. This latter is not unlike the theory held by Braid in his later years, for he too came to believe that a different level of consciousness existed, and that the operation of this part of the self could be held to explain at least some of the phenomena of hypnosis. Such ideas are much more acceptable now than they were before Freud's work became well-known.

As mentioned in the previous chapter, the Nancy school, led by Liébeault and Bernhcim, held the view that most of the phenomena of hypnosis could be attributed to the effects of suggestion. It is to the role of suggestion in the induction and maintenance of the hypnotic state that we now turn our attention.

Suggestion and suggestibility

Every normal human being is suggestible. If this were not so there would not, in all probability, be any commerce, art, or even science. The practice of medicine would also fall to very small proportions. At least one modern profession, advertising, has been built up around this fact of universal suggestibility and appeal has been made to all of the sense organs in an attempt to influence human behaviour. There is no race of mankind which is immune to suggestion and there seems to be little difference in the response of people living in the most varied cultures and in all parts of the world. This has been demonstrated over and over again, so far as the practice of hypnotism is concerned, by workers like Esdaile in India, Liébeault and Bernheim in France, Wetterstrand of Stockholm, Schrenck-Notzing of Germany, Bramwell in London and numerous authorities across the Atlantic, especially in the USA. The sex of the subject also appears to have little bearing on the degree of susceptibility to hypnosis.

It is common knowledge that suggestion is able to influence the emotions; we may be made to feel happy or afraid or depressed according to the type of suggestion which enters the mind. These emotions may also in their turn give rise to disturbances of bodily function such as diarrhoea or frequency of micturition when attending for an important interview or examination. The term 'sick with fear' has passed into our everyday speech, and equally descriptive ones can be found in the speech of other peoples as well.

The Hypnotic State and its Phenomena

There are however factors which tend to increase or diminish the power of suggestion. As an illustration of the former the increased suggestibility of women during pregnancy may be quoted. This has not only been observed by medical practitioners, such as obstetricians, but has even been commented on by patients themselves. Children are also especially susceptible. On the other hand, a decrease in suggestibility may sometimes be found in old people and in certain illnesses. The response to suggestion may also vary according to whether the subject believes or expects it to produce an effect. This state of mind may, in turn, depend upon the acceptance or rejection of a prior suggestion. For example, a physician practising hypnotherapy may be able to induce a state of hypnosis quite easily and cure his patient because the latter expects this to happen. This expectation may, however, largely have been brought about by the patient hearing stories of the wonderful cures wrought by the doctor. In many instances patients have been relieved of their symptoms by suggestions given without the aid of hypnosis provided they were acceptable and were given by an individual with the requisite authority and prestige.

Closely allied to belief and expectation is the power of the imagination in rendering an individual susceptible to suggestion. If a person is told to walk in a straight line across the floor of a room he will probably do so quite easily, but if he attempts to walk along a plank of wood one foot wide several feet up in the air, he may begin to wobble and lose his balance. Moreover, the more he struggles to exert his will-power to prevent himself from falling, the more unstable he will become. It is observations such as these which have led workers in hypnosis to declare that satisfactory suggestion and the induction of the hypnotic state has nothing whatever to do with the weakness of a subject's will-power, but rather depends on the ability of the operator skillfully to manipulate the imagination.

In the light of a vast accumulation of clinical and experimental evidence extending over more than 150 years, it can now be stated with a considerable degree of assurance that the persons who respond best to suggestive influences are normal people endowed with good mental and physical health. In fact, one might almost say that a test of 'normality' could be the ability of an individual to show some sort of positive response to hypnotic suggestion. Suggestibility must not of course be confused with gullibility. Those who have tried to hypnotize the insane and mental defectives have found that in practically every case it has been impossible to influence mental defectives and the same difficulty may arise with certain types of insanity. Bramwell (1930), who had a wealth of clinical experience in this matter, stated 50 years ago that his most refractory patients were those who had some form of mental disturbance.

It has been suggested by Milton Kline and others that the need to hypnotize patients will become less and less frequent as the barriers between doctor and the patient are removed. There is a fundamental truth behind this idea for, to a certain extent, it seems that present day hypnotic techniques have replaced the older doctor-patient relationship. The modern trend has been to debunk the physician in the eyes of the public, so that he no longer has the prestige of former days. As a result the intangible, yet sometimes all-important, healing properties of the doctor's presence, and his very words and manner, have lost much of their effect.

A dramatic historical instance of the hypnotic effect of a personality upon his audience can be seen in the way in which Maximilien Robespierre affected the members of the Paris Convention during the days of The Terror. It is said that the insignificant-looking Robespierre had only to turn his myopic eyes in the direction of the members of the Convention in order to reduce that body to a condition of servile compliance with his wishes. Great fear, like great love, will sometimes give rise to certain psychosomatic phenomena clinically indistinguishable from those produced by the most powerful hypnotic suggestion.

THE PHENOMENA OF HYPNOSIS

The hypnotic state is now believed to occur in varying degrees according to whether the subject is only lightly or more deeply affected. There have been numerous attempts to classify the 'stages' of hypnosis, but all of them must to some extent be artificial and arbitrary in character. Detailed descriptions of the various classifications may be found in the larger textbooks such as the classics of Moll and Bramwell.

In this chapter it will be convenient to consider the hypnotic state as divisible into light, medium and deep or somnambulistic stages and then to discuss the phenomena which occur at each level. It should always be kept in mind that these are arbitrary divisions and that many of the phenomena overlap from one stage to another and some may be completely absent in certain subjects.

LIGHT STAGE

The following phenomena may be expected to occur: a feeling of drowsiness and heaviness of the eyes and limbs (referred to be some as the 'hypnoidal stage'), inhibition of the swallowing reflex, and other muscular changes such as an inability to make certain voluntary movements. This last can be obtained in some subjects who are otherwise perfectly wide awake and experience no drowsiness at all. About 40% of people are able to enter this stage without difficulty.

MEDIUM STAGE

Here the feeling of drowsiness may be more marked and the changes involving the voluntary muscles much more noticeable. One of the most striking phenomena is catalepsy; a limb may be made perfectly rigid by suggestion and held for a long time in a given position without apparent effort or fatigue. Cases have been reported in which limbs have remained in fixed positions for hours on end, with no discomfort to the hypnotized subject. Not only may an arm or a leg be thus affected, but the process can be extended to other muscles of the body; in extreme cases the subject's whole body can be made so rigid that he can be supported quite well by supports placed only under his head and his heels, just as if he were a plank of wood. When a limb rendered cataleptic does finally return to its original position it does so slowly and gently, without any trembling or irregularity.

Another curious phenomenon is what is known as *flexibilitas cerea* (waxy flexibility). In this condition a limb may be moulded into certain rather bizarre positions at the joints because of the great increase in relaxation of the surrounding muscles. There is also an apparent increase in the strength of some muscles. This may be because any conscious restraint normally imposed upon muscular activity is removed during hypnosis so that the muscles are able to contract with their full force and to the maximum extent.

Certain sensory changes may be produced as well. Sensations of warmth and cold, heaviness and lightness, and paraesthesiae of all kinds may occur. Good surface analgesia and anaesthesia is often obtained; this may be of use to the surgeon or dentist.

Simple post-hypnotic suggestions may sometimes be given to good effect in this stage. These are suggestions which, although given during the hypnotic state, are intended to take effect *after* the subject returns to normal consciousness. They are frequently of considerable therapeutic importance. Some of their uses will be discussed in later chapters. About 35% of all subjects can enter the medium stage of hypnosis with ease.

DEEP STAGE (SOMNAMBULISM)

Although some authorities would put somnambulism into a class by itself, it will be regarded here as the end stage which is reached when the hypnotic process is deepened to the maximum extent possible. The state reached is usually considered to be identical with that occurring during 'sleep-walking'. During deep hypnosis all the phenomena already mentioned may be present, although usually to a greater degree. In addition, other characteristics and important effects occur; amnesia of events during hypnosis, recall of previously buried memories, regression to childhood, sensory hallucinations etc. These phenomena will now be considered one at a time.

Amnesia of events during hypnosis

This is usually complete in somnambulism, but the events may be recalled during subsequent hypnosis or the subject may be told to remember them in the course of the normal waking state. With very deep hypnotic states, however (the 'hypnotic coma' of Braid), it may be impossible to recover any memories of what has passed during the trance.

Recall of buried memories

A deeply hypnotized subject may be enabled to recall past events which have long been forgotten. This recall of buried memories may take place either during hypnosis or afterwards. It is of particular value to the physician treating functional disorders and psychoneuroses, for it is by this method that repressed material can be found in the deeper levels of the mind. This discovery led Freud to his concept of the subconscious and unconscious mind and eventually to the elaborate structure of psychoanalysis.

Occasionally there is considerable reluctance on the part of a patient to recall certain events which are distasteful to him. In order to overcome this difficulty Meares (1957) evolved an ingenious method of getting the patient to express the material in pictographic form. The patient is given a paint brush and told to paint whatever is in his mind on to a blank sheet of paper. This technique has proved of considerable diagnostic value, but resistance may still be present in some cases. Care is also needed in the interpretation of these paintings: as Ainslie Meares himself has emphasized, the symbols used by patients should not be hastily assumed to be of orthodox Freudian significance. A good deal of symbolism is highly personal to the patient himself and its meaning can be discovered only by reference to the individual who produces it.

Age regression

Closely allied to the recall of buried memories is the phenomenon of age regression. In the somnambulistic state it is possible to take the subject back step by step to earlier periods in his life. He seems able to re-experience or re-live former patterns and habits of his life and even, some-times, to act as if he were again an infant a few months old. In the course of experiments connected with age regression it has been found that not only does the subject act as if he were at the age suggested, but physiological reflexes appropriate to the period occur. For example, an extensor plantar response has appeared in adults regressed to the age of less than one year and the sucking reflex has also been revived in similar circumstances. Other confirmation of the reality of the experiences of age regression comes from the work of Kline (1960). He was able to demonstrate by means of the polygraph that there was no deception on the part of subjects who were regressed and questioned rigorously about their experiences.

Sometimes this phenomenon may be of great value in the treatment of psychosomatic illness. It is possible with some patients not only to trace the onset of certain disorders such as asthma but also to make them abreact* the experiences connected with the first appearance of the disease. It is then possible for the skilled hypnotherapist to reintegrate any distressing episodes into the main current of his patient's personality and then to couple this with 're-education' so that the symptom ceases to have any function and therefore disappears.

Some interesting, although highly controversial, work on age regression has been carried out by Kelsey (1953), who believes that memories relating to the trauma of birth, or even earlier, may sometimes be recovered during states of deep hypnosis. The idea that the mind receives impressions from a very early age indeed is not an entirely new one, in fact it has found philosophical expression on numerous occasions. John Locke in his famous *Essay Concerning the Human Understanding*, published in 1690, likened the mind of a newly born baby at the moment of birth to a blank sheet of paper upon which nothing was registered, but it is doubtful if the majority of modern philosophical thinkers hold the view that a newly born infant's mind is entirely devoid of any kind of sensory experience. The real truth of the matter is that the point at which mind emerges is still as completely wrapped in mystery today as it ever was in the past. In matters such as this which affect the very fundamentals of the self we can still only echo the words of St Paul; 'Now we see through a glass, darkly' (*I Corinthians* 13 v. 12).

---

*'Abreact', from the German word *'Abreagierung'*, coined by Freud and meaning 'to act out' or 'work off' something by re-living it in speech and feeling.

Although the validity of age regression as a phenomenon of the hypnotic state seems to be accepted by most workers in this field there are those who remain critical and sceptical. Barber, for example, believes that age regression can be produced as well in non-hypnotised as in hypnotised subjects. This view is at variance with the results obtained from certain other recent trials: Fellows and Creamer (1978) state that in their own experiments subjects of high hypnotic susceptibility produced better age regression than subjects of low susceptibility who were given appropriate 'motivational instructions'.

An interesting case of possible age regression was once encountered by one of the authors (G.N.). A somnambulist was regressed step by step from the age of twenty-one years down to an age between four and five. At the various age levels the subject was asked to write her name. When she was once again in her normal state of mind, she was asked to write her name as she thought she would have written it at these same age levels. On comparing the two sets of signatures there was considerable variation in style between corresponding groups, which may imply that in the first group she wrote her name while undergoing the experience of being the age which was suggested, while in the second the signature was no more than what might be expected of someone trying to simulate the greater immaturity to be found in the writing of a younger person. The phenomena of age regression may, in many instances, amount to no more than the recall of buried memories; this particular case may be one which illustrates to a high degree the faculty of hyperamnesia brought about by hypnosis in a subject who still remained psychologically an adult.

Sensory hallucinations

All the senses may be hallucinated during somnambulism. Hallucinations may appear during the course of hypnosis or be delayed until it is terminated and then occur in response to a post-hypnotic suggestion. Both positive and negative hallucinations may be produced but if the latter is suggested — the subject may be told, for instance, that he will not be able to see a certain object — it has been shown that first of all he must be able to recognize it so that the negative suggestion can then take effect.

Rapport

This is a peculiar condition which is present in the deeper hypnotic states. The hypnotized subject appears to be oblivious to the commands of everybody but the hypnotist and will obey only him. This condition of rapport is however transferable and may be transferred by the hypnotist to any other individual whom the subject is likely to trust. This is of some importance in medicine. A case history involving such a transfer is given on p. 192.

Increase in accuracy of time sense

Some remarkable experiments carried out by Bramwell, and later confirmed by other investigators, have demonstrated the uncanny accuracy in timing with which some somnambulists can carry out post-hypnotic suggestions. Weeks or even months have sometimes elapsed before the sugestion was put into effect and then it was often executed to the minute. There is apparently no calculation, subconscious or otherwise, in the subject's mind, but the act is performed as the result of an almost irresistible urge which has the force of an obsession. From this it is clear that great care should always be taken when giving post-hypnotic suggestions and none should be made which may be difficult to fulfil.

Post-hypnotic suggestion

The effects produced by post-hypnotic suggestions are usually more dramatic if they are given during deep hypnosis. The subject then has associated amnesia and is rarely able to remember the true reason for the performance of the actions which are due to the suggestion. If asked why he did such a thing he will nearly always rationalize and give anything but the correct explanation. Suppose, for example, a somnambulist is told that he will remove his left shoe ten minutes after 'he wakes up'. He may say, when questioned as to his reason for so doing, that his foot hurt because of a painful bunion when in fact none exists.

OTHER PHYSIOLOGICAL CHANGES

Apart from a possible alteration in the direct current output from the body the hypnotic state itself is not productive of any change in physiological function. In this respect it again differs from sleep. The various phenomena which have been mentioned are solely the result of suggestion. They are more dramatic and effective than if given during normal wakefulness merely because of the hypnotic state. The method of induction may, itself, play a significant part. If 'sleep' suggestions are given for example, we may expect to find evidence of drowsiness or lethargy. Whether the induction is verbal, by fixed gazing, or by any other method, it is inevitable that some suggestion must be present. How the suggestion is interpreted by the subject's own mind is, of course, a personal matter, so that physiological manifestations accompanying the hypnotic state may vary from individual to individual.

There are two possible ways of effecting chemical and physiological changes during hypnosis, by direct suggestion and through emotional stimulation. A few typical examples follow of the results obtained by the use of each method.

DIRECT SUGGESTION

Experiments have shown that it is possible to increase *metabolic activity* and *pulmonary ventilation* by giving resting subjects suggestions of work; conversely, these rates may be diminished in subjects who are lifting weights if suggestions are given that the weights have become lighter. The *respiration rate* and the *acid-base balance* have also been altered by direct suggestions to breathe slowly or rapidly. Cohen and Cobb (1939) report that a case of hysterical hyperventilation was cured by a direct hypnotic suggestion to breathe normally.

Sensations of heat and even *blister formation* may be obtained in some subjects. The former is fairly common and a well documented case of blister formation has been reported by Hadfield (1917). In his experiment, the appearance of a blister on the subject's arm was suggested and the limb in question was bound up in a sealed bandage. Twenty-four hours later a large inflammatory area appeared at the site indicated.

The effect of hypnotic suggestion on *gastro-intestinal secretions* is interesting and is closely linked with Pavlov's discoveries. If the intake of various kinds of foodstuffs is suggested, it is found that the type and amount of enzyme secretion and the degree of gastric acidity produced are those characteristic of the type of food indicated. Other experiments relating to the inhibition of hunger contractions have clearly demonstrated that under hypnosis such suggestions are much more effective than they would be if given during the normal waking state.

Renal function has also been investigated under hypnosis and workers like Marx (1926) and Völgyesi (1950) have reported that diuresis has been obtained by suggesting an intake of water and also by suggesting the application of heat to one of the kidneys. In these cases the specific gravity of the urine was low, so that it resembled the diluted urine which would normally be excreted following the drinking of a large quantity of fluid.

Theoretically, we would expect only certain physiological functions of the body to be susceptible to modification by hypnotic suggestion. If this were not so, physiological and biochemical chaos would result from the use of indiscriminate suggestions. Experimental confirmation has however been provided by the work of Grassheim and Wittkower (1931) who attempted to reproduce the specific dynamic action of protein by giving their subjects non-protein meals and, at the same time, suggesting that they were consuming foodstuffs composed of protein. In spite of these suggestions the test meals did not give rise to any specific dynamic action. On the other hand a typical specific dynamic action curve resulted if protein meals were given even when the subjects felt definite hunger from accompanying suggestions that they had eaten no food at all.

EMOTIONAL STIMULATION

It is common knowledge that emotional disturbances frequently give rise to physical symptoms. Anger will make a person go red in the face and send up his blood pressure; fear, on the other hand, will result in an abnormal pallor and a cold clammy skin. The effect of suggestion, even in normal consciousness, is often quite marked. During hypnosis a greater effect may be anticipated.

One of the most frequent systems to be affected by emotional disorders is the *cardiovascular*, and a hypnotized subject who is given suggestions of anxiety or anger will show a corresponding increase in the force and rate of the heart beat. This has been verified by ECG. Hypnosis by itself has little if any, effect on blood pressure, but if suggestions aimed at arousing emotions of fear or anger are given a definite rise in pressure will follow, as occurs when similar emotions are experienced in the waking state. Conversely, any psychogenic factors involved in the aetiology of a case of hypertension may be counteracted by suggestions of calm and tranquillity.

The *blood sugar* level has also been altered by hypnotic suggestion having a strong emotional content. Mohr (1925) reported the cure of a case of glycosuria through calming suggestions, while Koster (1951) treated patients with diabetes mellitus by the same method. Koster also reported that in some cases hypnotherapy either abolished the need for insulin or else decreased very considerably the dose required. Conversely, hyperglycaemia and glycosuria have both occurred following suggestions involving stress and anxiety.

The effect of suggestion on the composition of the *gastric juice* was the subject of an experiment by Heilig and Hoff (1925). They first told a group of volunteers that they were eating a certain food with great pleasure and relish, and found that the gastric acidity became increased as a result. When the same subjects were told that they had a marked dislike for the food they were consuming a decrease in gastric acidity occurred. Similar findings have been reported by other investigators.

Another example of a biochemical change resulting from an emotionally charged hypnotic suggestion is the alteration of *abnormal blood calcium* levels. Glaser (1924) describes a case of anxiety neurosis in which the serum calcium was reduced by over 2 mg/dl when suggestions of calmness and relaxation were given. Similar findings have been recorded by other writers.

An interesting confirmation of a traditionally held belief concerns studies on the *secretion of bile*. If suggestions arousing the emotions of fear or anxiety are given the flow of bile is increased. Historically, it was for centuries believed that mental states were closely linked with changes in the bile, and Evans has put forward the interesting suggestion that, because of this, emotional disturbances may be aetiological factors in certain types of cancer. This is based upon the observation that a recognized carcinogen (methylchol-anthrene) is a derivative of human bile and that, according to Woolf and Woolf, alterations in the chemical constitution of bile have been shown to occur following psychological disorders.

Probably one of the most significant papers in this field has been published by Yujiro Ikemi et al. (1959) on the influence of hypnotic suggestion upon the anti-bacterial activity of human blood. They tested this anti-bacterial property against two common micro-organisms, *Staphylococcus aureus* and *Escherichia coli*, before and after hypnotic suggestions of fear. In almost all cases there was a marked reduction in the size of the bacterial colonies obtained on blood culture following these suggestions. A marked increase in the leucocyte count was also obtained after a similar suggestion. If these findings can be substantiated by further experiments they may provide a scientific explanation for the well-known clinical observation that patients severely ill with acute infectious disease have, nevertheless, recovered because of the operation of psychic and emotional factors. It is a matter of common knowledge that when animals fall sick they will often creep away to a place of safety and comparative comfort and remain there passively waiting for recovery, or death. This ability to be calm and passive in the presence of illness seems in many instances to be all that is required in order that the inherent natural healing forces of the organism should take effect. It is something which many of us appear to have largely forgotten, the recovery of which could be facilitated through appropriate hypnorelaxation.

THE ELECTRO-ENCEPHALOGRAM

The findings of the EEG are of considerable importance in helping us to arrive at any proper understanding of the hypnotic state. The EEG wave pattern in hypnosis does not have the characteristics of that in ordinary sleep but is usually indistinguishable from that of the normal waking state, even when induction is achieved by the method of 'talking sleep'. All that we can conclude is that the condition is a state of 'altered consciousness'.

Barker and Burgwin (1949) during the course of their experiments found that if a subject already hypnotized was given strong suggestions of relaxation, sleep, and loss of sensory contact with his surroundings, 'sleep' patterns could be obtained on the EEG. The alpha waves, normally present during consciousness, could be made to disappear or diminish in amplitude and frequency. In some cases continued suggestions of sleep, coupled with repeated suggestions that a subject would become drowsy and less and less aware of his environment, were sufficient to bring about normal sleep, thereby terminating the hypnotic state. Similar results have been reported by other authors.

Most EEG studies of hypnosis have been inconclusive. Sometimes the hypnotic condition gave rise to EEG tracings with theta waves resembling those found in a light sleep, while in others no change was noticed. Such conflicting reports seem to indicate that the psychological state we term 'hypnosis' is not a static one but is one which is dynamic and capable of fluctuation. This would explain the variations in response to treatment which all experienced hypnotherapists encounter. It is very probable that some subjects who are presumed to be hypnotized are in reality merely asleep.

SOME PITFALLS IN THE INDUCTION OF HYPNOSIS

There are a number of factors which may prevent the successful induction of the hypnotic state in persons who might have been expected to be influenced. These factors will now be considered in relation to the hypnotist, the subject and the environment.

THE HYPNOTIST

Although all hypnotic phenomena are now recognized to be subjective in character and not to depend upon any magical powers possessed by the hypnotist, his personality does matter a great deal in the successful induction of hypnosis and in the treatment of patients. The doctor who intends to practise hypnotherapy must first of all be adaptable and possess considerable confidence in his own ability. He must have a good practical knowledge of medicine, not only as a science but also as an art in its application to the needs of human beings. He should be patient and show a sympathetic understanding of the problems of his subject. He must be able to assess fairly accurately the personality of the subject. He must also, in the majority of instances, avoid any appearance of being domineering, for most of his patients will respond better if they are 'led' rather than 'pushed'. An authoritarian attitude may sometimes be highly successful in the induction of hypnosis but for medical purposes the right approach is usually along much more gentle lines. This does not mean that the physician does not need authority. In the vast majority of cases this and prestige are required, but they are not to be displayed in a flamboyant or domineering manner; rather should they appear as deep reserves of psychic power which are felt more than seen and which can always be called upon when necessary.

In addition, the medical hypnotist must not be easily disconcerted. If any particular suggestion is not obeyed by his patient he must not become discouraged or he will 'lose face'. He also needs to have considerable enthusiasm for his work; a lack of interest is soon detected by his patients. The successful practice of hypnotherapy also demands a good deal of hard work. Satisfactory treatment by verbal suggestion does not depend upon merely talking to the patient, as Krafft-Ebing pointed out many years ago. Many intangible, yet vital, factors which accompany the spoken word also exert much influence and may make or mar attempts at successful hypnosis.

Medicine is an exacting taskmaster and in no branch is this more apparent than in the practice of hypnotherapy. The medical hypnotist needs to be physically and mentally fit if he is to be of real use to his patients. The practitioner who is ill or tired is in no position to treat successfully those who come to him for help. Indeed, he may very likely make his patients worse rather than better if he undertakes treatment under such circumstances, for during hypnotherapy it is as easy to convey negative suggestions, such as doubt and disbelief, as it is to convey positive ones of confidence and well-being. Hesitancy, doubt and indifference on the part of the doctor may be unwittingly communicated to his patient. The physician's words and suggestions then lose their force and therapeutic value, and the patient may be in danger of becoming more entrenched in his symptoms than ever. It is not unknown for hypnotherapists to give up the practice of their profession because they have lost the exuberant confidence they possessed in their younger days and yet provided their health is good and their interest remains there is no reason why such a situation should arise. When one has seen the undoubted benefits obtained from medical hypnosis over a number of years it is possible to marvel at the latent healing powers residing in psychological forces, rather than be depressed at any failures of the method.

Although no doctor who is interested in the subject need fear that he will not make a good hypnotherapist, it is possible that the modern training of medical students may be a barrier to the success of treatment by suggestion. The explanation of this lies in the application of the 'scientific method' to the teaching and practice of medicine. If our minds are trained to believe in a narrow and rigid relationship of cause and effect it is possible that we may be handicapped when dealing with the principles of suggestion. For example, let us take the common method of inducing hypnosis by verbal suggestion. The hypnotist may give suggestions such as the following: 'Your eyes are getting heavier . . . you are feeling sleepy and drowsy . . . your arm feels heavier . . .' etc. At the same time as he utters these words he may have other thoughts in his mind: 'My patient is not at all tired, therefore why should he feel sleepy or his eyes feel heavy. He has no neurological disease, so why should his arm feel any different? ' If such an ambivalent attitude is present in the hypnotherapist, this may be transferred to the patient. The good hypnotist, when he makes his suggestions, expects them to be acted upon but is not disconcerted if they are not. In a scientific sense it is like 'putting the cart before the horse'.

It is also possible that with some patients the medical hypnotist may secure better results if he himself has had some experience of entering the hypnotic state. This is simply because he may then be in a more favourable position to interpret clearly to his patients the subjective feelings and sensations which accompany the induction of hypnosis.

Last, but by no means least, practical experience is as invaluable to the hypnotherapist as it is in every other branch of medicine.

THE SUBJECT

Just as psychological factors related to the hypnotist may determine the success or failure of hypnotherapeutic measures, so may similar considerations relating to the subject. For the purpose of medical hypnosis it is nearly always essential that the patient should be free from apprehension concerning this method of treatment. He should be able to feel that the doctor can be trusted implicitly and that no possible harm can result. If he has any misgivings about the normality or morality of hypnosis or is afraid that he will be under the control of the hypnotist his objections should be met as far as possible by a reasoned and patient explanation. He must be reassured that the submission to hypnosis is an entirely voluntary act on his part and that he does not lose his own free will as a result of so doing. The patient's own viewpoint should never be overridden in a rough-shod manner but should receive sympathetic consideration. An ideal relationship is that of doctor-patient combined with the roles of teacher-pupil. If the medical practitioner is willing thus to adapt himself it will be found that in the vast majority of cases any fears on the part of his patient will soon be overcome.

Nevertheless, with highly nervous patients, it may sometimes be advisable to administer a short-acting sedative shortly before the induction of hypnosis is attempted: 2 milligrams of diazepam could be given about half an hour previously. In the most refractory cases where there is a good deal of resistance to the usual techniques of induction the patient may be given a small intravenous dose of a suitable hypnotic. This method, which was first introduced by Horsley, has often proved effective in cases which would otherwise have proved extremely resistant. From time to time other drugs, like chloroform and heroin, have been reported as possessing hypnotic effects.

THE ENVIRONMENT

This also is important. The ideal is a quiet, restful room with a comfortable armchair and couch. The environment should be so arranged that it produces the maximum possible degree of mental relaxation. The colouring of the surroundings should be restful and there ought to be no distracting noises. Care must also be taken to avoid draughts and any degree of heat or cold which is liable to cause discomfort. Before attempting the induction of hypnosis, enquire of the patient whether or not he is quite comfortable. Even such apparently trivial details as a tight collar or some slight irregularity in the back of an armchair may be quite sufficient to nullify all attempts at inducing the hypnotic state. It should be remembered that the patient's mind frequently becomes much more aware of such things at first, so that they exert a disturbing effect seemingly out of all proportion to their importance.

Another factor which must be taken into account is whether or not to permit the presence of a third party in the room at the time treatment is being carried out. As a rule most patients prefer not to have anyone else present, but it is advisable to find out beforehand what their wishes are and to conform to them whenever possible.

BIBLIOGRAPHY

BARBER, T. X. (1962) Hypnotic age regression: a critical review. *Psychosom. Med., 24*, 286-299.

BARBER, T. X. & CALVERLEY, D. S. (1966) Effects on recall of hypnotic induction, motivational suggestions and suggested regression: a methodological and experimental analysis. *J. abnorm. soc. Psychol., 71*, 169-180.

BARKER, W. & BURGWIN, W. (1949) Brain wave patterns during hypnosis, hypnotic sleep and normal sleep. *Archs. Neurol. Psychiat., 62*, 412.

BRAMWELL, J. M. (1930) *Hypnotism, its History, Practice and Theory*, 3rd ed., pp. 66, 114-39. London: Rider.

CHERTOK, L. & KRAMARZ, P. (1955) Hypnose et électro-encephalographie, la semaine des Hôpitaux de Paris. *Path. Biol., Paris, 31*, 5.

COHEN, M. E. & COBB, S. (1939) The use of hypnosis in the study of the acid base balance of the blood in a patient with hysterical hyperventilation. In: *The Inter-relationship of Mind and Body, Res. Publs. Ass. Res. nerv. ment. Dis., XIX*, 318.

EVANS, Griffith (1930) Resonance in Christian healing. In: *New Horizons of Healing*, ed. W. Wood. Worcester: Arthur James.

FELLOWS, B. J. & CREAMER, M. (1978) An investigation of the role of 'hypnosis', hypnotic susceptibility and hypnotic induction in the production of age regression. *Br. J. soc. clin. Psychol., 17*, 165–171.

FREUD, S. (1924) *Collected Papers*. London: Hogarth Press.

GIDRO-FRANK, L. & BOWERS BUCH, M. K. (1948) A study of the plantar response in hypnotic age regression. *J. nerv. ment. Dis., 107*, 443.

GLASER, F. (1924) Psychische Beeinflussung des Blutserumkalkspiegels. *Klin. Wschr., 3*, 1492.

GRASSHEIM, K. & WITTKOWER, E. (1931) Suggestive modifications of the specific dynamic action of protein. *Dt. med. Wschr., 57*, 141.

HADFIELD, J. A. (1917) The influence of hypnotic suggestion on inflammatory conditions. *Lancet, 2*, 678.

HEILIG, R. & HOFF, H. (1925) Beiträge zur hypnotischen Beeinflussung der Magenfunktion. *Medsche Klin., 162*.

HERNÁNDEZ-PEÓN, R. & DONOSO, M. (1957) Influence of attention and suggestion upon subcortical evoked electrical activity in the human brain. *Proc. 1st Internat. Congress. Neurol. Sci. Brussels, 3*, 385-396.

IKEMI, Y., AKAGI, M., MAEDA, J., FUKUMOTO, T., KAWATE, K., HIRAKAWA, K., GONDO, S., NAKAGAWA, T., HONDA, T., SAKAMOTO, A. & KUMAGAI, M., (1959) Hypnotic experiments on the psychosomatic aspects of gastro-intestinal disorders. *Int. J. clin. exp. Hypnosis, 7*, 3.

KELSEY, D. (1953) Phantasies of birth and prenatal experiences recovered from patients undergoing hypnoanalysis. *J. ment. Sci., 99*, 415.

KLINE, Milton, V. (1960) Hypnotic age regression. *Int. J. clin. exp. Hypnosis, 8*, 1.

KOSTER, S. Sept. 6th, 1951. Paper read before the International Congress for Psychotherapeutics at Leiden.

MARCUSE, F. L. (1959) *Hypnosis – Fact and Fiction*. Harmondsworth: Penguin.

MARX, H. (1926) Untersuchungen über den Wasserhaushalt. 2: Mitteilung. Die psychische Beeinflussung des Wasserhaushaltes. *Klin. Wschr., 5*, 92.

MEARES, Ainslie (1957) *Hypnography – A Study of the Therapeutic Use of Hypnotic Painting*. Springfield, Ill.: Charles C. Thomas.

MOHR, F. (1925) *Psychophysische Behandlungsmethoden*. Leipzig: Hirzel.

MYERS, F. W. H. (1887) The subliminal consciousness. *Proc. Soc. psych. Res., 7*, 298.

ORNE, M. T. (1970) Hypnosis, state or role. In: *Hypnose und Psychosomatische Medizin: vortrage vom Funften Internationalen Kongress für Hypnose und Psychosomatische Medizin; Mainz*, 22–23. Stuttgart: Hippokrates Verlag.

VÖLGYESI, F. A. (1950) *Hypnostherapie und Psychosomatische Probleme*. Stuttgart: Hippokrates.

VÖLGYESI, F. A. (1963) *Menschen- und Tierhypnose*. Zurich: Orell Fussli. (Eng. trans. 1966 *Hypnosis in Man and Animals*. London: Baillière, Tindall & Cassell.)

WAGSTAFF, G. F. (1977) Post-hypnotic amnesia as disrupted retrieval: a role-playing paradigm. *Quart. J. exp. Psychol., 29*, 499–500.

WYKE, B. D. (1960) Neurological mechanisms in hypnosis. Some recent advances in the study of hypnotic phenomena. *Proc. dent. med. Soc. Hypnosis*.

CHAPTER 4

THE INDUCTION OF HYPNOSIS

Before describing a few of the most widely used techniques of induction, let us consider a few practical points of general application.

In the first place the medical hypnotist should not restrict himself rigidly to any one particular technique, although he may discover that one method of approach usually gives him better results than others. If so, there is no reason why he should not make this his principal one and use alternative methods should the personality of any particular patient seem to require something different.

Secondly, patients should never be told, either directly or indirectly, that they are not good hypnotic subjects. Even should one hypnotist fail to elicit a response from a patient another practitioner may easily succeed. Furthermore, it is impossible to tell how many attempts may be required before a good response is obtained. Vogt of Berlin is reported to have obtained somnambulism in two of his cases only after 500 and 700 attempts respectively. For practical purposes, however, most practitioners would probably be on fairly safe ground if they made four or five attempts before deciding to discontinue their efforts. This opinion is by no means a universal one, and authorities like Forel and Moll have emphasized that many more attempts than this might be necessary in refractory cases.

Thirdly, the medical hypnotist should be very careful in his method of trying to assess the depth of hypnosis achieved. He should avoid direct enquiry for fear of implanting a negative suggestion into the subject's mind in case the desired response may not have been obtained. He should not, for instance, say 'Did you feel the prick of the pin?' after a suggestion of analgesia. If the area of skin involved is not entirely analgesic such a question may raise doubts in the subject's mind. If it is essential to ask him for this information it is usually better to say 'Will you let me know when the pin begins to feel blunt?'. The practitioner should also watch his patient closely the whole time, for then he may gain from the reactions of the latter the knowledge which he seeks without the necessity of having to ask for it. Any desirable information concerning the depth of hypnosis should be obtained in a tactful roundabout way so that the possibility of arousing counter-suggestions is reduced to a minimum. For most medical purposes a rigid measurement of depth is not necessary. It must also be remembered that depth frequently depends upon a proper conditioning of the patient, so that a number of sessions may be required to reach a medium or deep stage. In this respect it resembles the induction in certain subjects where a number of attempts may be required before the smallest degree of hypnosis is achieved.

A common question about the induction of the hypnotic state is 'Should a patient be told he is submitting to hypnosis if he does not already realize it?'. Generally speaking if the patient is at all nervous about the matter, it is better to say that the treatment is designed to help him relax more completely so that by co-operating fully with the doctor he may recover from his illness. One of the difficulties which the medical hypnotist has to overcome is the popular view that hypnotism is something sinister and makes a person completely subservient to the will of another. It should be explained to the patient that he has within himself the power to get better and that the doctor is merely the instrument for enabling that power to be mobilized.

The idea should be conveyed to the patient — by the demeanour and speech of the practitioner and by the environment — that hypnosis is essentially a pleasurable experience. The medical hypnotist should always study the effect of gesture and manner of speaking when trying to induce the hypnotic state. Success may sometimes depend upon the tone of voice or the way in which words are spoken rather than upon the actual words themselves. It is this personal factor which makes mechanical aids, such as gramophone records, largely out of place in the practice of medical hypnotism, although the first of the methods of induction about to be described does make use of certain physical contrivances in the initial phases. Nevertheless, it may on occasions be an advantage to have records of soothing music played softly in the background, to lull any apprehension of the patient rather than as a stimulant to his emotions. For this purpose music has been employed by many hypnotherapists from the time of Mesmer onwards. In previous centuries the importance of music in the healing art had already been recognized by the priest-physicians of ancient civilizations.

PHYSICAL METHODS

These consist essentially of monotonous stimulation of one or other of the organs of special sense. Those commonly used are sight, hearing and touch.

The method of inducing hypnosis through sight is by getting the subject to gaze steadily at a light or a bright object for a few minutes. This light or object is placed in such a manner that looking at it places a slight strain upon the eyes, which are compelled to turn in a slightly upward direction. In some cases, after a time varying from about thirty seconds to a few minutes, the subject's eyes will become rather misty and tired and the lids begin to flicker and close. It is important that they do not become too strained, and at the first indication that they are becoming tired and are about to close the hypnotist can sometimes help matters by telling the subject to shut his eyes and then giving suggestions of heaviness and sleep. This method of fixed gazing at a bright object was first used by Braid and is sometimes called 'Braidism'. Care should be taken to avoid this technique in patients who suffer from migraine or headaches due to 'eye-strain'.

Other physical methods which have from time to time been employed are monotonous sounds such as the ticking of a clock or a metronome, galvanism, and the rhythmic stimulation of cutaneous nerves by repeated passes made up and down the body. This last was frequently resorted to by Esdaile and his hospital orderlies as a means of producing hypnotic anaesthesia in his patients prior to operation.

Although physical methods have often been resorted to in the practice of hypnotism, it is difficult to be certain what proportion of the successful results obtained have in fact been due to an element of suggestion. Even Braid later came to regard all physical methods merely as forms of indirect suggestion. Some authorities are of the opinion, however, that certain methods of sensory stimulation, such as monotonous passes down the body, stroking the head, or gentle pressure on the forehead, may *themselves* produce a hypnotic condition in the absence of any kind of suggestion.

PSYCHOLOGICAL METHODS

Verbal suggestion may be used alone or combined with physiological methods in order to obtain a heightened effect. Since some variation of these methods is met in practice, the procedure of one of them will be described in some detail.

The patient is first of all given a suggestibility test. He may be told to stand up straight with his feet pressed tightly together and with his head tilted slightly backwards; then he is told to close his eyes. The hypnotist then notes whether, after a few seconds or so, there is any tendency to fall backwards or to wobble. If there is, the patient is instructed to sit down comfortably in an armchair; if there is not, suggestions of falling backwards are given and the patient may also be asked to imagine that he is standing high in the air on a narrow plank. The hypnotist may also place his hands lightly across the subject's shoulders and say that when he removes their supporting influence the latter will begin to topple backwards. In the vast majority of instances there will be a positive response to this test of suggestibility — with or without the addition of active verbal suggestion — and the patient is then ready for an attempt at the actual induction of hypnosis.

As the essence of successful hypnotic induction lies, to a great extent, in the ability of the operator to manipulate the imagination of his subject, it may be useful to make a point of finding out beforehand something about the profession or occupation of the subject. One of the authors, for instance, can recall trying the 'falling test' on a professional soldier and meeting with complete failure.

Instead of using the 'falling test', the subject may be told to clasp his hands together and then given firm and rapid suggestions that he will be unable to undo them. Initially this may be combined with firm but gentle pressure of the hypnotist's own hands so as to reinforce the impression made on the subject's mind that his hands are indeed tightly clasped and his fingers so locked together that he cannot release them.

Other tests which are commonly used are the Rorschach inkblot test and the odour-suggestion test. In the former the subject is told that some people think the inkblot resembles such-and-such an object, and the hypnotist names one or two of the most common responses. He then mentions other objects which, for most people, would bear no resemblance at all to the shape of the blot and asks the subject if he can also see these objects in the inkblot. If the subject is very suggestible he will probably accept these ideas with little or no resistance.

In the odour-suggestion test, a number of identical opaque bottles containing various perfumes appropriately labelled are given to the subject to smell. He is then presented with a similar number of identical bottles, all of which contain only water, but which are again labelled differently. Once more he is told to smell the contents. The degree of suggestibility is determined by the number of odours which he claims to detect in the second group of bottles.

The Induction of Hypnosis

If a positive response to these, or any similar tests, is obtained, the patient is then told to sit down comfortably in the armchair with his hands loose in his lap and his eyes closed, and to commence rhythmic breathing. As he breathes he is told that he will feel his eyelids become heavier and his arms begin to feel more relaxed. After a few minutes he is given further suggestions that as the regular breathing is continued he will feel himself becoming drowsy and, at the same time, more and more relaxed. He is also told that he will become less and less concerned with things other than the voice of the hypnotherapist which he will still hear quite distinctly. Suggestions of sleepiness and relaxation are continued in a persuasive but rather monotonous tone of voice until it is apparent that the patient is indeed in a drowsy condition and shows evidence of bodily relaxation.

At this point it is possible to commence the treatment of most types of functional disorders, for the patient's mind is then in a sufficiently receptive condition. Some forms of the psychoneuroses may also be treated successfully at this stage, and Chapter 6 contains case histories illustrating the details of treatment.

Although the induction of hypnosis is here described as following a suggestibility test it should be stated that many hypnotherapists omit such tests entirely and commence with suggestions of relaxation while the patient is sitting in the chair or reclining on the couch. Sometimes the patient may be asked to stare into the eyes of the physician or at a small light, for a minute or so, just to fix his attention while the preliminary suggestions are given. He is then told to close his eyes and to commence regular breathing. When suggestions are given of physical changes such as drowsiness, numbness and relaxation, it is important to allow sufficient time for these to occur. This applies especially to subjects hypnotized for the first time. Later, as they become more accustomed to entering the hypnotic state, these physiological changes take place more rapidly. If the person can achieve somnambulism the whole process is speeded up and more dramatic changes such as catalepsy and anaesthesia may be produced quickly. It should be emphasized, however, that some somnambules may not enter a deep stage until several attempts have been made.

For the inexperienced hypnotist the following technique of inducing hypnosis by counting has been found very successful: the majority of patients will enter the hypnotic state quite readily by its use. The patient is seated in a comfortable chair and told to look at a light. The room is best darkened but this is not essential. The patient is told, 'Look at the light, steadily but comfortably. Now imagine that all the muscles of your body are becoming relaxed. You now feel yourself sinking deeper and deeper into the chair ... now you begin to feel lovely and sleepy ... sleepy ... You feel you are entering a pleasant, drowsy and dreamy state. Listen to my voice as I speak to you. You are getting more and more sleepy, drowsy and sleepy; now your eyes are beginning to close and you feel yourself becoming more and more relaxed. That's right, close your eyes and listen to me as I count up to ten. I shall count slowly to ten — as I do so you will become more and more sleepy and drowsy ... heavy and sleepy. That's good; now you hear me counting to ten and as I do so you feel yourself becoming more and more sleepy and relaxed ... sleepy ... relaxed. ...'

The hypnotist counts slowly and deliberately from one to ten, preferably making the counting coincide with the patient's inspirations, and, as the number ten is reached, it will often be found valuable to say quite authoritatively 'Now you sleep!'

Needless to say, there are various modifications of the above technique and the reader will learn, as he becomes more experienced, to use several methods of induction so that he can choose the one likely to be most suitable for the needs of his patient.

THE 'CONFUSIONAL' TECHNIQUE

This is reserved for those subjects who, because of a critical mental attitude, are unable to accept suggestions of a straightforward nature. If, for example, it is suggested that the right arm is becoming heavy such an individual may think that there is no reason why it should do so, since nothing has been done to it; the sensation in the right arm therefore remains unchanged. This resistance may be overcome in some subjects by adopting what is known as the 'confusional' technique. Instead of being told 'Your right arm is beginning to feel heavier than the left one' and then leaving it at that, the following suggestion may be given. 'Your right arm is becoming heavier. At the same time your left arm feels lighter and the right foot feels numb. Now your right arm feels lighter still while the left is becoming heavier and heavier and begins to fall. The left hand is also feeling numb and cold. At the same time you notice how warm your left foot is getting, while your right arm is becoming so heavy that you cannot lift it without considerable effort. All this while your left hand continues to feel warmer and warmer and, as it does so, it gets lighter and lighter and begins to lift in the air.'

If suggestions such as these are made for five or ten minutes it will be found that the subject's mind often becomes less critical and more resigned to accepting the desired suggestion. The effort of trying to adopt a critical attitude towards all of the conflicting suggestions proves too much: eventually the line of least resistance is adopted and criticism is suspended.

INDIRECT METHODS

Sometimes, when faced with patients whose minds are forever jumping from one idea to another so that securing their attention for even a brief period is impossible, an indirect approach may succeed. Such a person may be asked to carry out some familiar routine task such as typing a letter, in order that his mind may be directed into a channel where little or no resistance is likely to be encountered. There is then a distinct possibility that an appropriate suggestion will induce a condition of hypnosis.

One of us (G.N.) employed this technique successfully with a highly neurotic secretary who was completely unable to respond to any of the more usual direct methods. The patient was instructed to copy out some business correspondence in Pitman's shorthand just as if she were at work in her office. She was told that what she wrote would be read to check it for accuracy and then, after a trial demonstration, the induction was commenced. This was accomplished by counting slowly from one to twenty and making suggestions of relaxation, sleepiness and eye closure. She was then told that when she felt she was becoming so sleepy that it was impossible to keep her eyes open she could let them close and discontinue writing. By this means a satisfactory depth of trance was achieved in about ten minutes and the rest of the session proceeded without further difficulty. If this technique is going to succeed it usually does so within a short space of time. If it is prolonged there is the possibility that the patient will become so absorbed in what he is doing that external suggestions will pass him by.

The following case illustrates the unintentional induction of hypnosis in a third party (the attendant nurse) while a patient was undergoing hypnotherapy. During treatment of the patient the nurse was engaged in writing up some notes, a task upon which a large part of her conscious mind was concentrated. At the same time she had to be aware of conditions in the clinic so that she could render assistance if required. As the induction proceeded there was a sudden knock on the door and the nurse jumped up from her seat to answer it. Shortly afterwards she complained of a severe headache and a feeling of strangeness and bewilderment, as if things were unreal to her. She also said that the interruption at the door had come as an unpleasant shock to her, but that she had jumped up automatically without wishing to do so. As it seemed fairly certain that she must have unconsciously absorbed some of the suggestions given to the patient, it was proposed to rehypnotize her and remove these symptoms. However, she was reassured that the headaches and other unpleasant sensations would completely disappear. This they did after a few days. Patients have sometimes been successfully hypnotized in this manner without their knowledge or consent when a failure might have been anticipated from a more direct approach. Whether such techniques, deliberately employed, can be justified on ethical or legal grounds is another matter.

ELECTRONIC METHODS

For a long time it has been known that musical sounds of a certain pitch were able to shatter objects such as wine glasses. Indeed one celebrated singer is reported to have been able to do this at will as a kind of party trick by singing the exact note which would produce the effect. This phenomenon presumably depends upon the precise frequency of the musical note. In the field of medicine, sonic or electrical frequencies have been similarly used for the purpose of diagnosis and treatment of disease — medical radiaesthesia is an example.

The flashing of lights at certain frequencies has also been noticed from time to time to produce changes in the mental state, usually towards a condition of somnolence. Kroger and Schneider (1959) have made use of this phenomenon for inducing hypnosis by means of an electronic device which could be set so as to reproduce the frequency, amplitude and waveform of the brain pulse by controlled photic stimulation.

It seems likely that in the future various electronic instruments may be tried out as an aid to hypnotherapy. Such methods are really the modern equivalent of those older ones already mentioned which have now become a part of the history of medicine. The rhythmic passes up and down the body by the mesmerists, the metronome and the swinging pendulum were probably more uncertain in their results than are their newer counterparts which are designed to correspond with what we now know of the physiology of the brain from EEG investigations. On scientific grounds we should expect that if the electrical discharge pattern of the brain during hypnosis can be reproduced by mechanical means a way is open for facilitating induction of the hypnotic state.

DEEPENING THE HYPNOTIC STATE

In most cases the greatest depth is not reached at the first attempt. It has been found by experience that, for most people, the greatest depth is usually attained somewhere between the fourth and the twelfth sessions. In order to deepen the hypnosis, suggestions of increasing drowsiness are made, for up to thirty minutes or so if necessary. Suggestions of muscular and sensory changes, such as catalepsy and analgesia, may be continued concurrently. With some subjects it may be found useful to employ the 'fractional method'; this consists of inducing hypnosis for a short period then waking the subject, then re-inducing hypnosis, repeating the process several times. In this way a deeper state may sometimes be achieved at the end of an hour's session than if a continuous procedure were adopted.

Another useful technique for deepening the primary induction of hypnosis is a modification of the so-called 'Yo-yo' method. It is rather similar to the 'fractional' method just described but the subject is not completely awakened. The procedure is as follows. The patient is made comfortable and the room darkened. He is told to look at a lamp, a light, or any suitable object at some distance from him. The following suggestions are given:'Breathe quietly and regularly; as you breathe begin to feel all your body relax; your arms begin to hang limply and your neck muscles begin to feel very relaxed; now your eyes begin to feel heavy and you feel drowsy, heavy and sleepy – that's good, very good. Now close your eyes and listen carefully. I shall count from one to ten slowly. You will listen very carefully and at ten you will feel more sleepy, heavy and drowsy.' The hypnotist then counts slowly from one to ten. Then, with the patient resting quietly, the hypnotist says something like 'I am now going to count from ten down to one; as I do so you will open your eyes, look over at the light and I will then begin to count from one to ten again – but the next time I do so you will feel much more relaxed, much calmer and more drowsy. As I say ten you will go into a deep, very drowsy, sleep state.'

The hypnotist again counts slowly from one to ten and this manoeuvre is repeated several times. If this technique is successful the hypnotic state is not interrupted during the whole procedure. The patient is also rendered more confident by the use of this method for he is enabled to take a more active part himself in the actual induction of hypnosis.

Whatever the technique employed, however, it is important to tell the subject before 'awakening' him that on the next occasion he will respond even more quickly and readily. This is in the nature of a post-hypnotic suggestion and should be given as a routine.

TERMINATION OF HYPNOSIS

There are several ways of doing this and they vary from blowing on the subject's face to simply telling him to 'wake up'. So long as the subject understands what is required of him it matters little what method is used provided the following points are borne in mind. First of all, before bringing a patient out of the hypnotic state, it is extremely important to remove any abnormal suggestions which may have been given. For example, if sensory or muscular changes have been suggested these should be specifically removed by appropriate counter-suggestion. The patient should also be given general suggestions of fitness and well-being as a routine measure. Secondly, it is desirable to terminate the hypnosis slowly. The majority of patients enjoy the feeling of rest and relaxation which they have experienced and may resent an abrupt ending to this pleasurable sensation. It is therefore best to adopt some formula such as 'I am now going to count three slowly, and as I do so you will wake up. You will feel refreshed and any slight drowsiness which may still be present will rapidly disappear.' If the counting technique has been used as a method of induction it is as well to count in the reverse order when waking the patient. This would tend to eliminate any confusion as to what was expected of him. The same consideration should apply, on theoretical grounds at least, to all methods of inducing and terminating hypnosis: if a particular signal, such as a touch on the hand, is used to bring about the hypnotic state, a different one should be employed for its termination.

In the vast majority of cases the patient will 'wake up' without the slightest difficulty. Very occasionally there may be some reluctance to do so; in such cases the instruction to wake up should be repeated slowly, distinctly and emphatically. If in spite of all efforts the patient still refuses to awaken, there need be no cause for alarm, for if he is left alone the condition will pass into normal sleep from which he will wake up in the usual manner.

SELF-HYPNOSIS AND AUTOGENIC TRAINING

With proper training, a considerable proportion of people become able to induce the hypnotic state themselves without the assistance of a hypnotist. As a rule it is necessary for them to receive instruction in a suitable technique and to undergo hypnosis a few times with the help of an operator. If the same technique is repeated a number of times and the subject has become used to the experience of entering a state of hypnosis, it will

The Induction of Hypnosis

be found that the chances of producing the condition through autosuggestion are quite good. Autohypnosis is particularly useful where the effect is required at some later date, for a visit to the dentist or for a confinement. Persons who through practice become expert in self-hypnosis are then able to give themselves therapeutic suggestions in a wide range of circumstances. Some of the indications most commonly met with are attacks of angina pectoris, palpitations, headaches, functional gastrointestinal disturbances, insomnia, obesity and local pain. As the late Milne Bramwell once stated, the patient is enabled to 'gain increased control over his own organism'.

In the case of somnambules it is often wise to adopt a formula which is not too simple or easy for the induction of self-hypnosis. This is to prevent the subject unwittingly giving himself suggestions which might induce a state of somnambulism at the wrong time or in undesirable circumstances.

In 1959, Schultz and Luthe devised a series of simple exercises accompanied by autosuggestion to induce relaxation. Examples include concentration on a particular limb and the repetition of phrases such as 'my right arm is becoming heavy' or 'My right arm is becoming warm'. Later, similar suggestions can be applied to other parts of the body. These are designed to promote feelings of muscular relaxation and may be aided by concentrating on slow and steady breathing. After each exercise is terminated the patient should give himself appropriate countersuggestions to ensure that he is not left with a feeling of excessive relaxation, drowsiness or heaviness. Schultz and Luthe state that the patient should not exceed one minute or so of passive concentration during the exercise. R. P. Snaith (1974), on the other hand, believes that the duration of a session should be longer — fifteen minutes — since patients may become discouraged if no obvious result is obtained after one or two minutes. He also warns against employing the method in certain circumstances, for example whilst handling dangerous implements or driving a motor vehicle. This is in keeping with the degree of care which is necessary on the part of any hypnotherapist in order to ensure that his patient is not left in a state of mind which could be harmful to him or to others in meeting the contingencies of everyday life.

It would seem that any form of self-hypnosis or autogenic training could have a good deal in common with the practice of certain types of Yoga. For instance Wyke (1960) cites exponents of the Bengal school of Kriya-Yoga who 'place themselves in the classical lotus posture of immobility and then meditate upon a bright light that they imagine to appear at the nasion as a manifestation of the cosmic force called "Kundalin".' He bases this belief on the alterations in brain-wave patterns seen on an EEG.

WAKING HYPNOSIS

A condition of which the medical hypnotist should be aware is that of 'waking hypnosis'. Here there is no drowsiness or any resemblance to normal sleep. The subject is wide awake and conscious of all that goes on around him but may nevertheless exhibit marked hypnotic phenomena such as catalepsy, anaesthesia and functional paralysis. In such cases a hypnotist accustomed to the drowsiness most subjects display might be unaware that his subject is in fact deeply hypnotised.

The doctor should also bear in mind that some individuals may be so suggestible that they enter a deep hypnotic state without any direct attempt being made to hypnotize them. Such occurrences are not infrequent during public exhibitions of hypnotism, especially when there are large numbers of young people present. One of us (G.N.) has seen this happen when giving lecture-demonstrations to audiences composed mainly of students and undergraduates. Erickson (1941) has also reported an interesting case of a girl who was actually hypnotized and treated without her knowledge by the pretense of carrying out treatment on her friend who was present at the same time. Similar indirect techniques have been described by H. Rosen (1951).

DEFENCES AGAINST HYPNOSIS

All experienced hypnotherapists have at times met resistance to the induction of hypnosis on the part of their patients. The most commonly encountered defence mechanisms, in the authors' experience, are restlessness, talking, pretence and normal sleep.

RESTLESSNESS

There may be a general restlessness of the whole body, or merely a twitching of the fingers or movements of the feet or legs. The symptoms are those of anxiety and are most frequently seen if the induction is a gradual one with the emphasis on relaxation. A not uncommon symptom is the development of a nervous cough. The patient will make repeated efforts to clear his throat.

When dealing with such patients a quicker, more dramatic, method of induction may succeed where others have failed. Alternatively, if a particular movement, say twitching of the fingers, has been observed, this may be incorporated in suggestions of hand levitation. The suggestions should be well-timed and, if they are given at the true 'psychological moment', they may very well prove successful.

TALKING

Sometimes, when the induction of hypnosis appears to be proceeding smoothly, the patient will start to talk or ask questions. This is not necessarily a defence mechanism: a question may be prompted by previous inexperience of entering the hypnotic state. If doubts in the patient's mind are allayed by a sympathetic and acceptable answer no further difficulty is usually encountered. However, if the questioning or talking is due to the patient's fear that he is being influenced against his will, or that he is 'going under', then a quicker method may be tried so as to prevent such thoughts from arising in his mind. It may also help if the initial induction is attempted with the patient as a member of a group in order that the reassuring effect of being 'one of a crowd' is present from the start.

PRETENCE OR SIMULATION

Some patients who fear that they will lose their self-control should they allow themselves to be influenced by the suggestions of the hypnotist may pretend to carry out the suggestions. This is done in full consciousness so that any anticipated threat to the subject's ego is thereby averted. As a rule it is easy to recognize this defence mechanism, although it is possible that sometimes the conscious carrying out of a suggestion may really be due to a confusion in the subject's own mind. The authors have observed patients who performed certain suggested muscular movements because they 'thought they ought to do so', or because 'they were trying to help the doctor'.

The clue to the recognition of a true response to hypnotic suggestion lies in the manner in which the muscular movements are performed. Consider arm levitation. If an arm is raised in response to hypnotic suggestion it moves slowly and rather jerkily. Suggestions usually need to be repeated several times. If the action is a simulated one the movement is quicker and smoother and may seem almost to have anticipated the suggestion itself.

This particular kind of defence mechanism may be dealt with either by ignoring it or by making use of the 'confusional technique' already described. If the method of induction is not changed the simulated movements may be allowed to remain but the hypnotherapist should try skilfully to turn them against the subject. This can sometimes be achieved by getting the subject to concentrate his mind more and more on the movement suggested and watching carefully for the effect produced. If this is done it may be found that eventually any movement suggested assumes the character of one performed under true hypnosis.

NORMAL SLEEP

Occasionally, if suggestions unacceptable to the patient are given, he will fall into a state of normal physiological sleep. In this way he can avoid having to experience any inner conflict due to unpleasant ideas implanted in his mind during hypnotherapy. Unless the physician becomes aware of this all his efforts at suggestion will be wasted. If the 'sleep' is really a passive state of hypnosis, the patient will usually respond to a suggestion involving some motor activity such as the raising of his hand or arm. In cases of doubt, therefore, this is the test to employ.

CONCLUSIONS

It should be stressed that there is nothing unethical in trying to overcome psychological resistance to hypnosis, assuming that whenever the hypnotherapist sees any patient, apart from certain emergencies, the latter has already given full and free consent to hypnotic treatment. The doctor will bear in mind the high ethical standards demanded by his profession, and will see to it that he does not betray the trust of his patient. In all attempts to overcome resistance, the sole motivation of such efforts should be a desire to help the sufferer recover from his illness as speedily as possible.

Some patients who have persistent misgivings when being subjected to hypnotic techniques protect themselves either by completely refusing to be influenced by any method or, if they are already hypnotized, by refusing to respond to any suggestion they find objectionable or unacceptable. The surest bulwark against objectionable suggestions is a strong and virile religious faith. This has always been recognized, but further support for this fundamental truth has been dramatically forthcoming in recent years from many who have withstood 'brain-washing' techniques even when subject to marked physical discomfort.

POSSIBLE DANGERS OF HYPNOSIS

Apart from the question of diminished moral responsibility already discussed in Chapter 2, it has been suggested that repeated hypnosis may lead to an excessive liking for the hypnotic state, and that this may be undesirable. It is quite true that many subjects testify to the pleasant feelings of calm and relaxation which occur during hypnosis and occasionally they may be reluctant to terminate the condition. Far from being in any way harmful, use is sometimes made of this pleasurable experience by prolonging it for therapeutic purposes often with very beneficial results. The authors have treated hundreds of cases without the slightest reason to suspect that repeated hypnosis may lead to undesirable effects, and their own experience has been amply confirmed by workers in other countries.

There is considerable evidence to suggest that hypnotherapy in skilled hands is one of the safest procedures in medicine and carries the minimum of risk to the patient, but the physician should nevertheless be on watch for any untoward or unexpected reaction. One of the authors (G.N.) was once confronted with the unexpected occurrence of epileptiform convulsions soon after hypnosis had been induced in a patient. This particular subject had given no personal or family history of epilepsy and was of higher than normal intelligence. In this case, which was originally reported in full to the Society for Clinical and Experimental Hypnosis of New York, one possible explanation of the phenomena was that the patient, who had already in the past received a course of electroconvulsive therapy (ECT), may have unconsciously associated light finger pressure on the forehead with the application of electrodes. It is a matter of historical knowledge that at one time convulsions were not uncommon during the induction of hypnosis and they were widely expected to occur.

Should such phenomena supervene the best thing to do is to deepen the hypnotic state although the natural tendency may be to lighten it and so bring the subject out of the condition. At the same time firm, positive, reassuring suggestions of calmness and relaxation should be given as was done in the case just mentioned. The patient will then almost invariably respond and will be none the worse for his experience, of which he will generally remember nothing.

The practice of hypnotherapy must not be expected to be entirely free from emergency situations although these should be considerably less frequent than in surgery or general medicine. Whenever the unforeseen occurs it is, of course, essential that the doctor should keep control of himself so that his judgment remains unimpaired.

In the past it has been believed, although without good reason, that hypnosis should be avoided in the treatment of psychotic patients or in those with a pre-psychotic personality. Recently, however, Wolberg and other psychiatrists using hypnosis in the United States have testified that in their own experience the employment of hypnotherapy in such cases does not constitute a hazard. It is true that the actual treatment of schizophrenia by hypnosis may be difficult and often unsatisfactory but this is no valid reason why the method should not be tried.

For many years it has been the custom for writers on hypnotherapy to warn against the employment of direct suggestion for the removal of offending symptoms. However, it has become apparent that direct symptom removal is frequently resorted to by practising medical hypnotists, with little apparent harm to the patients. It should, however, be emphasized that the treatment of frank psychiatric conditions, with or without the use of direct suggestion, should be undertaken only by one who has special skill and training in psychological medicine.

For all practitioners there may be a small, but real, hazard of inducing a subsequent unwanted hypnotic state by using almost any technique if the operator is not alert to this possibility. Some years ago, for instance, a motorist, after being placed in a hypnotic trance by means of a metronome, drove across a red traffic light. The reason he gave, when brought before the Court, was that the action of the windscreen wipers of his car had produced the same effect upon him as had the metronome shortly before. Due to the rhythmic motion of the wipers he fell into a state of trance which he was quite unable to resist. The possibility of such dangers must always be foreseen by the hypnotherapist and appropriate steps taken to protect his patient against them.

Similar considerations apply to the giving of post-hypnotic suggestions. Great care should be taken to avoid any suggestion, whether direct or indirect, that cannot be acted upon because of the changed circumstances of the patient or his environment. Although this particular hazard is not likely to be encountered during the practice of hypnotherapy it has occurred during the use of hypnotism for so-called 'entertainment'. For example, a hypnotised person may be told to perform a certain seemingly innocuous action on a given day in three months' time. If on the day in question he is elsewhere so that it is impossible to carry out the suggestion, a state of anxiety, sometimes amounting to an obsession, may ensue because of this failure to comply with an urge arising in his conscious mind.

However, not all who are engaged in research into the nature of hypnotism are convinced that a post-hypnotic suggestion is always more powerful than one which is given in the normal waking state. M. T. Orne (1972) states that in certain laboratory studies the effect of post-hypnotic suggestion decayed more rapidly than did simple requests made to control subjects who were not hypnotised. 'Data such as these', he writes, 'suggest that in some circumstances hypnotic suggestion may actually interfere with the performance of some experimental tasks'.

Another rarely recognised danger may be one that faces the hypnotherapist himself. It does seem possible that a patient's symptoms may, during hypnotherapy, be transferred inadvertently from the patient to the one who is treating him. If the therapist is not fully in control of the situation – for example if his own attention is wandering or he is day-dreaming – it seems just possible that a patient's own thoughts and feelings may, in certain circumstances, be implanted in the mind of the hypnotist. Although one cannot be dogmatic about this since there still remains a vast amount that is unknown about the workings of suggestion, this possibility is one that should not be lightly discounted. Some years ago one of us (G.N.) did meet with a hypnotherapist who appeared to have succumbed to this particular hazard.

BIBLIOGRAPHY

BENSON, H., BEARY, J. F. & CAROL, M. P. (1974) The relaxation response. *Psychiatry, 37*.

DAS, N. N. & GASTAUT, H. (1957) Variations de l'activité électrique du cerveau, du coeur et des muscles squelettiques au cours de la méditation et de l'extase Yogique. *Electroenceph. clin. Neurophysiol.*, Suppl. *6*, 211–219.

ERICKSON, M. H. & KUBIE, L. S. (1941) The successful treatment of a case of acute hysterical depression by a return under hypnosis to a critical phase of childhood. *Psychoanal. Quart., 10*, 583.

KROGER, William S. & SCHNEIDER, Sydney A. (1959) An electronic aid for hypnotic induction: a preliminary report. *Int. J. clin. exp. Hypnosis, 7*, 2.

MARINESCO, G., SAGER, O. & KREINDLER, A. (1937) Études électroencéphalographiques: le sommeil naturel et le sommeil hypnotique. *Bull. Acad. Méd., 117*, 273–276.

ORNE, M. T. (1972) Hypnosis, state or role. In: *Hypnose und Psychosomatische Medizin*, ed. D. Langen, p. 23. Stuttgart: Hippokrates Verlag.

ROSEN, Harold (1951) Radical hypnotherapy of apparent medical and surgical emergencies. *J. Personality, 1*, 3–4.

SCHULTZ, J. H. & LUTHE, W. (1959) *Autogenic Training*. New York: Grune & Stratton.

SNAITH, R. P. (1974) A method of psychotherapy based on relaxation techniques. *Br. J. Psychiatry, 124*, 473–81.

VOGT, Oskar, quoted by Bramwell, J. M. (1930) in: *Hypnotism, its History, Practice and Theory*, 3rd ed. London: Rider.

WYKE, B. D. Neurological mechanisms in hypnosis. Some recent advances in the study of hypnotic phenomena. Lecture given at Royal Soc. Med. 7th March 1960. *Proc. dent. med. Soc. Study Hypnosis.*

CHAPTER 5

HYPNOSIS IN GENERAL MEDICINE

This chapter will be largely devoted to the technique and value of hypnosis in the psychosomatic field of medicine. A good deal of experimental work has now been undertaken in this country and elsewhere with regard to the role of hypnosis in this branch of medicine. Much of this work has emanated from the USA. We must in particular mention the work of Martin Orne of Philadelphia, T. X. Barber of Massachussetts, William Kroger of California and the redoubtable Milton Erickson of Arizona, who has been active in the field of hypnotherapy for over 40 years. Clinically, Erickson enjoys a unique position in the field of hypnotherapy. It is difficult to define the reason for his pre-eminence, for there have always been good hypnotists, including stage-hypnotists, but his genius has possibly been his skill in writing and his masterly use of hypnotic technique in psychopathology and the psychodynamics of psychiatry. Harold Rosen of Maryland and the late Leslie LeCron of Carmel deserve much credit for their work in this branch of psychotherapy. LeCron wrote several books, which were popular with his friend and colleague Bordeaux. All along the southwest coast of America interest in hypnosis has increased; much work has been accomplished by Ivor Birkland of Seattle, Clagett Harding of Portland, Krippner of San Francisco and many others from Los Angeles to San Diego. Philadelphia psychiatrists practising hypnotherapy flourish under the leadership of Orne, and large groups, many with an interest in psychosomatic medicine research, practice all over the States. Although the major contributions have undoubtedly come from the USA, hypnotherapy has for several years been of international interest, particularly following the publication of *Hypnosis in Modern Medicine*, edited by J. M. Schneck.

The Australians Meares and Collinson have established considerable reputations. In Japan, Ikemi has taught many students and produced a team of research scholars who are indefatigable in their efforts to shift the image of hypnosis away from mystery and magic and to present a fair and unbiased viewpoint to interested colleagues all over the world.

One or two research projects have been undertaken in England, such as the work of Maher-Loughnan on asthma, and articles on hypnosis have found their way into the pages of the *Lancet* and the *British Medical Journal*. The work of Wyke at the Royal College of Surgeons has already been stressed. In Scotland many groups of hypnotherapists have been established; indeed, they will be the hosts for the next conference of the International Society of Hypnosis, scheduled to take place in Glasgow in 1983.

With the advent of the Royal College of Psychiatry in England, it has been found in practice that far more sympathy has been accorded to the use of hypnosis in cases of psychosomatic illness. The Royal Society of Medicine in London now includes a section devoted to hypnosis and psychologists have turned their attention to the clinical and research possibilities. The British Society of Clinical and Experimental Hypnosis has met several times and started a Journal with the aim of teaching their colleagues the use and value of hypnosis in various fields. Much research remains to be undertaken in the field of suggestion, but since the first edition of this book was published almost exactly a quarter of a century ago our understanding of hypnosis — its uses and limitation, what it can do and what it cannot — has increased enormously.

REACTION TO STRESS

Stress is undeniably a significant factor in many illnesses. Hypnosis could be expected to help counteract stress in two ways: as a prophylactic agent, and in the cushioning of shock (Selye's general-adaptation-syndrome). Selye and Fortier (1950), describing alarm reactions in animals, demonstrated three stages in the response of the animal to stress of either a physical or psychic nature—reaction, resistance and exhaustion. The animal would first show resistance to stress. If the resistance was strong enough the animal recovered, but should the stress be continued for any length of time then exhaustion supervened and the animal was in grave danger of developing an irreversible somatic effect. An attempt has recently been made to link up the work of Selye with Pavlov.

Pavlov (1928) was able to demonstrate conditioned reflexes in animals. If stress becomes conditioned, the animal cannot continue without some manifestation of a shocked central nervous system or an effect upon the soma. One animal might show an anxiety reaction whereas another could develop acute otitis media or a similar inflammatory condition anywhere in the body. There is experimental work by Pavlov to support this contention.

Alexander (1940), one of the pioneers of mind-body medicine, elucidated the role of psychic dysfunction in the genesis of physiological change. The work of Mirsky et al. (1949), showing an increase of pepsinogen in the urine of humans subjected to acute emotional distress, paid a direct compliment to Mohr's earlier work in demonstrating glycosuria in the psychically stressed patient. The glycosuria could as dramatically be abolished by increasing the person's emotional stability.

The research of Heyer (1923) showed that digestion could be affected by direct hypnotic suggestion. Together with Heilig and Hoff's work (1925) on kidney dysfunction and gastric acidity it gave added proof that hypnotic suggestion is a powerful weapon in the hands of the research phsyiologist. Hypnosis appears to provide the most suitable method of exploring unconscious motivation and for the study of psychosomatic reactions under research conditions.

Papers by Luria (1932), Erickson (1944) and Wolberg (1947) have described the process of inducing an artificial conflict during hypnosis. The conflict proceeded to a psychosomatic reaction which could be abolished by removing the induced conflict. Work of this nature suggests the value of hypnotherapy in relaxing the individual and thus raising the threshold for fear, shock and stress, thereby increasing the individual's capacity to withstand any further emotional difficulty.

Such relaxation techniques may influence or even arrest the progress of organic disease. This could be accomplished by an auto-hypnotic technique, for if the patient has acquired the conditioning necessary to put himself into a light hypnotic state, he could theoretically protect himself against continued stress or shock; hence the value of the hypnotic state in psychosomatic medicine. In those cases where the disease process is an established fact both patient and doctor will find hypnosis of great value for imparting relaxation and a general sense of well-being.

It is not implied that hypnotherapy should ever replace recognized medical and surgical techniques for the various conditions which follow, but certain conditions in the general medical field appear to offer greater scope for treatment by hypnotherapy than others. Hypnosis can be used as an adjunct in the treatment of these complaints.

CONDITIONS WHERE HYPNOTHERAPY WILL BE FOUND OF VALUE

ASTHMA, HAY-FEVER AND ALLERGIES

Asthma will be discussed on pp. 124–125 and the treatment explained. Adult asthma is possibly more complicated to treat with hypnosis, for there appears to be a more 'infective' basis to chronic asthma in the grown-up. Constant asthma attacks will undermine the somatic part of the syndrome and bronchitis and emphysema may come to be associated with the asthmatic condition.

The physician should treat adult asthma from two viewpoints. The patient's psychology must be explored and any intercurrent infection should be treated by physical means. Certain patients will accept the psychogenic part of their illness without question and are ready to agree to all suggestions given. If these patients are good hypnotic subjects, the prognosis can be excellent. However, should resistance to psychotherapy be experienced at a superficial level, the prognosis should be guarded: treatment might have to be prolonged.

Ideally, patients should be treated by a combination of hypnotherapy and medicine. The real problem is often the need to break a vicious circle: in the chronic asthmatic there is seen an attitude of expectancy and of awaiting the next attack. The condition has become a habit and much anxiety is experienced by the chronic sufferer, particularly if the patient finds that medicines are not always the answer to his problem.

In hay-fever there is an apparent sensitiveness of the upper air passages and conjunctivae. The sensitivity is ill-defined and is said to be associated with the proteins of pollen. Timothy grass is usually said to bear the brunt of the responsibility. Be this as it may, hay-fever attacks may be aborted by suggestion during light or deep states of hypnosis and very often the attacks can be overcome for many years by the use of hypnotherapy, which sometimes pinpoints actual traumatic events occurring before the first attack of hay-fever.

> A man aged 25 had suffered continuous hay-fever attacks for many years; they first appeared in childhood. He was a somewhat moody person, given to his own company, with few interests.
> The hay-fever had a definite connection with hay and grass. He said that attacks often occurred when he passed a particular part of the road where he lived. There was long grass at this point and he could associate some vague memory of playing in the grass with first getting an attack.

Under deep hypnosis he remembered the following facts. At the age of 3½ he was playing with his sister, aged 15. She must have upset him in some way, for he attacked her with a toy and cut her arm. He could see the blood running down her arm. When his father came home that night he was beaten for the offence and told never to attack girls again. He abreacted this incident with a good deal of anxiety.

He also remembered playing in some long grass with other children two years later. The girl in charge of the party was about 15. She ordered the patient to come home and he 'felt like hitting her'. He immediately suffered a feeling of being choked, became frightened and rushed home by himself. The doctor was called and the boy was confined to bed for over 14 days. He was given injections (probably penicillin) for several days. It was further elicited that his attacks commenced at the age of 5. When these facts came to consciousness, it was possible to control the 'hay-fever' and he has not had an attack in over six years. He remains somewhat shy and introspective, but has made greater efforts to interest himself in hobbies, and has recently been going to dances and has joined a club.

The writer has had one attack of 'hay-fever' in his life. It was under circumstances of frustration together with a constant feeling of being behind in his work, on one of the hottest days of summer. The 'hay-fever' required antihistamines and auto-hypnosis to overcome it. The attack actually lasted for only a few hours but the effects were felt for more than 24 hours. Every effort was made to avoid bed and to continue with ordinary life; so often hay-fever can be made into a chronic disease by pandering to each attack and thereby conditioning the patient as in asthma (see p. 149).

Sufferers from hay-fever often complain bitterly: 'Nobody really has time for me. It may be only a 'cold' to the doctor but it's an awful bind for me'. What the person is saying is true. There are many secondary symptoms that people have to wrestle with, hence the enormous numbers of 'cures' sold over the counter by pharmacies. It is possible that 20 minutes spent daily in relaxation and meditation could be the equivalent of many tablets of aspirin, vitamins and antihistamines swallowed by the patient; auto-suggestion might be more positive than any medication. But how many people have 20 minutes which they can devote daily to relaxation? Allergies seem destined to strike at those people who tell us that they cannot afford the time to indulge in their misery. They honestly believe this to be the case. One is forced to the conclusion that in such cases of psychosomatic illness the sufferer becomes the slave to his soma: 'the tail is wagging the dog'. Many GP's will recognize this syndrome.

The patient is often quick to accept the tail-wagging analogy. The physician's objective then becomes the control of his patient's psyche. This can best be achieved during hypnotic treatment. One valuable suggestion takes the form: 'You will find it more valuable to you to wag the tail that previously wagged you.' Every person suffering hay-fever or allergy should be taught auto-hypnosis just as surely as all pregnant women should be taught how to relax for childbirth: a few minutes spent in perfecting the technique of auto-hypnosis may save a patient hours of 'allergic' misery.

ANOREXIA

True anorexia nervosa occurs as a voluntary restriction of food caused by an emotional upset. The patient must find a rational explanation for this upset if the vomiting is to cease.

There is a 'secondary' or 'simple' anorexia due to the belief that the stomach is disordered when it is not. This is an anxiety reaction which occurs mainly in girls or young women. Anorexia nervosa may proceed to extreme starvation. Death may occur from cardiac failure or intercurrent disease.

In the simple type, patients may fear gastric disease and become more and more particular in their diet. Medical practitioners continually encounter the 'faddy' patients who, for example, cannot eat meat or drink milk, suggesting that certain foodstuffs make them 'sick' or 'ill'. These patients can generally be made to overcome their dislikes by simple suggestion, but some cannot be persuaded to add to their meagre diet. Hypnotherapy has been used successfully in overcoming these fads and probably achieves its success by imparting a feeling a confidence, abolishing anxiety and re-educating the patient.

Many cases of anorexia produced their symptoms as a revolt against too dominant a parent, more often the mother. This is well illustrated by babies who battle with their tense and anxious mothers until the age of five or six, when they suddenly 'discover their appetites'. Girls reaching puberty may sometimes develop anorexia due to fears of pregnancy and ignorance of how babies are born. The dynamic interpretation of anorexia nervosa is best left to the trained psychiatrist or analyst. Unfortunately, cases of anorexia nervosa are becoming increasingly common and although much research has been undertaken into this condition, the mortality rate has increased to 15% or even more. Sargant has claimed success after treatment with chlorpromazine using heroic doses, but his 'cures' have not always been maintained. Chemotherapy has been most disappointing and may even have increased the mortality rate. It is very rare that males suffer from this condition, but they are best treated by suggestion and analysis. One of us (G.A.) was very successful with two cases involving similar dynamic problems. Both had phantasised themselves as girls and had been afraid of pregnancy. They had always been doubtful of their gender and hypnosis was valuable in reassuring them of their ultimate manhood.

If hypnosis can be used at a deep level it may be life-saving. Certain psychiatrists doubt whether hypnotherapy is of the slightest value but it has proved clinically to be as good as, if not better than, other methods of psychotherapy. Long involved psychoanalysis does not appear to be any more successful than simple reassuring psychotherapy combined with suitable chemotherapy for anxiety. If hypnosis is used, dynamic interpretation is a necessity and the patient should be allowed to verbalise under deep hypnosis. Some success has been achieved using hypnosynthesis (see page 130).

If the weight sinks below a certain critical level and vomiting and diarrhoea continue, hospital treatment becomes a necessity. Patients appear to be 'psychotic' in their attitude to their body image. One patient weighed less than 30 kg, yet was always looking forward to wearing her bikini on the beach: 'all the boys will want to date me for a drink in the evening'. The conscious and unconscious seem to reassure and at the same time to deny each other.

Some patients develop symptoms in late life. These cases might be described as 'simple' anorexia.

> A married woman aged 31 complained of exhaustion, panic feelings, nausea and difficulty with feeding for more than 8 months. While she was awaiting psychoanalysis, early treatment was considered a necessity by her doctor and she consented to have treatment by suggestion.
>
> She had first experienced nausea while motoring to the town where her parents lived. By recall under medium hypnosis she remembered her conversation with her husband on that day. She had discussed whether she might be pregnant and said that during the conversation she felt fearful and alarmed that she might be. At this moment she wanted to vomit and since then had become more and more particular about her diet.
>
> The past history showed that she had been brought up by an obsessional father and she showed fear and reluctance in speaking about him. He was particularly difficult in the home; demanding, and insulting to his wife and children. She remembered seeing him

strike her mother. He continually made hypochrondriacal statements during meal times and was constantly complaining of 'indigestion' and 'heart-burn'. When she wished to marry, her father opposed this on the grounds that she was 'marrying beneath her'. After she was married she came to live in the south. She would visit her parents two or three times a year, always facing these visits with tension, panic and anxiety. She became pregnant, but just before the twelfth week she aborted. She immediately began to lose weight, became more panicky and could not eat without fear of vomiting.

The patient had been a nurse before her marriage. Her fears of pregnancy (revealed by dreams) were discussed and these fears were later understood by the patient as anxiety associated with her father's conduct to her mother and her own difficult childhood. Hypnosis abolished a good deal of her tension and was used to recall forgotten memories, which made her considerably less aggressive against her father. Her dreams were incorporated into the analysis and later she learnt how to interpret them for herself.

She was seen on ten occasions. She began to eat her food without nausea and she added many articles of food to her diet; she had been unable to eat many of these foods since childhood. She began to put on weight and became less tired and exhausted. She became pregnant and arrangements were made for her to be delivered with the aid of hypnosis.

In the most protracted and serious cases of anorexia nervosa it is always worthwhile supplementing psychotherapy with hypnosis. Simple anorexia should be treated by the general practitioner: treatment appears to be accelerated by the use of hypnotherapy.

CHRONIC DYSPEPSIA

Much of the GP's time is taken up with patients complaining of indigestion, flatulence and nausea. These patients go on complaining for years, while the practitioner continues to give powders, diets and medicine in the belief that there exists no greater relief for the condition. If the dyspepsia is allowed to continue the patient becomes convinced that nothing can be done to give him permanent relief. Many patients use their symptoms as a defensive mechanism to protect themselves against their environment or the frustration engendered by unobtainable ambitions.

Many dyspeptics continue to ulceration and it is with this particular type of peptic ulceration that hypnosis might be expected to help. Undeniably some of these cases will require psychiatric treatment, but the hypnotherapeutic approach offers an accelerated means of learning the particular emotional difficulties assailing the patient and attempting to deal with them. These patients are frequently restless, excitable and incapable of throwing off the cares and troubles of their daily task. Hypnotherapy may be used to teach them how to achieve some degree of hypnosis themselves, thereby largely abolishing their symptoms. Many patients treated in this way have found immense benefit from learning the art of relaxation.

Direct hypnotic suggestions of well-being, restfulness and increased confidence can be most beneficial to these patients, for many of them will complain of subjective symptoms – 'inferiority complexes', self-consciousness and shyness – and will show a tense restlessness well known to the general practitioner.

In the treatment of dyspepsia it is essential to enquire fully into the history of the patient and make an assessment of the personality. Many dyspeptics will complain of emotional difficulty in childhood, of their self-consciousness and shyness and of how they have noticed that emotional problems 'take it out on my stomach'. The patient generally realises that psychological difficulties might be responsible for his symptoms. By the time the patient is seen by the hypnotherapist he is ready to accept any treatment in order to break the habit of 'my mind being constantly on my stomach'. But the chronic character of a condition which may have been treated for many years by tablets, medicines and powders, has conditioned the sufferer, so that it will be a hard task to break the vicious circle of expectation of dyspepsia. General practitioners know well the patient who cannot eat anything of an acid, pippy, heavy or stodgy nature and who seems to boast of his digestive foibles. This attitude of mind is difficult to overcome.

> A man of 42 was seen complaining of 'nervous indigestion'. He admitted to shyness, lack of confidence and panic attacks. He gave a 20 year history and had been to almost every hospital in the London area. Repeated investigation by X-ray, barium-meal, etc. failed to reveal any cause for his indigestion and he was constantly told to 'live with it'. He had been married for 15 years, during which his wife gave him the same advice. He also complained of various fears. He feared a collapse while travelling anywhere and could not go to football matches or to the cinema. These phobias had only begun within the last few years.
>
> He eventually saw a psychiatrist who treated him with drugs for six months, but he made little progress. He had always wanted hypnotic treatment, but most of the doctors he had seen advised against it.

He was seen for hypnotherapy over a dozen times. He was a good hypnotic subject but continually denied that he was deep enough. Only extreme dominance during the hypnotic state could persuade him that he was going to get better and would worry less about the symptom. He was curiously reluctant to accept the fact that he could overcome his indigestion, but with a good deal of patience it was possible to get him to add certain items to his diet. He had previously not eaten an apple or an orange for 20 years. During the whole of the treatment he showed an obsessional need to keep his symptoms and when last seen he was on constant doses of a sedative drug.

The only fact revealed during hypnosis was that he first noticed his symptoms during a film, which he later associated with an occasion when he saw an ambulance at the door of his house waiting to take his mother to hospital with suspected acute appendicitis. He remembered also that his symptoms became worse when his wife was ill with a chest infection. However, he showed some insight at the last interview, when he stated: 'I allowed the symptoms to control me and I suppose that 20 years is too long a time to be able to forget them.' Hypnosis used in the first place might have helped him to 'gain control of his organism'.

Contrasted with this case are many instances of relief of dyspepsia and ulceration by psychotherapy and hypnotherapy. If rapport is satisfactory, no more than 20 to 30 one-hour sessions should be necessary. During this time it will be found that the patient will add more and more to his diet and eventually admit he is eating foods he would never have dreamt of eating before treatment. Particularly if hypnoanalytical techniques are used, each session produces a greater degree of understanding, relaxation and re-education, until the patient discovers the symptom has simply been masking difficulties of environment or marriage or frustrations of career. As the patterns of childhood and adolescence are more readily understood, the digestion ceases to be the focal point of the emotions. Re-education by hypnosis and a superficial analysis of emotional difficulties may even prevent a subsequent continuation to frank ulceration.

Both authors have treated cases of ulceration in the worrying type of individual with good results. It is with this type of patient that hypnosis will be found of much value. Many of them are suggestible individuals with a high degree of intelligence and insight and are eager to co-operate fully in the therapy planned for them when introduced to a method which offers them adequate relief from their constant pain and allays fears of a recurrence of their symptoms.

MIGRAINE AND TENSION HEADACHES

Migraine, which some authorities claim is a rare illness, is characterized by paroxysmal attacks of headache, usually with nausea and sickness and often preceded by disorders of vision. In general practice the tension headache is more common than classic migraine. Every now and again, however, someone will consult his doctor with a typical history of 'migraine attacks'.

The condition appears to be more common in women. Although certain textbooks suggest that migraine attacks are rare after the age of 30, many older patients will be seen complaining of one-sided headache and nausea, suggesting a diagnosis of migraine. A family history of migraine is common and often mothers suffering from migraine will bring their children for treatment.

Some authorities speak of an 'allergic' reaction and there seems to be some evidence of a relationship between cyclical vomiting in childhood and later migraine. Worry and anxiety are predisposing causes. Other causes sometimes mentioned are gastric disturbances, ocular defects, fatigue and menstruation. It will often be found in practice that there is no apparent cause for the attack.

Patients suffering from these attacks often have a 'migraine personality'. They are intelligent, over-anxious, tend to bury their stresses and are over-dependent in their relationships with others. The treatment of these patients is difficult and very often unsatisfactory. Hypnosis should always be employed for those cases resistant to medicinal treatment. Many migrainous patients are capable of reaching a deep state of hypnosis. Direct suggestions of well-being should be given. It will be found in actual practive that many cases involve associated anxiety symptoms. Patients will readily agree that their attacks are often related to stress or nervous reactions of some sort.

A man of 55 changed his occupation from gardener to night watchman. As a watchman he was expected to keep a record of hourly events throughout the night. He described typical headaches which developed over the right eye, with some nausea. The attacks were severe enough to keep him away from work. Spectacles ordered for him did not help. Although it is tempting to call this problem 'migraine' it is far more likely to be a tension headache. However, he was incapacitated and had to stay off work. There was no vomiting, and other expected symptoms of the classic migraine syndrome were not experienced.

This was a conflict not difficult to deal with by hypnosis and re-education. The headache stopped when certain adjustments were made to his work schedule.

It would appear that this condition is attributable to two factors: a spasm of the cerebral arteries, and a neurosis. In many cases there is a typical history of tension and anxiety resulting in a crippling attack of migraine which renders the patient incapable for one or two days. Often vomiting will relieve the attack. Patients often show well marked neurotic features.

As in asthma, epilepsy, stammering and indeed any condition characterized by spasm, all degrees of the condition will be met with. The more neurotic the patient, i.e. the less the individual can accept the illness, the greater will be the subjective reaction.

The following case history of a patient treated for migraine illustrates the factors associated with a psychogenic illness translated into headaches of a migrainous nature. Release of the psychic trauma caused the attacks to disappear.

A married woman aged 35 complained of constant attacks of one-sided headache and vomiting severe enough to make her extremely ill for 24 hours; she would lie on a bed prostrate with pain and sickness. These attacks were becoming more severe as time went on.

She had been married twice, having divorced her first husband. She claimed he had been a sex-pervert and said: 'He always wanted me.' He would come home in the morning and afternoon and demand sexual intercourse. She was apparently frigid and therefore resented this behaviour. If she resisted, however, he would lock the door and beat her until she agreed. For a long time she was unable to leave him as she feared that he would follow her and do her serious harm. Later she was able to get a court order against him and he had gone back to his parents' home.

She had married her present husband about 4 years later and almost immediately afterwards began to have migraine attacks. She disagreed with her own doctor that the attacks were 'psychological' in origin and when seen by a psychiatrist still claimed that there was something organically wrong with her brain or stomach. She denied that the attacks could be associated with troubles occurring so long before.

After telling her story she seemed less tense and it was decided to use a hypnotherapeutic approach in order to abreact the sexual trauma from her mind. She would not consciously accept the psychiatrist's explanation for the migraine attacks, that the sexual act had become to her a cruel and savage one fraught with pain and misery and that her migraine attacks were a defence against submitting to the act, which had become a revolting one for her.

Fortunately the patient was seen some years later after her doctor sent a personal note saying that she had been free of all attacks since hypnosis had first been attempted. It is sometimes most difficult for patients to return to their first hypnotist. This may be something to do with the search for 'magic' which most people admit to on first seeing a hypnotist. In general practice, however, it is much easier to keep check on patients and follow-up can reveal interesting data for research. When this patient decided to return for treatment, she had been free of all 'migraine attacks' for nearly 4 years, i.e. since hypnosis had first been attempted. It was decided to make a more detailed investigation of the deeper psychological conflicts which might be expected to be revealed after some years of freedom from migraine.

As would be expected, the sexual assaults by the first husband were simply 'cover' memories for earlier sexual traumata. She recalled by regression under hypnosis that as a child she played with the genitals of a boy-friend and had been discovered. 'Life became one long headache after my father beat me. I was only 7 at this time'. She could remember many subsequent events, such as quarrels, which made her 'hold her head'. She agreed that her first marriage could have been a repeat of her parents' marriage. She went further and could see, while in the hypnotic state, her father beating her mother. She said: 'I must have allowed my husband to beat me to repeat their pattern of behaviour.' As insight was acquired, she explained that, after breaking off hypnotic treatment for 3 years, she had been treated with behaviour therapy, but slowly realized that she had to find a method of building up a new way of life. She knew that her headaches were the result of early conflicts and could only be dispelled by her understanding of what had led to their genesis. By regression using hypnosis (not a difficult manoeuvre) she was able to dispense with the unconscious thought 'life to me is one long headache' (Livingstone 1958).

As early as 1937 Eisenbud advocated hypnoanalysis for the full-blown attack of migraine. Many analysts have used their methods in those cases seemingly resistant to other forms of treatment. More recently Basker (1979) has published details of his use of hypnotherapy and claims useful results.

Auto-hypnosis should always be taught in the hypnotic treatment of migraine. In good hypnotic subjects the approach is not difficult, the patient being conditioned to count to 5 or to take five deep breaths. Preliminary conditioning is achieved by post-hypnotic suggestions. The following case outlines the treatment.

> A woman aged 42 complained of headaches from an early age. She described the headache as a severe, 'boring' pain over the left eye. There was no vomiting but she would be compelled to go to bed for at least 24 hours. 'Nobody knows the agony I suffer,' she said. The attacks occurred almost every 14 days. She remembered seeing her mother in similar attacks, and her own daughter, aged 12, occasionally complained of the same symptoms.
>
> At the age of 7 she had been sent to an orphanage, both her parents having died quite suddenly. She was not unhappy there but could not get on well at school. She was always highly strung and excitable. During this time she found that she could avoid 'nasty things' by an attack of migraine.
>
> She later married but the marriage was not successful. Her husband was inadequate sexually, always tired and interested only in his garden. She attributed much of her troubles and the continuation of the migraine to her husband's attitude. She proved to be a good hypnotic subject and rapidly learnt how to hypnotize herself. She was somewhat unusual, for she would prefer to enter the hypnotic state with her head resting on her elbow. Considerable success was achieved with post-hypnotic suggestions that she would be able to count to five slowly and repeat to herself: 'One, my eyes are heavy; two, they close; three, even if I tried to open them I could not; four, I'm sleepy and drowsy; five, I sleep.' With this technique she has warded off all attacks. She is happier and more relaxed than she ever has been and can even forgive her husband some of his inadequacies.

For those patients intolerant of drugs and injections who find life particularly tiresome, treatment by hypnotherapy offers a useful method of treatment.

There appears to be a distinct migraine personality; in childhood shy, obedient and stubborn, he later becomes over-conscientious, perfectionist and inflexible, being generally intelligent, sensitive and ambitious. Such patients may suffer feelings of inferiority and take on greater responsibility as an over-compensation. They are thus under constant stress. They cannot overtly express their repressed childhood emotions of rage, hostility and envy which are thus turned inwards, later to produce the symptom of a migraine headache.

ULCERATIVE COLITIS

Much evidence has accrued that cases of non-specific ulcerative colitis are associated with stress. It can often be demonstrated that the disease commenced with a history of emotional trauma producing an internal conflict. Many patients will agree that any emotional upset affects their bowels with either an attack of diarrhoea or obstinate constipation. So many times analysis of the events leading up to the patient's present symptoms reveals ill-repressed aggression, humiliation and inferiority generally directed against, or associated with a parent (more often the mother). Frankel (1954), Groen (1947), Lindemann (1945) and Portis (1949) have all stressed the sense of inferiority and humiliation that appears to go hand in hand with the disease.

The following case, although described nearly 30 years ago, is given in full. It has been possible with the help of the general practitioner involved to follow up this patient, who is now 60 years old. No apologies are necessary for quoting a case from so long ago, since it is rarely possible to have such a length of time to follow up a patient. Indeed, hypnotherapists often see a patient and give him treatment which appears to be most satisfactory and then, suddenly, the patient breaks off treatment. Psychiatrists often tell us the same thing and one can reasonably be sure that physicians and surgeons have had the same experience! Sometimes we hear that the patient has relapsed after our treatment and has gone elsewhere for other treatment, such as acupuncture, yoga, transcendental meditation, or simply group therapy, or to a society of individuals cured of their own illnesses and helping others, such as Alcoholics Anonymous, Obesity Anonymous or Depressives Anonymous.

It may be argued that many people seeking hypnotic treatment are disappointed when no 'miracle' rapidly occurs and thus tend to seek a 'cure' from the next miracle-worker they can find.

A male patient aged 30 suffered continued pain, diarrhoea and pyrexia. In November 1951 he developed sharp pains across the upper abdomen, starting in the morning and persisting all day. The pain varied in intensity and was not affected by food or respiration, but was made worse by sudden movements. He had pale, loose, offensive stools. The bowels were open about twice daily. He gradually got weaker and noticed a temperature of 99° to 102°F (37° to 39°C), associated with headache. He said that he had always been introspective. He was admitted to hospital on 13 November 1951.

The past history revealed that in 1939 he was investigated in hospital for persistent diarrhoea. All investigations proved negative, and he was diagnosed as 'chronic diarrhoea. ? cause'.

In 1941 he had a recurrence of diarrhoea and was considered to have tuberculous peritonitis. He was treated for 10 weeks in a sanatorium and showed a marked improvement.

In 1944 he was re-admitted to hospital with diarrhoea and *Shigella sonnei* was found in the stools. When in hospital in 1951 he was described as 'an ill-looking man with a sallow complexion'.

Investigation showed:

Haemoglobin	8.9 mg/dl
WBC	6850
Polymorphs	78%
Eosinophils	1%
Lymphocytes	15%
Monocytes	6%
Stool	No pathogens isolated
	Benzidine test negative
Gastric test	Achlorhydria
Agglutination test for dysentery	Negative

A barium enema was consistent with a diagnosis of ulcerative colitis affecting mainly the ascending and transverse colon. Barium meal and follow-through showed a lesion involving the terminal part of the ileum and caecum. The caecal pole was deformed and the mucosal pattern deranged. The terminal part of the ileum was narrowed. The appearances were 'suggestive of Koch's or Crohn's disease'. Sigmoidoscopy: 'Mucosa slightly fragile, no other abnormality. ESR—10 mm/hour.'

While in hospital, and following the gastric test, he passed four loose stools in 8 hours and on the evening of 4 December 1951, after an interview with a psychiatrist, passed 4 ounces (100 g) of dark red motion, and during the next 2 days more red blood.

The psychiatrist reported that 'he is a shy, sensitive, methodical person who stands up to responsibility badly' and that 'the recent attack may be related to his having become a father and having been overworking, or possibly to the death of a friend'.

In view of the history and the radiological appearances, it was considered advisable to perform a laparotomy to ascertain if tuberculosis or Crohn's disease was present.

On 3 February 1952 he was admitted to a surgical bed and a laparotomy was performed. The report follows.

'Right hemicolectomy. Right paramedium incision. The last 10 inches of the ileum was thick, red, indurated and dilated. Ileocaecal region very thickened. Ascending colon also thick and red. Mesenteric glands large and soft. About 18 inches of terminal ileum and right hemicolon removed with adherent omentum and mesenteric glands. Ileo-transverse end-to-end anastomosis.

Specimen showed gross polypi of the large gut and a low ulcerated polypoid mucosa of the ileum.

Pathological report — appearances consistent with early Crohn's disease.'

On 13 December 1953 he was admitted to the surgical ward again, this time for excision of a fistula-in-ano. On 1 January 1954 he was discharged to the care of his own doctor with a note: 'In view of the persistent diarrhoea and recurrent pyrexia, it is thought that the original pathology must be still active and he should have a barium enema as an out-patient.'

On 9 March 1954 a letter from the surgeon stated: 'He now has an extension of the disease involving the last 6 inches of ileum.... sooner or later a further resection must be done.'

The patient decided that before subjecting himself to further surgery, he would like to be treated by hypnotherapy. Permission was granted by the surgeon.

He was seen on 9 March 1954 for the first treatment. At this time he looked pale and ill. Apart from the obvious depression about his illness, his tension and anxiety, he claimed that his illness must be organic and did not believe that psychological troubles could affect his bowel, but he added that any treatment was preferable to continual surgery. He feared he would 'have no more bowel to cut away'. Treatment took place from 9 March to 1 June 1954, and comprised fifteen visits.

He was hypnotized at the first visit and said later that the hypnotic state had rid him of tension. It 'made me feel I was going to get well. I realized that the illness could be "nervous".'

During treatment he recalled four 'episodes' which had caused him great distress.

(1) The realization that his father had married again and that he had half-brothers and a half-sister. He stumbled upon this fact by accident at the age of 11 and it caused him a great deal of insecurity and produced inferiority symptoms. He dated his bowel troubles from this time but admitted that during early childhood, between the ages of 3 and 8, when he was afraid or annoyed he 'dirtied his pants with his faeces'. He added: 'I always seemed to worry with my bowel.'

(2) He went through a stormy and aggressive courtship. He had a good deal of trouble with his wife's parents because they felt that she was marrying beneath her — he said he would feel tense every time he visited his in-laws.

(3) During World War II his wife was attracted to another man and he suffered some humiliation on this account.

(4) He had allowed a friend, ill with cancer, to stay in his home, but had been in conflict with himself over whether or not he should ask him to leave. His wife had just had a baby and he knew the work entailed was too much for her. A few days after he had asked the friend to leave the latter died from his illness. The patient thought he was to blame and felt guilty about his friend's death.

All these traumatic episodes had caused diarrhoea and fever. He showed obvious reluctance and abhorrence when first he spoke of them. Each disturbance was abreacted under deep hypnosis. Later he could speak of them without emotion and said that he understood how they could have made him ill.

Pertinent questions to be asked in this case are:

(1) Did the psychogenic factors cause or aggravate the disease of the bowel?

(2) If the pathology is allied to psychological causes had the process become irreversible?

(3) What was the condition of the last 6 inches of the bowel following treatment by hypnotherapy?

(4) Was the condition simply one of 'spasm' induced by stress and followed by inflammation?

The patient still has slight pain and flatulence. It has not been possible to control the diarrhoea. He can achieve deep auto-hypnosis and is conditioned to counting to five for this purpose (see section on migraine). He has put on over 5 pounds in weight and is certain that he will be able to carry on without surgery.

The prognosis in this case is considered to be good. Adequate unsight has been afforded the patient who stated on the last day he was seen: 'I now have a rational explanation of what seemed to me to be a visitation.' He was no longer defeatist in his attitude to his illness and the subjective improvement was marked.

He has been followed up for fifteen years and no further surgery has been necessary. He has had further marital problems but emphasizes that his bowels no longer take the brunt of his troubles. He has learnt to live with stress and refuses to transfer emotional problems into symptoms.

Patients can often control psychosomatic illness by post-hypnotic suggestions and increased insight. They should always be taught autohypnosis for this purpose. For nearly twenty years since this patient was first treated with hypnoanalysis, he has had no further trouble with his bowels. He has suffered problems, as all of us do, but at no time has he seen or needed to be treated by a surgeon or physician for this particular condition.

Care should be taken in these cases. The symptom may be masking a deeper psychological disturbance and some cases of mucous colitis, treated by symptom removal, have resulted in psychosis. If, during hypnotherapy, the patient shows agitation, treatment should be left to the expert. It is as well to ask the patient, at every session, whether he is being upset or disturbed by the analysis. The actual state of hypnosis should be as deep as possible to withstand the shock of too rapid an insight. Indeed the best technique to use in many of these cases is a state of complete tranquillity. The room is darkened and the patient is covered with a blanket. Talking is allowed, indeed any method of recall is tolerated, but often a state of peace and relaxation followed by a few minutes' suggestion at the end of the session may be found the most beneficial technique of all.

DIRECT SYMPTOM REMOVAL

By and large, it is wrong for a therapy which is marked by its value as an abreactive and re-educative agent to be used directly for the removal of one symptom. However, in certain cases and in certain circumstances the use of hypnosis for direct symptom removal can be tolerated. The following are examples of some cases well suited to this simple and rapid treatment.

A girl of 16 could not go to dances, for when a dancing partner took her in his arms she always felt like giggling and squirming. The condition was thought to be associated with her having been held down as a child while her feet were tickled. Hypnosis was used on one occasion only. Suggestions were made along the lines: 'Your partner takes you in his arms; you feel yourself dancing, and there is no discomfort or tickling; you will never again be worried or think about this.' The symptom was abolished.

A singer complained of a 'frog in the throat'. She would get a nervous cough (habit spasm) when broadcasting or on the stage, which caused her considerable embarrassment. She was hypnotized once only and has had no further trouble.

A woman schoolteacher aged 60 complained of a painful tongue for over 5 years. Constant treatment at hospital and elsewhere was valueless. The diagnosis was said to be avitaminosis with glossitis. Hypnosis was used on one occasion only and the following suggestion made: 'You will no longer worry about your tongue, the pain will go away and you will feel more happy and less anxious than you have been for years.' This resulted in the relief of pain. No cause for the pain was ever discovered and no new symptom has been reported to the physician.

A man of 45 complained of severe headaches. He said he had been a merchant seaman during the war and had been swimming in the water after his ship was sunk when he saw a large spar floating towards him. He thought it would hit him on the head, panicked and felt he would be drowned. He was picked up some time later. Abreaction of this fear incident in a single session stopped his headaches.

A school mistress aged 45 said she was always losing her voice. She agreed that it seemed to occur when she was worried. The children she was looking after were 'a bit of a handful'. Hypnotic suggestion that her voice would return at seven o'clock the same night proved to be a remarkably accurate forecast. Two years later she had another attack and the same treatment was successful. Previous to hypnosis she had had to remain away from school for a week or more at a time. One year later her husband telephoned from over eighty miles away to say that his wife had again 'lost her voice'. Suggestions were made to the wife over the telephone that she should lie down, count five and relax, and that after 5 minutes her voice would return. These were successful. She has had no further trouble since leaving the teaching profession. No new symptom was created by overcoming the aphonia and the cause for this was obvious from the first time she was seen.

An elderly woman complained of excessive cigarette smoking. So heavy was her smoking that she would have five or six cigarettes alight at the same time in different rooms. Two hypnotic sessions of 10 minutes each, with the following suggestions, stopped the smoking: 'You are feeling less anxious and restless. You will feel calm and happy and there will no longer be any necessity for you to smoke. You will never want to smoke in the future; it is a habit and will mean nothing to you again.' A light state of hypnosis only was needed in this case.

There is a good deal of evidence that many cases of excessive smoking have relapsed after direct treatment by hypnosis. Many patients, however, can be helped by hypnoanalytical methods aimed at the root of the problem. Often it will be found that patients with a supposed neurosis associated with giving up this habit are repressing important psychological problems at a much deeper level of the psyche. Early feeding problems and strong frustration of the 'oral' phase of infancy are two possibilities; these are personality factor which will require deep penetrative techniques. Hypnosis will be of limited help to these patients and they will have to be treated by psychiatrists.

A girl of 21 was seen with a history of functional amenorrhoea. She was convinced that she was pregnant and was excessively nervous and worried. Sexual intercourse with her fiancé had taken place a few days after the end of her last period. Her general practitioner had reassured her that she was not pregnant. Under deep hypnosis she was told that her period would start on the following day at 10 a.m. This happened, to the minute. Although she was only 7 days late with her period she had reacted in a neurotic manner, threatening to 'do something to herself'. It was noticeable that immediately after hypnosis was terminated she left the room smiling and obviously completely happy.

A girl aged 10 was seen because her mother said that she was jealous of her younger brother. The girl said that she could not understand the jealousy, but agreed with her mother that it was interfering with her schooling and preventing her concentration. Direct hypnotic suggestions abolished the symptom and she became immediately happier, improving markedly at school.

A dental student claimed that she 'knew her work backwards but went to pieces in the practical'. She failed her examination purely on account of her anxiety. Medium hypnosis helped her to face this examination for the second time with great confidence, and indeed her friends chided her on her apparent lack of interest, believing at the time that because she was so relaxed and cheerful, she could not be taking the examination seriously. She passed.

There is a condition in the musical profession known as the 'pearlies'. The derivation of the term is unknown. This condition is commonly experienced by violin players, i.e. those using bows, although any member of an orchestra may suffer similar symptoms.

A musician aged 30 feared that he would lose his position in a well-known orchestra. Three years before, he had experienced 'bumping' of his bow on the strings of his violin, followed by a sudden tightening of the muscles (muscular spasm) of his bowing hand and arm. This occurred during a quiet and melodious part of the music. However hard he tried he could not overcome the bumping and subsequent spasm. He discovered that alcohol helped him, but he needed increasing amounts of spirit.

As a child, he had to play to friends when they were visiting his parents. His father was very proud of him but never *told* him how clever or brilliant a player he was. He had always been a 'day-dreamer' and was 'highly strung and imaginative'.

Direct hypnotic suggestions that he would no longer worry about his playing, particularly his bowing, and would not require alcohol to overcome his handicap were entirely successful.

The last condition is extremely common and can attack any member of an orchestra. The great master can suffer from the complaint as well as the most junior member of the orchestra. Tablets and medicine are valueless.

Some years ago a well known international golfer complained of 'shanking' his shot when anywhere near the green. Fortunately, the hypnotist was a golfer himself and recognized this particular difficulty. It is not uncommon with golfers and is allied to the 'pearlies' (see page 79). Due to nervous tension and anxiety, the player of any game tends to 'tense-up' and may complain of sprains and tears of ligaments and muscles. He is naturally also subject to spasm. In this particular case the patient was always suspect when he played an iron shot but could hit further than most with a wood. Subsequent hypnosis and psychological explanation, together with a few sessions of analysis of his marital problems, cured his 'locking' in mid-air. He had been the butt of much coarse Freudian ribaldry at the Club-house after a match.

The author of this chapter (G.A.) was fortunate in seeing an example of 'the pearlies' during another game — snooker.

During an international match on television an unfortunate competitor, struggling for his country against the redoubtable Fred Davis, the captain of the English team, was within an ace of beating his rival. However, he was obliged to take a rest to play the white ball and pot a simple looking blue ball. All the other colours were well within his compass and if the blue could be potted the game was over. The cameras settled on the young man. Suddenly it was noticeable that something was very wrong. In taking deliberate aim with the rest, the player suddenly broke away from the table. He then started again to place his cue in the rest and again seemed to be in desperate trouble. Then came the voice of the commentator: 'Oh my goodness; he's got his trouble again, he's been to see all sorts of people, there isn't a psychiatrist who can help him.' It was then obvious that he had an attack of the 'pearlies' and was doomed to a life of chronic anxiety with his snooker balls. One feels that he had probably seen all the best hypnotists, for some of these problems are very complex and are not easily treated. Needless to say he missed the blue, gave away 5 points and the British captain potted the remaining balls to win the match.

The author (G.A.) is indebted to a colleague, Dr H. M. Thomas, for another example of the 'pearlies', a case of 'telegraphist's glass arm'. The patient was a very good hypnotic subject and benefitted from hypnotic treatment. Previously he had seen many doctors and consultants. Neurologists were particularly puzzled by the symptom. Wherever spasm of muscles can occur in the body, together with the necessary conflict, and 'need for the gain', we should be warned of this interesting condition.

Many cases treated by direct hypnosis are described by earlier writers. Reiter mentions the case of a schoolgirl suffering from acute anxiety after seeing a plane crash on her school. She was successfully treated by three sessions of hypnosis.

Individuals uncertain of the value of this therapy have tended to condemn the practice of using hypnosis directly. Brill, a colleague of Freud, tells the story of a man who was unable to go on a journey without knowing that a hypnotist was at the other end to dispel his headache on arrival. No other means of relieving the headache had been discovered and he was apparently resistant to all other forms of medicine. The original hypnotist was Krafft-Ebing, who had hypnotized this man when he was 14. He had obviously used hypnosis wrongly in the first place. He should have analysed the reason for the headache and used hypnosis as a psycho-cathartic, i.e. abreactive, instrument.

Patients will be seen in general practice complaining of annoying symptoms, such as blushing, lack of confidence, inferiority, etc. When asked if they are complaining of any other symptoms they will deny them, saying only that they blush often, have no confidence, are shy in company, etc. Thus one patient was worried because his hand would shake while he was writing if there happened to be a superior in the room; a girl complained of a fainting feeling in church; another girl felt frightened of thunder storms. All these symptoms were abolished by direct removal after the therapist was convinced that they were serving no 'useful' purpose and, by dealing with them in this way, there would be little fear of his patient developing another conversion symptom.

Analysts and psychoanalysts will find themselves attacking the concept of treatment by direct suggestion. They prefer to search for the psychological dynamism behind each symptom. Thus the Freudian will see Reiter's schoolgirl as previously experiencing traumatic sexual experience of an emission and the subsequent detumescence of the erect penis. This may or may not be accurate, but we could agree that under hypnosis the girl saw the actual experience, fantasy or real, and by reliving this episode with her analyst, she was enabled to come to terms with a previous trauma which she had found impossible to accept. In other words, the process of hypnosis allows a repressed incident to come to unconsciousness and to be abreacted with subsequent relief of the symptom. It is not always necessary to seek for further repressed material, particularly with children, but this must obviously be left to the judgment of the analyst.

At this point some readers may criticise this handbook, believing that too much analysis has crept into its pages. It is a feature of the hypnotherapist's life and work, given the current acceptance of psychosomatic medicine, that the concepts of psyche and soma can no longer be separate. Once the hypnotic state is induced in a person, a conscious and unconscious mechanism must have occurred. Any psychotherapeutic manoeuvre must be dependent upon a relationship between hypnotist and hypnotised known in hypnotic circles as *rapport*. In Psycho-analytical terms this relationship is more often described as transference and counter-transference (see chapter on Hypnoanalysis and Hypnosynthesis): each school of thought understands exactly what it means in its own circles. A subtle change in psychological attitude must commence and the physician will want to understand more of the inner conflicts which might inflict themselves upon the psyche of the patient. As we broaden our own psychological vision, our patients, particularly our hypnotic patients, may wish to come with us. This is easier to accomplish if we remove the blind spots (beautifully named – 'scotoma' – by Stekel) from our minds and seek to see more of our own motivation. As we embrace a larger philosophical understanding for ourselves we shall want others to enjoy a new-found freedom of thought and action. This understanding of our own emotions, and their acceptance, will lead to the happiness of both ourselves and our patients. Happiness is the fulfilment of oneself, a greater knowledge of life in every sense. This must be the aim. It demands that all hindrance to freedom of thought and expression must be done away with. This then is the object of hypnotherapy and psychotherapy. Text-books of hypnosis should not merely be concerned with ego-strengthening but should embrace a wider philosophical concept of human behaviour.

But it must also be realised that when patients present with one specific symptom it may be indicative of gross psychiatric illness. An example of such a case was a patient sent for hypnotherapy who had complained of pain in his side for over 15 years. Exhaustive examinations, including X-ray investigation with barium meal and eventual laparotomy, revealed nothing abnormal. Under hypnosis the patient stated that he had lost his position with his firm after 20 years and was in acute financial difficulty. He had refused ECT treatment and expected hypnosis to be a miracle and rid him of his pain. Under deep hypnosis he began to realize that his pain was a defence mechanism — while he had the pain he was not the failure that he had always considered himself to be. His wife refused to visit the psychiatrist treating him with hypnosis in order to discuss her rôle in his treatment — she sent a message to say that she was 'fed-up with his illness and he could do more for himself if he pulled himself together'. The patient then broke off treatment and a few days later took his life by hanging himself.

Many symptoms can be of superficial origin; it will depend upon the experience, intuition and confidence of the physician treating the patient whether deep or superficial psychotherapy is undertaken. Under certain circumstances, for instance where long involved and tedious psychotherapy is out of the question, it will be found of great value to hypnotize the patient and attempt to combat the symptom by positive suggestions as outlined in previous chapters.

THE EXPERIMENTAL FIELD AND TREATMENT BY HYPNOTHERAPY

CHRONIC PEPTIC ULCER

The proved peptic ulcer case demands more patience and longer therapy than does the dyspeptic. If the ulcer patient is a good hypnotic subject he will be helped considerably and healing will be hastened by hypnotherapy. Relapse can be prevented by adequate analysis at a superficial level.

The relationship of the emotions to digestive malfunctions has been described by many writers, but little original work has been done on the treatment of acute peptic ulceration by hypnosis. Raginsky (1948) has outlined the treatment of a case of duodenal ulceration by this means and he mentions papers by Alexander (1936), Dunbar (1938), Mittlemann (1942) and Wolff (1943).

Hamilton Moody (1964) has described the investigation and comparison of peptic ulcer cases treated by hypnosis and by medical treatment.

All the 20 patients studied were between the ages of 25 and 45; the small group was carefully chosen and as carefully investigated. Moody found that those patients treated by hypnosis and relaxation did better than the medically treated group.

It is research of this description which is so vitally needed in the study of hypnosis and illness. In general practice, research in diseases such as diabetes, rheumatoid arthritis and ulcerative colitis should not be difficult; much good work has been done by the Royal College of General Practitioners in this respect. Other psychosomatic illnesses will be discussed in this chapter. The technique for the research into duodenal ulceration by Moody outlined above should be taken as a standard model for research in these diseases. Control and experimental groups might be obtained in a large general practice or group practice; one doctor conversant with hypnotic procedure and possibly one other, together with a radiologist, could form the necessary team.

DIABETES MELLITUS

Much experimental work is taking place in the treatment of diabetes. Newer insulin compounds are being used which cut down the required number of injections and indeed medication can now be given by mouth in certain selected cases.

When insulin was first discovered by the work of Banting, Best and McCloud, great hopes were aroused for the *cure* of diabetes. Unfortunately it was not to be. More recently we have been faced by the same state of affairs in rheumatoid arthritis and tuberculosis, when much was expected of cortisone, streptomycin, ACTH, PAS, and allied substances.

It seems reasonable to suppose that when once Selye's adaptation syndrome comes into play and the body cannot adapt, the somatic part of the disease is there to stay, and antibiotics or synthetic endocrine substances are powerless to help, except in a general way by making the patient feel better. For too long the patient has been subjected to treatment against the symptoms of his disease. Nowadays it is known that the *person* must be taken into account. Hypnotherapy can produce a rapid insight for the patient and, by its power of relaxation and release of tension, helps both psyche and soma. If relaxation can be achieved it is reasonable to suppose that the body will be in a better state to absorb and use the endocrine or antibiotic substances of value in the particular disease.

The following case emphasizes how many cases of diabetes can be directly attributed to stress. Practitioners may know of similar ones.

A woman patient aged 45 was asked when she first experienced her diabetic symptoms. She told the following story.

Twenty years ago she had a growing suspicion that her husband was in love with his secretary. One day she came into his office unexpectedly and found the two of them in a compromising position. Her 'whole stomach turned over' and 3 days later she was removed to hospital in a diabetic coma.

She had been well maintained on injections of insulin until 15 years later when she suddenly felt again a deep resentment against her husband. She had never really forgiven him for the original incident, but her latent feelings now welled up and she felt 'terribly aggressive against him'. Once again she went into a diabetic coma and had to remain in hospital for a month. There seemed to be satisfactory evidence that her shock and misery actually had no foundation in fact, but it is reasonable to suppose that abreaction of the shock soon after the traumatic incident might have assisted her greatly.

Hypnosis has been successfully employed in the treatment of obesity caused by over-eating or neurotic trends and the technique might therefore be used in controlling the appetite of the diabetic patient, allowing him to feel happier about his enforced diet (Raginsky 1948).

Hinkle and Wolf (1949) experimented with a 15-year-old girl and during experimentally-induced stress ketosis was observed to continue to the point of clinical acidosis. Raginsky (1953) has said: 'In selected cases the use of hypnotherapy can reduce the quantity of insulin needed to keep the urine sugar-free and to reduce the frequency of attacks of ketosis. Hypnotherapy often induces an easier acceptance of the restricted dietary regimen.'

ESSENTIAL HYPERTENSION

The diagnosis of 'high blood pressure', particularly when suggested to the nervous, tense and anxious patient, causes in itself much unnecessary mental ill-health, suffering and doubt. It is not unusual to be confronted with a patient who states: 'My blood pressure is very high, doctors have always told me so.' Patients have even been known to telephone their doctors asking to have their blood pressure taken before accepting a new job.

It is fairly well understood nowadays that the blood pressure can vary between the time the patient enters and the time he leaves a doctor's surgery, and that a frown or puzzled look on the face of the physician while taking the blood pressure may register an extra 10 mm on the sphygmomanometer. Constant blood pressure recordings are to be condemned because of this suggestive element. If the blood pressure can be increased by fear induced by the wrong suggestion, it is pertinent to suppose that the reading can be lowered by the right suggestions. It is very well known that if a patient is rested both physically and mentally the blood pressure will attain its normal reading after a time. In the same way if a patient can be guarded against stress and shock the cardiovascular system, in particular, will be guarded. It has been known for many years that stress has a profound affect on the heart rate and blood pressure and modern research and teaching have illustrated that if the nervous patient is shocked by hearing that his blood pressure is too high, the knowledge will often add to the patient's anxiety.

Few doctors will deny that there can exist a *type* of patient likely to suffer hypertension. The aggressive, tense and 'explosive' individual, restless, frustrated and excitable, might be expected to 'wear out his arteries' before the more serene and less worrying person. In several papers Alexander (1939) describes the condition of essential hypertension as the result of a psychoneurotic condition and assumes it to be due to excessive and inhibited hostile impulses. Dunbar (1935) and Wolfe (1936) used hypnotherapy to destroy tension which they felt was acting as a defensive mechanism and explained this mechanism on physiological and psychological grounds. Analytically trained psychiatrists such as Binger and his co-workers (1945) seek to explain the synthesis of hypertension in terms of 'an unresolved conflict between dependency on the parent and aggression. The battle is eventually lost to the hostility of the parent figure and the patient accepts the defeat of his normal aggressive drives. He fails to adjust to his environment and becomes tense and depressed. Measurement of the blood pressure discloses evidence of a rise in systolic and diastolic pressures.'

Raginsky mentions that good results have been obtained in some cases of essential hypertension, especially in the younger and middle age groups, following abreaction by hypnosis. In support of this contention the following case is of interest.

> A man aged 40, who had seen active service in Burma as a sergeant in World War II, complained of dizziness and buzzing in the ears, particularly in the mornings. Certain other symptoms caused his doctor to measure his blood pressure. The reading was 160/100. He was given bed-rest for 14 days and later the reading was 150/95. After 6 months he complained of the same symptoms as previously

and, as he seemed anxious and depressed, the case was sent for opinion to a psychiatrist.

It was elicited that during the fighting in Burma, his division was cut off by the Japanese and they were forced to lie in fox-holes ('the box') for several weeks. During a lull in the firing he sent a corporal to reconnoitre. The corporal never returned. He had been worried about this incident and felt sure that he had caused the death of the corporal, who was also his friend. He thought he should have gone himself.

After abreaction of this traumatic episode the patient stated that he had been able to relax for the first time in years. He was abreacted on three occasions and there has been no recurrence of his hypertensive attacks.

Much evidence is accumulating that certain cases of hypertension can be helped by hypnotherapy and autohypnosis. Research in the field is open to the general practitioner, for he deals with the disease in its early stage.

In all the psychosomatic diseases mentioned in this chapter it is suggested that if patients can achieve medium or deep hypnosis, they should be left in this state for some time. Continuous hypnotic 'sleep' is of the greatest benefit to patients, and Voisin, writing over 60 years ago, claimed to have relieved psychotics as well as psychoneurotics by this method. The patient is hypnotized and told to awaken fresh and alert at a specified time some hours later, or after he has rested and feels relaxed. If specific suggestions to the contrary have not been given, the hypnotic state is terminated spontaneously, usually after thirty minutes or so, or hypnosis gives way to ordinary sleep and the patient wakes in the usual manner.

MULTIPLE SCLEROSIS

The primary lesion in this puzzling disease is of medullated nerve sheaths within the brain and spinal cord, with associated secondary neurological and vascular reactions. The foci of the disease are scattered thickly throughout the nervous system. The lesions invade the grey and white matter indiscriminately. Little is known of the aetiology of the disease and no treatment seems to be of the slightest avail. Many patients display associated emotional difficulties and the fugitive character of the signs and symptoms of the disease suggest that hysterical phenomena are common concomitants of early disseminated sclerosis.

It should not be forgotten that the course of this illness is insidious and deceptive, i.e. a chronic course characterized by remissions and, in the spinal type of the disease, the duration may be twenty-five years or longer. Because of these remissions and chronicity, follow-up and assessment of any treatment becomes difficult. The hypnotherapeutic approach is entirely experimental and the cases treated by this means have not been followed up for more than a few years. Marked subjective improvement has occurred following a course of hypnotherapy. Patients have shown progress in that their symptoms become less worrying and frightening to them. They appear to gain greater control over their disease. It must be remembered that the relieving of anxiety in this condition is of vital importance.

An attractive married female patient aged 30 was seen complaining of tiredness, bad temper, depression and inability to walk any distance without the support of a stick.

Her first symptoms occurred in 1946. Following this, she had episodes of diplopia and blurring of vision. She was first admitted to hospital in 1952 and from that time had been in hospital on four occasions. Careful clinical investigation, which included a Lange colloidal gold curve, established beyond any doubt the diagnosis of multiple sclerosis.

She was discharged the last time with a report that she had had a further attack of retrobulbar neuritis and there was diminution of power in her legs. The lower limb reflexes were absent and the plantars were extensor. Joint-position sense in the toes was severely diminished, as was the vibration sense. She was treated with sedatives which she claimed were just given to reassure her; she knew tablets could not help her. She said that her admission to hospital made her much worse, for her movements were restricted by bed-rest and she had 'forgotten how to walk'.

The history revealed that she had had an unhappy childhood. Her father died when she was young and her mother was sadistic and bigoted in her upbringing. The patient recounted how she was made to kneel several times a day to her mother, i.e. on any occasion that she was naughty. The 'punishment' was instituted for the most trivial things. She also remembered on many occasions being awakened early in the morning, to be told by her mother: 'If I die it will be your fault.' This conduct terrified her. She never answered her mother back but would have liked to have done so on many occasions. This made her aggressive, frustrated, uncertain, fearful and anxious.

There was one unforgettable incident, when her mother forced her to enter deep water to retrieve her brother's ball. The child screamed that she would be drowned but was forced on into the water. At this moment she saw a wasps' nest. This alarming experience resulted in a deep fear, not of water, but of wasps. Abreaction, under light hypnosis, later overcame the phobia.

Discussion of her mother's sadism and understanding of its possible cause was helpful to her. Abreaction and revivification of several of the traumatic incidents she recounted destroyed her tension and aggression. As insight was achieved she became more and more relaxed and the subjective improvement was remarkable. She became less introspective, accepted membership of an amateur theatrical society and acted in a play. She interested herself in social work and now walks over a mile without support.

Three months after her hypnosis treatment she showed left temporal pallor and some diminution in the power of dorsiflexion of the left ankle. The lower limb reflexes were absent whilst postural and vibration sense were still severely restricted.

The overcoming of introspection, the abolition of tension and anxiety, the revivification of the traumatic episodes caused by her mother and their destruction by abreaction under medium hypnosis, and finally insight into the reasons for the aggravation of her illness, have led to a marked improvement in her health. The improvement could well be a remission of the disease process. The patient will not accept this; she feels that her improvement cannot be explained on these grounds. The case will be followed up for several years. She can achieve autohypnosis, practises assiduously, and is seen for half-yearly reinforcement.

Many sufferers from this disease will explain that when subjected to shock or stress they suffer an acute exacerbation of their symptoms. Three patients, all young females, gave a history of panic reactions as children and the desire to run away from their danger without being able to do so. Each described a feeling of being 'rooted to the ground'. They had all been locked in rooms and left in the dark for long periods as punishment for misbehaviour. They described their first symptoms of multiple sclerosis as a feeling of panic and difficulty in walking, first noticed at adolescence.

Patients suffering from this illness should not be allowed to languish in bed (Parsons-Smith 1954). They should be given encouragement and hope that by their own efforts they can become active and learn how to adapt themselves to their disability. In this respect the personal experience of one particular brave woman sufferer should be read by all physicians treating this disease (*Lancet* 1948).

Treatment by hypnotherapy should be undertaken early in the illness. The correction of an unsatisfactory environment, the overcoming of associated emotional problems and any concomitant anxiety reactions together with positive suggestions under hypnosis can lead to a surprising degree of early subjective improvement.

RHEUMATOID ARTHRITIS

Direct hypnotic suggestion will be found of use in this condition, particularly in those cases displaying the more chronic symptoms of the disease. For example, pain can often be controlled by suggestions given during hypnosis and it will be found in practice that the dose of drugs necessary to induce analgesia may be correspondingly lessened. Life can be made easier for the sufferer. The general practitioner is in the best possible position to use the technique.

Naturally, autohypnosis must be achieved, for daily visits are impracticable. The technique outlined in the section on migraine should be followed. The patient is hypnotized; in these cases it is particularly valuable to aim at a deeper state of hypnosis. The patient will not enter the hypnotic state while in pain. The suggestion is then made that he will be able to achieve the same state by himself by counting to five.

Several general practitioners and psychiatrists have claimed that patients can certainly be hypnotized while suffering pain. Ryde has claimed that patients with acute tonsillitis suffering great pain have entered a deep state of hypnosis and he has hypnotized athletes suffering strains and muscular spasms with success and great relief of symptoms for the patient. This agrees with the paper by Goldie (see pages 137-138). It will be found in practice that very few sessions are necessary and the patient learns to appreciate the hypnotic state, thus conditioning himself rapidly to the technique.

The value of hypnosis in these cases is sometimes proportional to the depth of hypnosis attained. Good subjects should always be taught autohypnosis and learn to give themselves helpful suggestions. These suggestions should be the usual positive ones: 'I will control the pain, I will never let the pain control me; every day I will feel more able to overcome my symptoms; I shall sleep well and wake alert and refreshed each morning'.

Johnson et al. (1947) found that certain patients express and discharge unconscious emotional tendencies through the voluntary muscles, just as in hysterical conversion. They assume that these muscle spasms and the increased muscle tonus may, under certain conditions, precipitate arthritis. It is suggested by the writer that many 'spasm' illnesses may commence in this way, e.g. epilepsy, ulcerative colitis, asthma, angina pectoris and other cardiovascular disturbances, and migraine; the reader will be able to think of several others.

Raginsky (1948) has said: 'Those who use hypnosis in the treatment of this psychogenic reaction know how productive it can be. Since results obtained in this particular field do not lend themselves to easy and simple reporting in the literature, the frequency of satisfactory results obtained should not be underestimated. As medical men learn to use this technique with due regard to the fundamental issues involved, much may be expected from this approach.'

Little can be added to these words. The practitioner is offered a technique to be combined with the newer chemical treatments as they are made available for general practice.

SUMMARY

When this chapter on general medicine was first written, just over twelve years ago, a plea was made that medical practice should become more psychosomatically orientated. Whether this is so or not the reader can decide for himself. One of us (G. A.) knew very well a surgeon who is now no longer with us. He was a brilliant after-dinner speaker and suffered a bodily catastrophe which robbed him of his speech. Heroically he battled on and watched his beloved rugger games from a wheel-chair. He died as bravely as he lived. Was it an accident that deprived this great humorist and speaker of his voice, was it 'psychosomatically' induced, or was it just coincidence? Psychoanalysts would have us believe that unconscious factors somewhere played a part in the choice (*sic*) of the speech centres as the victim of damage in one so dependent upon giving others laughter and joy with his witticisms. The surgeon in question, however, could seemingly never accept the psyche as having much to do with the soma.

A patient with a case of Hodgkin's disease, which was confirmed by biopsy of a gland from the neck of the sufferer, was told to 'go home and await the outcome'. At the time this appeared to be a fair suggestion. However, the general practitioner in the case was psychosomatically orientated and an expert hypnotist, having read as early as 1945 a paper published by an American author in 1929. The paper suggested that a chronic medical condition, such as has been described in this chapter, should be understood from the psychological aspect. A complete change of environment was advocated, as it was in the treatment of tuberculosis in Switzerland long ago. It was possible for this young patient (he was 21 at the time) to change his life style. He was told to get away from home and he did. He was told to seek new companions; he did, and by the age of 23 he was married. Later he was the father of three children, which gave him great pleasure; he told his GP that this fact alone had made a great difference to his life. He began to play Rugby and his wife became an enthusiast as well. He began to develop physically and mentally, put on a fair amount of weight and became captain of the rugby club 1st XV. In a few years he had become a broad, presentable and tall adult man. Reports of his progress were sent to his surgeon. Always a polite reply would be received, but very much to the point, the gist being: 'Death sooner and not later'. An article appeared in *The Lancet* doubting the prognosis of Hodgkin's disease, this being an illness leading invariably to death. It was headed 'Benign Hodgkin's Disease'. The surgeon, sent the article for his comment, sent back his usual polite letter. A précis would have read: 'Interesting, but your patient will die of Hodgkin's disease.' He would never be drawn into a discussion of mind and body, being in all fairness far more concerned with the body. The surgeon is now unfortunately dead, the boy with the Hodgkin's is going strongly. He is nearly 50, and the remission (if this is what it is) continues. He is in excellent health and coaches his old rugby team. He works hard and plays hard. Can we believe that Selye could have been right (see page 60: 'general adaptation syndrome')?

The general medical and psychosomatic field thus still offers opportunity for exploration and research, so we can answer the question we posed at the commencement of this summary. In the past 10 years many more of our colleagues have shown increased understanding and sympathy for our aims. The personality, temperament and emotions of the patient are now given much more emphasis in the assessment of illness and the doctor has a better understanding of the genesis of the conditions with which he is dealing. In all branches of medicine at the present time it is possible to detect a revival of interest in psychogenic elements as aetiological factors in the causation of disease. So much more can be accomplished for the sick patient by an all-embracing approach which assesses not only the somatic part of the illness but also the underlying psychological factors adversely affecting the individual. By a mixture of medicine, surgery and psychotherapy the battle may be more easily won.

BIBLIOGRAPHY

ALEXANDER, F. (1936) *Medical Value of Psychoanalysis.* New York: Moreton.
ALEXANDER, F. (1939) Emotional factors in essential hypertension. *Psychosom. Med., 1*, 175.

ALEXANDER, F. (1950) *Psychosomatic Medicine, its Principles and Applications*, pp. 270-1. New York: Norton.
ALEXANDER, G. H. (1940) Psychotherapy and the psychotherapist. *Psychosom. Med., 2*, 304.
ALVAREZ, W. C. (1948) *Nervousness, Indigestion and Pain*. New York: Hoeber.
ANDERSON, J. A. D., BASKER, M. A. & DALTON, R. (1975) Migraine and hypnotherapy. *Int. J. clin. exp. Hypnosis, 23*, 48-58.
BARBER, T. X., SPANOS, N. P. & CHAVES, J. F. (1974) *Hypnosis, Imagination and Human Potentialities*. Oxford: Pergamon Press.
BASKER, M. A. (1979) *Insomnia and Hypnotherapy*. Amsterdam: Elsevier.
BICK, H. (1967) *Hypnose in der Medizin und ihre Wellentheorie*, pp. 83-85. Munich: J. F. Lehmanns.
BINGER, C. A., ACKERMAN, N. W., COHN, A. E., SCHROEDER, H. A. & STEELE, J. M. (1945) Personality in arterial hypertension. *Psychosom. Med. Monogr. Suppl.*
BOWERS, M. K. (Ed.) (1958) *Introductory Lectures in Medical Hypnosis*, p. 25. New York: Institute for Research in Hypnosis.
BOWERS, M. K., JACKSON, E. N., KNIGHT, J. A. & LESHAN, L. (1976) *Counseling the Dying*, 2nd ed., p. 42. New York: Aronson.
CHEEK, D. B. & LECRON, L. M. (1968) *Clinical Hypnotherapy*. New York: Grune & Stratton.
CHERTOK, L. (Ed.) (1969) *Psychophysiological Mechanisms of Hypnosis*. New York: Springer.
CRASILNECK, H. B. & HALL, J. A. (1975) *Clinical Hypnosis: Principles and Applications*. New York: Grune & Stratton.
DICARA, L. V. (Ed.) (1974) *Limbic and Autonomic Nervous Systems Research*. New York: Plenum.
DUNBAR, H. F. (1935) Psychic factors in cardiovascular disease. *N. Y. St. J. Med., 36*, 423.
DUNBAR, H. F. (1938) *Emotions and Bodily Changes*. New York: Columbia University Press.
EISENBUD, J. (1937) The psychology of headache; a case studied experimentally. *Psychiat. Q., 11*, 592.
ELLENBERGER, H. F. (1970) *The Discovery of the Unconscious*. New York: Basic Books.
ERICKSON, M. H. (1944) The method employed to formulate a complex story for the induction of an experimental neurosis in a hypnotic subject. *J. gen. Psychol., 31*, 67.
ERICKSON, M. H. (1944) Hypnosis in medicine. *Med. Clins N. Am., May 1944*, 639.
ERICKSON, M. H., ROSSI, E. L. & ROSSI, S. (1976) *Hypnotic Realities: The Induction of Clinical Hypnosis and Forms of Indirect Suggestion*. New York: Irvington Publishers.

FENICHEL, O. (1954) The psychopathology of coughing. In: *Collected Papers*, 2nd series, pp. 237–243. New York: Norton.

FRANKEL, F. H. (1954) Ulcerative colitis. *Br. med. J., 1*, 1403.

FRANKEL, F. H. (1976) *Hypnosis: Trance as a Coping Mechanism.* New York: Plenum.

FROMM, E. & SHOR, R. E. (Eds) (1972) *Hypnosis: Research Developments and Perspectives.* Chicago: Aldine.

FROMM-REICHMAN, F. (1937) Contribution to psychogenesis of migraine. *Psychol. Rev., 24*, 26.

GENDEL, B. R. & BENJAMIN, J. E. (1946) Psychogenic factors in the aetiology of diabetes. *New Engl. J. Med., 234*, 556.

GHEORGHIU, V. A. (1973) *Hypnose und Gedachtnis*, p. 45. Munich: W. Goldman.

GROEN, J. (1947) Psychogenesis and psychotherapy of ulcerative colitis. *Psychosom. Med., 9*, 151.

GROSSMAN, C. M. & GROSSMAN, S. (1965) *The Life and Work of Georg Groddeck: The Wild Analyst.* London: Barrie & Rockliff.

HALLIDAY, J. L. (1942) Psychological aspects of rheumatoid arthritis. *Proc. R. Soc. Med., 35*, 455.

HARTLAND, J. (1971) *Medical and Dental Hypnosis and its Clinical Applications*, 2nd ed. London: Baillière Tindall.

HATOTANI, N. (Ed.) (1974) *Psychoneuroendocrinology.* Basel: Karger.

HEILIG, R. & HOFF, H. (1925) *Dr. med. Wschr., 51*, 1615.

HEYER, G. R. (1923) *Klin. Wschr., 3*, 492.

HILGARD, E. R. & HILGARD, J. R. (1975) *Hypnosis in the relief of pain.* California: Kaufmann.

HINKLE, L. E. & WOLF, S. (1949) Experimental study of life emotions and the occurence of acidosis in a juvenile diabetic. *Am. J. med. Sci., 217*, 130.

JOHNSON, A., SHAPIRO, L. B. & ALEXANDER, F. (1947) Preliminary report on a psychosomatic study of rheumatoid arthritis. *Psychosom. Med., 9*, 295.

LINDEMANN, E. (1945) Psychiatric aspects of the conservative treatment of ulcerative colitis. *Archs Neurol. Psychiat., Chicago, 53*, 322.

LURIA, A. R. (1932) *The Nature of Human Conflict.* New York: Liveright.

MAHER-LOUGHNAN, G. P. (1970) Hypnosis and auto-hypnosis for the treatment of asthma. *Int. J. clin. exp. Hypnosis, 1*, 18.

MELLET, P. G. (1973) Emotional aspects of asthma. *Health, 10*, 39.

MIRSKY, I. A., KAPLAN, S. & BROH-KAHN, R. H. (1949) Pepsinogen excretion in various physiologic and psychologic states, Paper read at Am. Psychosom. Soc. Convention, Atlantic City.

MITTLEMANN, B. & WOLFF, H. G. (1942) Emotions and gastroduodenal functions. *Psychosom. Med., 4*, 5.

MOHR, F. (1925) *Psychophysiche Behandlungsmethoden.* Leipzig: Hirzel.
MOODY, H. (1964) *An evaluation of hypnotically induced relaxation for reduction of peptic ulcer symptoms.* Ph.D. dissertation under the direction of Roy M. Dorcus, Ph.D., reviewed in the *Veteran's Administration* and published with approval of the Chief Medical Director, University of California, Los Angeles.
DE MORAES PASSOS, A. C. (1975) *Hipniatria: Tecnicas e Aplicacoes em Fobias.* Sao Paulo: Editora Manole.
PARSONS-SMITH, G. (1954) A summary of the modern concepts of the treatment of disseminated sclerosis. *Medicine ill., 8,* 4.
PAVLOV, I. P. (1928) *Lectures on Conditioned Reflexes,* Vol. I. London: Lawrence and Wishart.
PORTIS, S. A. (1949) Idiopathic ulcerative colitis. *J. Am. med. Ass., 139,* 208.
RAGINSKY, B. B. (1948) Psychosomatic medicine: its history, development and teaching. *Am. J. Med., 5,* 857.
RAGINSKY, B. B. (1953) Hypnosis in internal medicine. In: *Hypnosis in Modern Medicine,* ed. J. Schneck, pp. 28–55. Springfield, Ill.: Charles C. Thomas.
ROSEN, H. (1951) The hypnotic and hypnotherapeutic control of severe pain. *Am. J. Psychiat., 107,* 917.
SCHNECK, J. M. (1963) *Hypnosis in Modern Medicine,* 3rd ed. Springfield, Ill.: Charles C. Thomas.
SELYE, H. (1949) *Textbook of Endocrinology,* p. 837. Montreal: Acta Inc.
SELYE, H. & FORTIER, C. (1950) Adaptive reaction to stress. *Psychosom. Med., 12,* 149.
SERBAN, G. & KLING, A. (Eds) (1976) *Animal Models in Human Psychobiology,* p. 65. New York: Plenum.
TART, C. T. (1975) *States of Consciousness.* New York: Dutton.
TILLEARD-COLE, R. R. & MARKS, J. (1975) *The Fundamentals of Psychological Medicine.* New York: Halsted Press.
TINTEROW, M. M. (1970) *Foundations of Hypnosis: From Mesmer to Freud.* Springfield Ill.: Charles C. Thomas.
UNESTAHL, L. (1975) *Hypnosis in the Seventies.* Sweden: Veje.
WEITZENHOFFER, A. M. (1957) *General Techniques of Hypnotism.* New York: Grune & Stratton.
WOLBERG, L. R. (1947) Hypnotic experiments in psychosomatic medicine. *Psychosom. Med., 11,* 337.
WOLF, S. & WOLFF, H. G. (1943) *Human Gastric Function.* New York: Oxford University Press.
WOLFE, T. P. (1936) Emotions and organic heart disease. *Am. J. Psychiat., 93,* 681.

CHAPTER 6

HYPNOSIS IN THE NEUROSES

The idea that 'illness is a state of mind' is obvious to the thinking medical practitioner from the first time he enters his consulting room or surgery, fresh from the triumph of qualification. It is possible that he (or she) in that first flush of enthusiasm, facing his patients with the hard-earned knowledge of six years in medical school, as he examined, probed, investigated and subjected his patients to exhaustive tests, found 60 to 80 per cent of his sick patients were negative to each and every test. Why then were they sick?

The knowledge, gained so quickly in general practice, that organic disease is the smallest part of practice, dawns on the individual doctor either quickly, if he be 'functionally' minded, or slowly should he be more academic and 'organically' minded.

Moreover no young doctor, fresh from medical school, can fail to notice, after his first year of practice, that although he might be at risk for two thousand or four thousand patients he will see in his surgery a regular band of individuals visiting him weekly. These patients are his 'regulars'. He cannot avoid them. Few doctors in general practice suffer these 'chronics' gladly; they find their valuable time taken up by patients who cannot easily be treated.

Could any method of therapy be found to prevent these individuals becoming 'chronics'? Is there anything in the pharmacopoeia to prevent the early neurotic patient from becoming conditioned to his illness? Is there any way of overcoming the neurosis when it *has* become conditioned?

Possibly, before the Second World War there were doctors who considered that a dose of bromide or an adequate sedative could prevent a breakdown in a patient's nervous system. Since the war psychogenic and psychosomatic medicine has come to the fore and many articles on the nervous reaction, the autonomic system, stress and the like have appeared. General practitioners are now hard pressed to convince many of their patients that a bottle of medicine or a tablet will cure their backaches or headaches; many patients nowadays seem a step ahead of their practitioners. They admit that their fibrositis is made worse when they get worried. The doctor may find it difficult to reassure the patient that a tablet will effectively relieve this emotionalism. The patient may even read an article which tells him that there is no such thing as fibrositis and that it is far more likely to be a conflict in his mind than a slipped disc.

The doctor needs a weapon powerful enough to break a vicious circle of psychogenic illness. This weapon must necessarily be effective and rapid, positive and re-educative. General practitioners have not the time for long and involved psychotherapy. Thus it comes as no surprise that the last decade has seen an enormous variety of different schools of thought attempting to meet this need. Not all these schools are necessarily popular with the current psychiatric establishment, which has become hide-bound in its use of chemotherapy to tranquillize patients. On the other hand, the schools of Aversion, Sophrology, Gestalt, Transcendental Meditation, Behaviourism, Synchronicity, Client-centred Psychotherapy, Learning Therapy, Erikson's Identity Crisis, etc. have become self-centred. 'Fringe medicine' has given way to the 'Psychotherapy Supermarket'.

If we are not to find ourselves lost in a jungle of psychological supposition, we should remember that all psychotherapy is based on suggestion, and many of these 'supermarket' schools have as the most potent factor in their success (or failure) an element of suggestion. If the suggestion is 'positive' and supported by adequate rapport, or by the 'transference' first brought to our notice by Freud (see page 111), treatment can be exceptionally helpful and fairly rapid. Naturally, with the more chronic type of anxiety, much therapy may be needed and all the different schools described above would be hard-pressed to help their patients or clients, but superficial neuroses, which from time immemorial have been treated by suggestion or a bottle of medicine, will 'get better' in a spectacular fashion. Sick patients do get well via a large variety of different therapies, but Eysenck's suggestion, that the patient will get better whatever one does, is going a bit too far. Ordinary suggestion is most valuable but cannot be relied upon to counter a process which, if not dealt with rapidly and at the earliest opportunity, might lead to irreversible conditioning and thus to the chronic reaction of psychological and psychosomatic illness (see Chapter 5: Selye's 'general adaptation syndrome').

In this chapter will be outlined a method of approach to the common neuroses seen by every doctor in general practice. These vary between anxiety, hysteria, obsession and depression; each will have a little of its fellow for good measure. Nowadays, with a new tranquillizer every other day and ever more powerful methods of abolishing these symptoms, we must ask ourselves whether we should 'sweep the crumbs of the neurosis under the carpet' or take measures finally to rid the patient of his emotional over-emphasis.

THE ANXIOUS PATIENT

It must be stressed that anxiety is a state of chronic fear. It is the overaction of the mind in an ineffectual attempt to overcome a difficult environment. The individual may even create a physical reaction in an effort to defend himself against an impossible situation. Thus fatigue will often be complained about, particularly on slight exertion, but the fatigue is curiously selective and is often brought on by the patients having to do something they resent. They will talk for hours about their symptoms but may be worn out after five minutes' conversation with certain people. There is generally a loss of weight due to a lack of appetite and many patients complain of indigestion and nausea, which will have no relation to food. They will often speak of a 'blown out' feeling directly following a meal and some few minutes later may experience flatulence and 'heartburn'.

Symptoms associated with the urinary system are common. Patients will speak vaguely of pain in the bladder and the necessity of passing water too often. They seldom get up at night, however, and the polyuria is mainly diurnal.

The anxious patient will often draw the doctor's attention to his fears. He may complain of pain near the apex beat of the heart and show that he obviously considers this organ to be diseased. His whole attitude is one of fear and trepidation. He may speak vaguely of the signs and symptoms of tachycardia, of cardiac discomfort or palpitation, and a tight constriction of the chest which frightens him. He will be conscious of his heartbeats and a dropped beat may be felt and enlarged upon. These symptoms will often occur at rest and the doctor may even be called out at night to a patient who has had a panic attack causing momentary loss of consciousness. These panic attacks may be precipitated by a situation provoking an emotional reaction, often at an unconscious level.

Many younger patients seen in practice will complain of flushing and self-consciousness when in company. These vasomotor disturbances are very common in the anxiety reaction. Patients will say they blush and perspire in an exaggerated way and will further explain their symptoms as excessive shyness, inferiority and difficulty of concentration. They will admit that they cannot stop thinking about themselves, for this state is marked by excessive introspection.

Such patients may complain of many symptoms. They suffer headaches and are constantly changing their glasses and asking if their eyes need testing. They may present with abdominal pain in the right lower quadrant, simulating a 'grumbling' appendix; or pain over the left side with signs of a spastic colon. (It will be remembered that constipation and diarrhoea are common conditions seen in anxiety.) They will complain of pain in the head, but if the question of pain is pressed they will admit to feelings of discomfort rather than pain, a 'swelling' of the scalp, or 'a band tied round the head', etc. Pains may also be felt at the nape of the neck or in the shoulders. They are very likely to be caused by spasm of the muscles and the patients will admit that they get worse at times of stress and emotion. These spasms are invariably referred to, and often diagnosed as, 'rheumatic' pains or 'fibrositis'. Many older patients will describe the pain they experience in the shoulders or arms as 'a weight bearing me down'. One patient, as she gained insight into her anxieties, stated: 'The pain seemed just like a yoke I was carrying across my shoulders.' She paused and continued: 'It seemed as if I had the cares of the world on my shoulders!'

Buzzing and singing in the ears may be complained about and the older patient might produce an intractable tinnitus little affected by any form of treatment. They are curiously resistant to sedatives or analgesics, and if reassurance from an otologist is not enough, hypnosis may prove effective.

Giddiness is more than common and some years ago a general practitioner could be kept busy checking and rechecking blood pressure for this symptom. The habit is still indulged in by the doctor uncertain of a diagnosis and, if carried out upon the anxious patient, can be the cause of much misery and unnecessary suffering.

> An elderly woman was seen after her own doctor had retired from practice. She had been told 12 years earlier that she had high blood pressure and might collapse in the street, and that it would therefore be best if she always had somebody with her when she left the house. She took the advice too literally and had not ventured out since that time. Later investigation revealed very little wrong except her fear of sudden death.

The anxiety syndrome is not difficult to diagnose and any suggestion likely to exaggerate these symptoms should be avoided by the physician.

It is surprising, however, that much fear and subsequent ill-health can be traced to the patient's first memory of a hospital out-patient or casualty department, and even the consultant staff inadvertently cause misery by treating sensible and intelligent patients tactlessly.

> A lady sent to hospital for observation and investigation following a 'collapse' in her home overheard the physician telling his registrar: 'This might be a very interesting brain tumour. The last one we had like her was operated on in Bristol and died.' Reassurance by her general practitioner stopped her from leaving the hospital and enabled her to go through with the investigation, which fortunately proved negative.

Of the many nervous reactions suffered by the anxious patient, insomnia is the commonest and most wretched. In the anxiety type of case the patient finds difficulty in getting off to sleep. The sleep rhythm is broken and a vicious circle of defeatism is set up. Sleep would appear to be a conditioned rhythm. Once the habit becomes conscious and the individual is assailed by doubts of whether he 'will get off or not' the general practitioner will be hard pressed to restore this rhythm. Sedatives are valuable, but many patients dislike drugs for sleep, fearing that they may become drug addicts.

Actually, anxious patients sleep more than they think they do. They often complain that they twist and turn all night, whereas in reality they are having restless sleep with bad dreams. These patients are difficult to deal with, and hypnotherapy might offer relief.

> A woman patient, who complained of many fears of a hypochondriacal nature and showed chronic anxiety patterns, was much relieved when she was able to discuss her 'death wishes'. She was having a great deal of worry with her mother who was, she claimed, a hard, cold woman who never loved her. She was encouraged to relive her intense aggression against this lady under a medium state of hypnosis. She was able to remember occasions when she would have been pleased if her mother had died. She stated: 'I would be better if the whole family went away and left me'. She meant her mother, father and sister. She was told that love and hate were simply ambivalent feelings for those she loved and several sessions were spent in reassuring her that she would not be able to cause these people any great harm by her thoughts. She rapidly made a good recovery from her insomnia and was able to go further and deeper into her real problems.

Hypnosis in the Neuroses 101

The difficulty of recapturing the sleep rhythm can destroy the power of concentration and may affect memory. It is the combination of these symptoms which might produce in the patient added fear and anxiety until he begins to feel that he may be 'going off his head'.

Hypnotherapy is of value in such cases, for it can be used as a rapid form of treatment and might also enable the physician to dispense with treatment by tablets or medicines and the constant repetition of prescriptions. It should be remembered that patients must be taught autohypnosis so that they can continue with their treatment and so supplement the suggestions of the hypnotherapist. It must be appreciated, however, that many cases will be seen where every effort can be made to relieve the insomnia at an hypnotic level without avail. In practice, if the patient can be taken deeper into hypnosis, some attempt made to analyse death fears and the patient allowed to verbalize these fears, insomniacs can be helped to a regaining of their sleep rhythm.

TREATMENT OF THE ANXIOUS PATIENT

Every medical man is potentially a hypnotist. His relationship with his patient puts him in a powerful position. In the first few years after qualification the young doctor finds it necessary to guard against a superior attitude towards his patients. He must also learn that every patient needs a different approach. He may need to be severe with some, to cajole others. In the approach by hypnosis the interpersonal relationship is a most important factor.

In spite of the National Health Service where, to a certain extent, the family doctor has had to bow to masses of documents and lists of patients' requirements, many practitioners have retained a personal relationship with their patients. This relationship is unique. It is built upon mutual trust and a code of honour. The general practitioner then is in an ideal relationship from the hypnotic point of view, for hypnosis demands, for its successful practice, just such a relationship.

It is intended to study the case history of a patient treated by hypnotherapeutic methods in general practice. The case will be illustrated at some length for it is an extremely common one and many of these cases will be seen in the course of a year's work.

> An attractive married woman was first seen complaining of indecision and 'the inability to get anything done in my home'. She would stand for some time thinking of what to do and never come to a decision about anything. There was something worrying her.

She would appear to get panic attacks. She cried often and felt wretched and unloved. She was bad-tempered with the children and her marriage seemed in jeopardy due to her sexual frigidity. She was unable to feel emotion and complained bitterly of depression and a terrible feeling that everything was going wrong and would lead to a dreadful tragedy. Her husband was seen and admitted that he was extremely worried by her symptoms: she had always been highly-strung but in the past few years things had gone from bad to worse. He seemed an intelligent man dedicated to helping his wife. At the beginning of treatment she had nothing but praise for him, but gradually a different story emerged.

Fifteen years earlier she had been hypnotised for symptoms of anxiety: she had received eight treatments and had remained well for many years. This time, the first three treatments resulted in alternating outbursts of hysterical weeping and aggression. She tore a chair cover and threatened to throw a stool through a glass bookcase. She was obviously displaying spontaneous, abreactive phenomena. No attempt was made to hypnotize her and she desperately pleaded that hypnosis should be used to 'release her unconscious worries'. After several treatments it was established that she had many phantasies: several sessions were needed for her to recount these phantasies. Meanwhile she admitted that she had never loved her husband and married him 'on the rebound'. She said: 'I was in love with an American boyfriend and only married to get my own back on him when he rejected me.' This seemed an extraordinary tale as she had already had children by her husband and loved them dearly. A crucial situation developed when it was established that hypnosis had been used to feed back each traumatic episode she recounted. The hypnotherapist had forbidden her to dwell on the recall of past memories and discovered early on that she was an amnesic, i.e., he had induced amnesia while she was in the hypnotic state and because (as she explained later) she 'expected everything he told me to happen' she could remember nothing of what had been told to her therapist.

It was further established that she had been treated for 'migraines' which were the bane of her life. These attacks appeared to be the classical type of migraine which would force her to go to bed and stay in a darkened room. Most times she vomited and spent 24 hours recovering. Her therapist had 'cured' these attacks by hypnosis. She agreed that she was a perfectionist. She felt ruled by time and stated that she was obsessional and quite compulsive in her actions and thoughts. She said further that her sister was brighter than herself and her father had always loved her more. These symptoms had all been helped by hypnosis, but even so she had gradually become less confident and more frightened of what people would say and think about her. She could understand her own immaturity and several times admitted that she felt like a little girl. She had become more and more frightened of her husband and agreed that her parents had had the same effect upon her. She was quick to appreciate that the patterns of her life had been repeated: her puberty and adolescence and her feelings at her marriage were simply a repeat of the first five years of her life. She recognised early in the treatment the necessity for 'growing-up' and agreed that hypnosis had been invaluable in showing her the problems and particularly the conflicts she had to overcome. Gradually she realised that her regressive need to go back and relive her emotions at an abreactive level were no longer necessary. She was offered the choice between behaviourism and resynthesis using psychotherapy. She chose the latter as offering a more rational approach. She thought that a behaviouristic technique would leave certain fears hidden, for she was still certain in her own mind that much of what she spoke about to her hypnotherapist had not finally come to consciousness.

The following facts were elicited by dreams and recall at a face-to-face level. At an early age she had followed a man into a wood. He had held her up and let her slide gently onto his penis. Later fellation took place. It was noticeable that while telling this story she seemed to go into a 'trance' state, spitting all the time. As it appeared obvious that she was repeating what she had told her therapist under hypnosis, she was told, in a forceful voice, to stop play-acting and being hysterical and to tell her story as a woman: regression was useless at this stage. She came out of her spontaneous hypnotic state and agreed that she would tell her story. It became obvious to her that the man she said she followed into the woods was a cover for her father and she complained weeping that her father only loved her sister. Each time she was reminded that she had already abreacted all these traumatic events before (she was quite aware of this word 'abreaction', having learnt the technique from her therapist). A long history of sexual adventures was recalled, particularly at adolescence. She quickly grasped that she could not bear to feel rejected by a man and equated 'man' with 'father'. She became less and less obsessional and compulsive as she recalled her sexual problems, and began to understand that although hypnosis had helped her in overcoming her symptoms she needed to mature emotionally.

Of some interest in this case was the thought, which obsessed the patient for many months, that her anxiety and fear were the result of a single critical event. She believed that all her symptoms would disappear like magic when a certain something (she was not sure what) 'came to the surface'. As each traumatic situation was exposed the sudden insight became the 'nucleus' she was looking for. Her disappointment was intense when she realized that she felt better for two or three days and would then repeat the same old anxiety-phobic-compulsive-obsessional-hysterical patterns. Stekel, in his incomparable study of this syndrome ('Compulsion & Doubt': 1950) has shown us that long, detailed analysis in these cases is best avoided. This statement is partly borne out by the improvement in this patient for a number of years, but also pinpoints the increasing knowledge that hypnotherapy should be used in *selected* cases, preferably in general practice.

This interesting case is invaluable for the student in emphasising the wisdom of accepting each patient as a person and not as a symptom. It would have been quite impossible to label this lady's condition as any particular neurosis. The diagnosis, if one has to be made, is 'emotional immaturity' and has a little of each of the symptoms of the common neuroses for good measure! The therapist in this case could reasonably argue that he had adequately treated a very sick person and relieved her of symptoms which had made her life unbearable for many years. He then very correctly sent her to a colleague for psychiatric opinion.

All hypnotherapists should be aware that every session will show one characteristic — resistance. Simply put, this means that neurosis is a game. It is when the patient 'gives up the game', or knows that 'the game is up', that we can expect a great surging-forward and a lessening of the bothersome symptoms that make life so difficult for the victim and the psychotherapist.

In the case outlined above every conceivable form of unconscious resistance had been used and each in turn had to be patiently explained away. The patient wished constantly to be hypnotised, irrespective of her gain in dynamic insight. Late in treatment she admitted that she could achieve autohypnosis for herself! Each time she had to rid herself of another 'secret' she begged for hypnosis. When last seen she was showing a greater understanding of the many facets of her serious illness.

The technique of using hypnotherapy follows the early method of Freud (Jones 1953). It will be remembered that before evolving his method of allowing the patient complete rein to his thoughts, Freud would direct the conversation along the paths he devised and thought valuable. In the same way, when using hypnosis, it is found more valuable to direct the patient's thoughts and emotionally-taxed ideas along the paths which the hypnotherapist feels are valuable and will yield most material. In this way much time is saved and the patient learns to speak of the thought most valuable to the doctor. When the physician comes up against the barrier

Hypnosis in the Neuroses

which Freud describes in his early works, hypnosis is employed to stimulate and thus expose psychogenic factors. This barrier will be obvious after a small amount of practice with these cases. It was at this barrier that Freud, at first, would probe, where the patient seemed to be unable to think of anything further. Freud then noticed that if he remained silent the patient would invariably produce unconscious material of inestimable value for the psychotherapist. It is precisely at this stage that hypnosis, used in the first, second or deepest stage, can cut across the excessive time factor (for it sometimes takes patients weeks to recall psychic material to the conscious mind) and allows the physician to accomplish two things. He can stimulate and thus extract the unconscious emotional trauma and he can commence re-education both at the conscious and the unconscious level. By these means the patient regains insight more quickly than is possible with certain other techniques in psychotherapy (Wolberg 1953).

The anxiety reaction is always associated in its genesis with misplaced guilt feelings. It is worthwhile explaining this symptom complex to every patient suffering from chronic anxiety with or without depression. Hypnosis may be used to accelerate the overcoming of anxiety and to allow other symptoms, such as inferiority, insecurity and the like, to be dealt with by reassurance and explanation. Chronic anxiety is very often diagnosed, by those seeing the case for the first time, as depression. The G.P. should be in a position to give an adequate and accurate reading of his patient's personality and temperament: much subsequent ill-health might be prevented by doctors versed in the methods of hypnotherapy.

The anxiety reaction is the commonest symptom seen in general practice. All manner of phobias will be encountered, from the fear of storms, through the fear of all sorts of animals, particularly mice, rats and spiders, to sitting down thirteen at table. Many of these fears will need no treatment. Many of them are readily treated and helped by hypnosis.

Another case of anxiety will be described which illustrates the type suitable for hypnotherapy in general practice and outlines a method using medium hypnosis to analyse and re-educate the patient. Some cases will obviously be easier to handle than others. Some will be more resistant than others. Intelligence, suggestibility, constitutional adequacy and the desire to get better on the one hand, and the personality and knowledge of the physician on the other, will be important factors in the improvement and ultimate well-being of the patient.

An attractive young woman of 20 said that her parents were continually complaining about her conduct. She smoked excessively, was constantly grumbling, always felt tired and seemed to have no zest for anything except to quarrel and abuse them.

The girl said she was nervous of everything. She seemed to have no confidence, worried about getting to work in the mornings and feared that something dreadful would happen to her parents. She was quite contented when she was away from the house, but on returning in the evenings they 'all seemed to be on at me at the same time'. Lately she could not meet people and had lost faith in herself and everybody else. She gave her story sensibly and at some length. There was little in the family history of much consequence. A maternal aunt was said to be 'nervy'. She had one brother younger than herself, who was apparently stable. Her father was a 'quiet type' dominated by his wife. She was responsible for the discipline while he seldom interfered with the children. The girl had noticed a growing resentment of her father and felt guilty about this. She had been well until the age of six or seven when she began to have temper tantrums. The father could remember her rolling on the floor in a rage and she would be punished for this behaviour by her mother.

At about this time an alarming incident occurred. A man tried to touch her on her genitals, which frightened her and she could remember running home to her mother sobbing bitterly. A considerable fuss was made of the incident and she was taken to the police station and questioned. At this time she suffered further trauma. When her brother was born she had received no explanation as to where he had come from. She had to accept the bewildering fact that her mother came from hospital with a baby. She added that although she dearly loved her brother she had always been jealous of him. She could not concentrate at school. Her teachers said that she did not want to try and could have done better if she had, an opinion with which both parents agreed. At the present time she had no boy-friends and seemed to lead a solitary existence.

Treatment with hypnosis was started with emphasis on the desirability of abreacting the effect of the assault from her mind. Abreaction by means of hypnosis is simple and can be accomplished in the light, medium or deep stage. The patient is made to fantasize, i.e. relive the actual incident while relaxed, and suggestions are given as below. The American school terms this revivification. Hypnosis, together with the appropriate suggestions, causes an explosion of tension surrounding the earlier traumatic episode, without the concomitant effects seen in drug abreaction. Here is an added advantage, for most drug abreactions demand the presence of a nurse or orderly and can hardly be accomplished in general practice. In

Hypnosis in the Neuroses

hypnotic abreaction a nurse is usually unnecessary and patients rid themselves of unconscious tension and 'psychic energy' with the minimum of discomfort and the maximum of effect (Ambrose 1951).

This case was dealt with in three phases. The first two sessions were used for conditioning the patient to the hypnotic state and allowing free rein to her conscious thoughts. In the first sessions of 30 minutes each session the traumatic incidents were elicited and then she was taught how to relax and to enter a hypnotic state quickly and easily.

In this three-phase method the induction is accomplished rapidly. The patient is simply told to relax the legs and arms in a chair (or on a couch) and suggestions that he or she is getting drowsy, sleepy and heavy are given in a steady, monotonous but positive voice. A light or bright object can be held just above the eyes, but this is unimportant. No measurement of depth is required, and when it is felt that enough relaxation is achieved the following suggestions are given: 'You concentrate only on my voice, as I talk you feel yourself getting deeper and drowsier, as I count to five you will go deeper and deeper, but always conscious of my voice. Your mind is clear and you follow every word I say. You are beginning to feel happier and less worried. A tingling in your foot is felt – this tingling means you are gaining more confidence every second I talk to you.' (It is often useful to emphasize an abstract emotion by allying it in the patient's mind to a physical sensation, for it creates a reflex which can become conditioned during further interviews.) The patient is told: 'With this confidence you will feel less shy and more sure of yourself. You will feel less tense while at home and soon you will lose your fears and feel well, happy and confident.'

At this stage only direct suggestions have been given but they will produce a surprising degree of improvement. This improvement does *not* depend on the depth of hypnosis achieved, the slightest relaxation will give the same effect. Suggestions must be given in a positive and dogmatic way, *there must be no doubt in the hypnotist's voice (or mind) that the improvement suggested will be achieved.* The aim is to reach a certain degree of relaxation – the hypnotic state will follow automatically and is learnt by the patient as a conditioning.

The second phase of this case was dealt with in the three sessions of superficial analysis and further positive suggestions. The suggestions, however, in this phase were given to withdraw tension from the patient by causing her to relive the traumatic episode thought to be responsible for the girl's present feeling, i.e. her fear of men and her growing dislike of her father.

Placed in a medium hypnotic state, she was given the following suggestions:

'You see yourself as a small child of six walking along the road. You see clearly the man who frightened you so much. He comes towards you, and tries to touch you, you scream and hit him, you are frightened and tense and you feel in your stomach the terrible tension that you felt at this time. Now you are no longer afraid, all the fear leaves you, you sink deeper into the chair, and you feel more and more relaxed. Never, never again will you be frightened by this incident. You will be able to think of it without fear or worry. You will never worry about this again, and when you open your eyes you will feel a wonderful sense of relief and happiness. Your shyness of men will disappear. You will love your father, as you have always done, for he loves you deeply. When you open your eyes you will feel wonderfully happy and well.'

By the fifth session she reported that she felt more confidence, knew that she was going to be all right, listened to the recitation of the facts when she was attacked by the man and fully understood the implications of fear, jealousy and insecurity.

The sixth and seventh sessions were a repeat of the first five sessions, and she reported six months after the last visit that she was well. Her parents wrote one year after treatment to say that she was engaged to be married and seemed very happy.

This case is illustrated for several reasons. In the first place it is extremely common. The combination of sexual trauma with jealousy leading to insecurity and consequent deepening of an already present constitutional anxiety is well known and can be seen frequently in general practice. Cases of this description will be illustrated in the chapter on children and their treatment by hypnotherapy. Naturally, treatment given early will be of the greatest importance. If these cases are allowed to go on to adult life many years of introspective misery are the outcome. Hypnosis is a therapeutic approach offering hope of relief from the tension, fear and anxiety found in this type of emotional illness.

THE HYSTERICAL PATIENT

Hysteria always begins with anxiety. It is most unusual in practice to see a case of pure hysteria for, in such cases, there are likely to be symptoms of anxiety present as well. Hysteria is a negative response to difficulties in the environment. In the anxiety state a patient manages to carry on with

Hypnosis in the Neuroses

his normal activities. The hysterical reaction is marked by the individual being quite incapable of doing so. The hysteric cannot fit into the environment in which he finds himself. Therefore, he tries to change the environment to suit himself. A patient suffering from a hysterical reaction may also produce a functional paralysis, aphonia or a convulsive fit.

Slater has denied that a state of hysteria exists at all. The authors of this book have constantly deprecated the 'pigeon-holing' of patients. To suggest for example that one patient suffers anxiety, another depression and a third obsessions, is in our opinion valueless to the student. In the introduction to this chapter it was suggested that patients will present with a mixture of symptoms, but it should be well understood that, when describing the condition known as hysteria, we are following the habit of many years of teaching and, although condemning the practice, find it easier for teaching purposes.

Clinically the features of hysteria are threefold: (1) a physical manifestation without a structural lesion, (2) a calm mental attitude (*la belle indifférence*), and (3) episodic mental states showing fugues, somnambulism, amnesia, double personality and emotional attacks. One case may show all three phenomena.

These cases are extremely resistant to therapy of any kind. They have been described as 'the despair of all practitioners'. By the time they are seen by the specialist, the condition is chronic and treatment is tedious for it demands insight and purposive conduct from the patient.

The type of case frequently seen in practice is illustrated below. The actual technique varies little from that described in the section on the anxiety state, but more positive suggestions for the future behaviour of the patient must be given to the relatives of the hysteric. He can be helped very much by those around him, just as he can be made worse by ignorant and foolish people.

> A young woman aged 32 was complaining of constant headaches, painful cramp-like feelings in her abdomen and bouts of depression. She said that she had always suffered from period-pains and problems of a like nature. She had had several friendships with men but they had led to nothing. She admitted that she seemed afraid of men and bitterly added that she had never known her father. He had divorced his wife when their daughter was a teenager and her mother had been forced to be both mother and father to her. Hypnotherapy revealed a great deal of aggression towards the mother.
>
> Frustrated in her feelings to the opposite sex, the patient had overcompensated by using women as her 'loved objects'. There was

only a vague story that at school she had passionately 'loved' another girl younger than herself, but she readily agreed that the games-mistress was a very special person to her. However, women were just the same to her as men: 'they all let me down in the end'. She found it difficult to believe that the projection of her own fear of rejection was responsible for her difficult relationships with almost everybody, but with the use of autohypnosis she worked hard to find the solution to her supposed misfit in life.

As commonly happens, she had found hypnosis to be a haven of rest after hospital treatment, where she was diagnosed as 'agorophobic' and given medication. 'Nothing seemed to work', she said, but in the earlier days of her treatment with hypnosis she would add 'and you are not much better either'.

Hypnotherapy was used with a view to helping this young woman to emotional maturity. The fixation on the mother had to be broken and the patient's adjustment to others provoked. She had a very marked 'chip on her shoulder' and felt that everybody was to blame but herself. The first hypnotic sessions were valuable in building up rapport, helping her to look inwards and examine herself and not to be afraid of seeing herself in her true colours. Insight was accepted only gradually; much cheerfulness, patience and optimism were necessary at this point.

The patient made great headway when a young man (intelligent and good-looking, she claimed) refused to be 'rejected' by her and suggested that the efforts of her analyst would help her to adjust. He became a tower of strength and quite possibly little could have been accomplished without his constant reassurance that treatment would ultimately be successful. She was afraid of marriage and he had similar difficulties; together they were able to help each other to a greater psychological adjustment.

It was pointed out to her during treatment that she would often recite a long series of symptoms, but with a grin on her face *(la belle indifférence)*. She could never understand why she did this, but readily accepted that it was a symptom of her neurosis. She agreed that as a child she was prone to nightmares and sleep-walking and had always been described as 'spoilt'. She was an only child.

Under hypnosis she realised that her constant battle with her mother was a projection of her guilt feelings: she feared that she had driven her father away. Her fantasies were indicative of her need to gain power (in lieu of love) over both parents. She became far less resentful when this frustrated aggression was released. She was taught autohypnosis early in treatment and could give herself positive suggestion (ego-strengthening) when she felt that she could not cope. Gradually she gave up her need to dominate her environment with her symptoms and became a more rational person.

It should be remembered that of all the common neuroses treated by hypnosis, hysteria has the longest and most exciting history. Charcot and his followers, working at the Salpêtrière (see page 9), were able to show the redoubtable Freud the 'arts of their science' and Freud went home to Austria captivated by the extrovert antics of the great French neurologist. Indeed it was while 'practising' on a patient bequeathed to him by his friend Professor Breuer that Freud was able to help Anna O, a gross hysteric, by the new method of 'free association'. Repeated hypnotizing simply produced new symptoms, but because Freud used hypnosis incorrectly he discovered a whole new world. From the small beginnings of treating a hysterical patient the art of psychotherapy grew.

The general practitioner must be aware that he will create a transference situation by using hypnosis. He will have to understand his own counter-transferences. When dealing with the anxiety hysteric the breaking of the transference situation is most important. When the doctor sets out to achieve insight and subsequent relief of symptoms in some six to twelve interviews he must be fully conscious of this transference. In this respect the hypnotic method was once explained on the grounds that it achieves its results by 'a homosexual attraction of the patient to the hypnotizer' (Schneck 1950), and some psychoanalysts believe that the transference seen in any psychotherapeutic technique can only be adequately dealt with by their own methods (Brill 1946). There is, however, much modern opinion that this transference *can* be dealt with adequately during hypnotherapy, and is in fact of the greatest value in gaining rapport and added suggestibility for the benefit of the patient (Wolberg 1946; Wells 1944).

MILD PSYCHOGENIC DEPRESSION

The diagnosis of the depressive reaction is more difficult than the name warrants. For purposes of this handbook the type of depression to be described is that of the patient who presents in general practice complaining of feeling depressed. *He can give no adequate reason for this depression.* If his wife had just died and his son had eloped, we should speak of his resulting unhappiness as a *reactive depression* and time might be the healer in a case of this description. In a mild depressive psychosis, where the depression is spoken of as *endogenous*, we are facing a common illness, which is dangerous and difficult to treat. The true depressive will commit suicide if not treated and if he is allowed to do so.

Nowadays, with the whole gamut of tranquillisers and anti-depressants available, the figures for suicide have continued the fall started by the rather more barbaric method of electro-convulsive therapy (ECT). However, many patients treated with antidepressants get rid of their depression and are able to carry on until a relapse afflicts them, when the general practitioner once again arranges for another course of antidepressants. It may be true that some of these cases are resistant to psychotherapy and treatment might be contraindicated if the psychiatrist feels that probing will do more harm than good. But so often a patient who could be helped by psychotherapy is not fortunate enough to receive it. A general practitioner may even be visiting a sick patient when he notices another person sitting disconsolately in a corner looking the picture of misery, but never having approached a doctor for treatment. Many such cases can be the result of superficial fear or guilt feelings. If these are associated with puberty or adolescence, a little probing years earlier could well have revealed the trouble. But to probe now would possibly precipitate an acute manic-depressive psychosis. Although these cases are best left to the psychiatrist, many of them would undoubtedly be helped by a short and not too penetrating course of hypnotherapy. Simple suggestions given while the patient is in the first stage of hypnosis have proved most beneficial. It must be emphasized that the approach is along positive suggestive lines and no attempt is made to analyse at a deep level until it is obvious that the depression is lifting or the patient seems anxious to talk.

In general practice, mild depression seems to affect female patients more often than males. However, there still seem to be women who expect to be depressed when they reach the menopause. This 'time of life' is blamed for many things: if a woman loses her temper with her husband, the comment from her friends is often: 'It's her time of life, it always affects them that way.' Even in an age when oestrins and the Pill prevail, we still hear these asides from certain people, who seem to know much more than their doctor but nevertheless keep him busy if they 'get ill'. Naturally such people represent a small percentage of the population, but a small band of faithfuls is what keeps the G.P. busy.

However, mild depression does offer the physician scope for reassurance, autohypnosis and acquiring knowledge of the dynamics of depression. One must remember that in many cases depression is simply the frustration of a person unable to allow his true emotions to be released.

Sooner or later a reaction can be expected, in which depression will have its place: much psychosomatic illness goes hand-in-hand with depression. Even the common cold has been the subject of much conjecture and there seems little doubt that the depressed person is more at risk in suffering these annoying complaints. After all, the person suffering a cold is not only crying, but can 'cough out' his aggression at the same time! Our task then becomes the release of this aggression to allow a sense of 'emotional freedom' — a freedom from fear, guilt, and all of the so-called 'negative' emotions. How do we do this? Throughout this book the emphasis has been upon the release of emotion, the blocking of which causes tension. Hypnosis is still the safest and best tranquilliser of all. If insight can be made acceptable and if the patient understands that no progress can be made while the desire for 'illness' persists, we shall have an early success. The rule in such cases is to let the patient tell her story. Sympathy is shown and not too much probing is attempted. In this respect there is a great deal of evidence that patients left severely alone in the hypnotic state at any level of depth can be helped a great deal by meditation. The technique is as follows: The patient is made comfortable in an armchair or on a couch and covered with a blanket (which probably facilitates regression to childhood). The hypnotherapist sits by or at some distance from the patient — there should be no rule, but intuitively the doctor should feel what best suits his patient. Nothing is said, but if the patient speaks he should be allowed to do so without any comment. Cases of asthma and certain skin rashes have been helped considerably by this technique. The patient works out his (or her) salvation while in the state of hypnosis and the physician says nothing or very little. In these cases of depression this technique will be found to be of the greatest value.

Every patient who has received drug treatment for depression should receive psychotherapy once the depression has lifted. So many of these patients may be left and relapse is unfortunately the rule and not the exception. Often the patient will want to tell the doctor the cause of the depression but finds it difficult or impossible to do so.

A particularly intelligent author aged 55 was taken to a private nursing home acutely ill mentally. He was depressed, agitated and hallucinated. He was screaming and seemed terrified. After sedation and immediate ECT he rapidly became calmer and after ECT $\times$ 4 he was discharged from the home. He was still somewhat agitated and seemingly depressed and when first seen in private practice kept saying: 'You can help me doctor, oh please say you can help me. I'm not mad, am I? You are sure I'm not mad, I will get better won't I? I'm no use to anybody, I haven't written a word for weeks, nobody will employ me, I'm out of work, I shall never be able to work again. What's going to happen to me? I shall have no money.' Great sympathy was shown to him and the words: 'You are going to be quite well, you are not mad, you must tell yourself constantly that you are going to get well, your type of case always gets well,' etc., were constantly reiterated. The depressive must be told over and over again that he is going to get quite fit and well. Reassurance must be given in a firm, positive tone of voice.

No attempt was made to hypnotize this patient on his first visit. He was sleeping badly and was terrified of being alone. He spent his week-ends in the country with friends. He was afraid of not being able to sleep and it was thought advisable to give a sedative in a dose adequate to counter the insomnia. It was considered essential to see him several times until he was stabilized. He was seen again two days later. He was still agitated, but said he had spent the last few days with friends and felt a little better.

He proved to be an excellent hypnotic subject and made headway from the first treatment. He was given the post-hypnotic suggestion that at the next interview he would be able to speak freely, and in the second session he recounted how as a child he was brought up under strict discipline. He could remember lying awake at night sobbing. He contracted poliomyelitis with resultant shortening of his right leg and became a 'buffoon' at school to compensate for his handicaps. The other boys called him a coward.

By the fourth interview he was sleeping better. He told how his mother was over-indulgent and his father bullied her. He was the youngest child and his father had little time for him. He had no instruction and had never been taught anything about sex. He discussed his sexual problems at the fifth session. He was able to speak clearly of his masturbatory fantasies: he had sadistic ideas of small boys being beaten by bigger ones. He enjoyed swimming with good-looking boys and would sport and play with them in the water. He was a homosexual, but not overtly so. He had indulged in sexual intercourse on only one occasion and found it distasteful. After this session he was deeply hypnotised and told that he would feel 'cleansed' and would 'wake fresh and happy each morning'.

The sixth session was to be the turning point in the case. He was still masturbating but, further to this, he explained in a scarcely audible voice that sexually he was a misfit, a person who needed condemning not condoning. He admitted to being guilty of coprophagia. This confession was accepted as a matter of fact, no comment being made except to explain that the same reaction causing a man of 55 to masturbate could conceivably go further and make him do things he must not do. He was immediately hypnotised and told that he would no longer need to give way to sexual feelings that he was ashamed of, that all the anxiety associated with these acts would be overcome by talking about them, and that from this day he would feel clean and pure, confident and happy. Insecurity mechanisms and the desire for comfort were explained and illustrations were given of how people seek security by acts taking them back to their childhood in an endeavour to seek oral comfort. The bare outline of the anal complex was explained. The patient had (before treatment) read widely of the popular psychiatric authors and was fully able to understand the implications of the act of eating his own faeces, although previously he was unable to emotionalise the situation. It will be found in practice that the hypnotic state greatly enhances insight by allowing emotional understanding where previously intellectual understanding was all the patient could manage. At the seventh interview he was greatly improved. He had begun to write again and a friend thought he was well enough to accept an important position abroad.

He was seen a further three times until he left for overseas, having succeeded in his application for the position. Later reports described him as well and enjoying life to the full.

It is important that patients suffering from any form of depression are not left on their own. They should always be with somebody and preferably a person whom they trust and who can constantly reassure them that they will get better. So often, in mistaken sympathy, these patients are told to 'pull themselves together'. This is impossible and if the advice is given too often it may precipitate a crisis. The patient, in desperation, may eventually *prove* that he could not do so.

It must be fully understood that it is hypnotherapy that is used in these cases. Hypnosis is in many cases valueless without analysis, but the word 'analysis' should not deter the practitioner. Psychoanalysis is not implied and is, of course, an extremely specialized form of therapy.

With hypnotherapy a deep analysis is not always to be commended and much can be accomplished by at times simply directing the patient, and at other times allowing the patient to guide the doctor in the approach. The method demands that the patient has an average intelligence and that the inter-personal relationship between the doctor and patient is adequate. It must be impressed upon the practitioner that great care is needed in the management of these cases. Deep analysis is to be deprecated but treatment using the methods outlined above has been rewarding and much can be accomplished by care, sympathy and re-education during hypnotherapy.

Analytically it might be argued that the hypnotist is afraid of his own depression and tries to avoid this problem in his patient. It should be understood that many patients may be pushed into temporary depression by any psychotherapy. The so-called 'honeymoon' period of analysis, when the patient temporarily substitutes a feeling of elation for one of depression, is known to every psychiatrist using psychotherapy of any description. It is the phase when depression returns that worries and frightens many physicians uncertain of their ability to contain the varying emotions of the patients. The rule must be once again to let the patient verbalize, to see the patient two or three or more times weekly (not difficult in general practice) and attempt to deepen the hypnotic state. If notwithstanding these attempts and the use of a suitable antidepressant the depression persists, then the services of a psychiatrist should immediately be sought.

THE OBSESSIONAL – COMPULSIVE PATIENT

These patients are most difficult to treat. They represent, however, an excellent field for the general practitioner in his approach by hypnotherapy. The same rules applying to the depressives apply here. It is unsafe to push analysis deeply and although many of these cases present with a story which appears to offer an excellent chance for deep analysis, they can be harmed rather than helped if the method of treatment outlined in the previous chapter is not followed. It is fair to add that several psychiatrists with a good deal of experience in this field have deprecated the use of hypnosis in this condition. However the authors feel that a hypnoanalytical approach using the technique of verbalization and interfering as little as possible can be used with success.

An *obsession* is a persistent irrational thought which the patient knows is irrational and which he can do nothing about. This thought leads on, in many cases, to a *compulsive* act which the person cannot help but carry out.

These symptoms will often serve to fulfil the personality needs of the patient, for the constantly recurring thought or action may be the patient's way of keeping more disturbing, terrifying or guilty thoughts out of his mind.

People showing this neurosis are often fussy, perfectionistic, penurious and meticulous in an exaggerated way. They keep their houses spotless and are desperately worried at seeing an ashtray or journal out of place. They are individuals who constantly reiterate 'punctuality is a virtue ...' or 'it is the principle of the thing'. They plead that they are tolerant and open-minded but in fact are usually bigoted, biased and superstitious. These patients show a true superiority reaction, they feel superior to most of us and ill-tolerate analysis which may show too suddenly that they are only human after all. This sudden insight may precipitate a breakdown and produce a frank psychosis. If analysis is attempted the above facts should be kept in mind but with experience hypnotherapy will be found valuable in overcoming the shock of too rapid an insight.

The mechanism of this disorder is very often a fear reaction inadequately repressed (Henderson & Gillespie 1941). There is later an attempt at getting rid of the neurosis by a displacement of affect, i.e. constantly recurring thoughts abhorrent to the individual are kept out of the mind by a symbolic act or thought. The emotional energy associated with the fear-provoking incident is displaced into the obsession or compulsion, thus relieving the mind of an unpleasant memory.

The general practitioner is offered an interesting field in hypnotherapy. By allowing the patient to talk and by facing these half-forgotten incidents with a sympathetic attitude and explanation, backed by suggestions under light or medium hypnosis, an excellent method of treatment is accomplished. The rule here is an active approach, not a passive one. The general practitioner should allow the patient to lead while he guides. Hypnosis is useful for stimulating forgotten memories and for re-educative purposes and its undoubted value lies in its power of symptom removal (Gindes 1953). Abreaction by hypnotherapy should always be attempted even under the lightest hypnosis and if the patient shows improvement should be repeated on several occasions. Constant reassurance is a necessity and visits of two or three times weekly should be aimed at. Recently, a case was seen in practice that required over two hundred sessions.

> An intelligent man over 50 years of age complained of the need to tap when in the street or in his home. He had a fear of contamination, gross fear of sudden death and anxiety associated with numbers, e.g. multiples of five occasioned him great distress when seeing cars, omnibuses, etc. He complained of sexual fears which necessitated special compulsive acts.
>
> He had consulted several physicians, but was told: 'Learn to live with it; gradually you will grow out of these habits.' He first experienced the problem in his early teens and had lived a life of difficulty controlled to a great extent by his compulsive acts. He would have to open a door in a particular manner and tap five times if he failed to open it in the self-prescribed manner. He had a curious compulsive way of walking downstairs. A sudden thought that a disaster would overtake him necessitated his walking up three stairs and

going down two. Sometimes, he would literally be several minutes in trying to get down the stairs without constantly having to go back again.

When first seen he was a pathetically ill man. He demanded constant reiteration by his doctor that he would get better. He never achieved a deep state of hypnosis and would describe his depth as 'pleasant relaxation'. Analysis was attempted with the greatest emphasis on his interpretation of his dreams. Early in his treatment this became somewhat difficult as he was inclined to adopt an obsessional-compulsive attitude to them. However, he was a good subject for deeper analysis, and at the end of each session an attempt was made to deepen his state of hypnosis and suggestions were given along the lines of greater composure, less attention to his compulsions, a greater ability to control his thoughts and suggestions that his dreams would aid him to rid himself of his nervous fears.

Early in treatment he became completely impotent and this occasioned him some alarm. His wife was seen and appeared to be a somewhat bitter, difficult person with little or no psychological insight. She criticized her husband and at first found it difficult to accept that he was ill. She refused to be sent to a psychiatrist, maintaining that their problems of marriage were her husband's fault and not hers.

Gradually, the patient became more able to control his symptoms, but it was noticeable that throughout treatment he persisted with 'the taps', particularly in the street. However, where previously he felt guilty of his behaviour, he began to accept his compulsions and discuss his fears openly. At one time he was unable to mention the word 'death' and was always seeking reassurance that he was not going to die. His dreams showed gross fear of hell and strong religious problems which had to be handled with great tact. He was always attempting to get the analyst tied up in a prognosis. He would continually ask how long treatment would take and add, 'I must be very ill if you won't tell me.' He complained of discomfort in his stomach, bowels and lower abdomen. During his first year of treatment it was found that his blood pressure was 200/100 and it was necessary to institute hypotensive therapy. This gave him added alarm and the doctor was hard-pressed to reassure him. He paid much attention to a guilty feeling towards masturbation, maintaining that his real worry had been induced by his father. It transpired that he had been told that 'to play with himself' was dangerous and would lead to 'terrible consequences'. It was only after many sessions that he was able to bring to consciousness that his father had actually said: 'If you masturbate, you will damage yourself.' He took this too literally and had worried unconsciously that this was going to be true. Later during relaxation he was able to bring to consciousness that he had slept with his mother. He had contrived to put his big toe near her genitals and she had said angrily (probably because of her own feelings of guilt) 'You must never do anything like that again.' Dreams at this point released a symbolic interpretation of his big toe being a penis (a well-known symbol). Later, when the patient was 17 years old his mother had had a mental breakdown (depressive breakdown?) and eventually died in the mental hospital to which she had originally been admitted. The guilt of her death was abreacted while in the hypnotic state.

It is doubtful whether straightforward analytical treatment would be possible in a case of this description. He had been constantly (according to the patient) refused psychiatric help and had simply been offered drugs or medicines. Being a knowledgeable person he could not accept that drugs would ever 'cure' him, indeed it is often found with this particular psychoneurosis that the patient becomes afraid of drugs just as he is afraid of death, etc. When offered hypnoanalysis, he was most grateful and proved an excellent subject for long analysis under a cover of dreams and hypnosis.

Some years ago Rosen (1952) described a specialized hypnotherapeutic technique. The patient recalls his emotion 'of the moment' and he must feel this emotion with great intensity.

Following this emotional recall, Rosen found that, of seven patients subjected to this technique, all of them abreacted a particular personal experience quite dramatically. He then treated this released emotion along dynamic lines. He does not explain why this abreaction occurs. Using the same technique one of us (G.A.) has had the same experience with six patients. After the abreaction each of these patients showed relief of tension and a greatly accelerated integration of their personality patterns.

It cannot be too often reiterated that we shall frequently see *all* the symptoms described in this chapter in one and the same patient. The 'pigeon-holing' of patients has been explained on the grounds that it makes teaching easier, but even in the so-called 'normal' person (if that person ever exists) a little anxiety, hysteria, depression, obsession and compulsion may be seen: James Boswell speaks of Dr. Johnson tapping his stick against each third railing as he walked. Even the genius is not above showing many of the neuroses we have discussed. Indeed it was the 1978 Nobel Prize Winner for Literature who wrote: 'At first the intellectuals sat on chairs and stared. After a while, they began to discuss sex. Schopenhauer said this ... Nietzsche said that. Anyone who hadn't witnessed it would find it difficult to imagine how ridiculous such geniuses can be' (I.B. Singer: 'A Friend of Kafka').

It is even possible that the so-called 'neurotic' helps the doctor to a greater understanding of himself and allows us to qualify for a deeper philosophy than we could acquire in other ways.

BIBLIOGRAPHY

AMBROSE, G. (1951) Techniques of abreaction. *Br. med. J.*, 2, 496.
AMBROSE, G. (1976) The dynamics of bisexuality. *Proc. Cong. Int. Med. psychosom.* Paris.
BRIGGS, G. J. F. (1975) Aggression in symptomatology. *Proc. Br. Soc. med. dent. Hypnosis*, 1, 1.
BRILL, A. A. (1946) *Psychoanalytic Psychiatry*, pp. 140–156. New York: Knopf.
ELLENBERGER, H. (1970) *The Discovery of the Unconscious.* New York: Allen Lane.
FERBER, A., MENDELSOHN, M. & NAPIER, A. (Eds) (1972) *The Book of Family Therapy.* New York: Grune & Stratton.
FENICHEL, O. (1954) The drive to amass wealth. In: *Collected Papers*, 1st ed., 2nd series, p. 89. New York: Norton.
FOUCAULT, M. (1971) *Madness and Civilization*, trans. R. Howard. London: Tavistock Publications.
FRANK, J. (1963) *Persuasion and Healing.* New York: Schocken Books.
FREUD, Anna (1973) *Normality and Pathology in Childhood.* Harmondsworth: Penguin.
FROMM, E. (1971) *Man for Himself.* London: Routledge & Kegan Paul.
GIBSON, H. H. & CORCORAN, M. E. (1975) Personality and differential susceptibility to hypnosis. *Br. J. Psychol.*, 66, 513.
GINDES, B. C. (1953) *New Concepts of Hypnosis.* London: Allen & Unwin.
GRAY, W., DUHL, F. J. & RIZZO, N. D. (1970) *General Systems Theory and Psychiatry.* Edinburgh: Churchill.
HADFIELD, J. A. (1967) *Introduction to Psychotherapy.* London: Allen & Unwin.
HENDERSON, D. K. & GILLESPIE, R. D. (1941) *A Textbook of Psychiatry*, 5th ed., pp. 507-16. Oxford University Press.
JACOBY, R. (1975) *Social Amnesia, a Critique of Conformist Psychology from Adler to Laing*, p. 121. Boston.
JANET, P. (1907) *The Major Symptoms of Hysteria.* New York: Macmillan.
JANOV, A. (1973) *The Primal Scream.* London: Sphere.
JONES, E. (Ed.) (1974) *Sigmund Freud: Life and Work.* Harmondsworth: Penguin.
JUNG, C. G. (1968) *Analytical Psychology: Its Theory and Practice.* London: Routledge & Kegan Paul.

LAING, R. D. (1970) *The Divided Self.* Harmondsworth: Penguin.
MEARES, A. (1974) *A System of Medical Hypnosis.* New York: Julian Press.
MEARES, A. (1957) A working hypothesis as to the nature of hypnosis. *Archs Neurol. Psychiat., Chicago, 77,* 54.
NARANJO, C. & ORNSTEIN, R. E. (1973) *On the Psychology of Meditation.* London: Allen & Unwin.
RYECROFT, C. (1971) *Wilhelm Reich.* London: Fontana/ Collins.
ROSEN, H. (1952) The hypnotic and hypnotherapeutic unmasking, intensification and recognition of an emotion. *Am. J. Psychiat., 109/2,* 120.
ROSS, M. (1979) Bisexuality – fact or fallacy. *Br. J. sexual Med., 6,* 49.
SCHNECK, J. M. (Ed.) (1963) *Hypnosis in Modern Medicine,* 3rd ed., p. 169. Springfield, Ill.: Charles C. Thomas.
SEDGWICK, P. (1973) Illness – mental and otherwise. *Hastings Centre Studies, 1,* 3.
SKINNER, B. F. (1973) *Beyond Freedom and Dignity.* Harmondsworth: Penguin.
SMITH-MOORHOUSE, P. M. (1969) Hypnosis in the treatment of alcoholism. *Br. J. Addict. Alcohol, 64,* 47.
STEKEL, W. (1935) *Sadism and Masochism.* London: Bodley Head.
STEKEL, W. (1950) *Compulsion and Doubt.* London: Nevill.
STEKEL, W. (1950) *Conditions of Nervous Anxiety.* London: Lund Humphries.
STEWART, H. & FRY, A. (1957) The scope for hypnosis in general practice. *Br. med. J., 1,* 1325.
THORNTON, E. M. (1976) *Hypnotism, Hysteria & Epilepsy: an Historical Synthesis.* London: Heinemann.
WATTS, A. (1973) *Psychotherapy East & West.* Harmondsworth: Penguin.
WELLS, W. R. (1944) The hypnotic treatment of the major symptoms of hysteria; a case study. *J. Psychol., 17,* 269.
WOLBERG, L. R. (1946) *Hypno-analysis,* pp. 257–87. London: Heinemann.
WOLBERG, L. R. (1953) *Therapy through Hypnosis.* London: Elek.

CHAPTER 7

HYPNOANALYSIS AND HYPNOSYNTHESIS

There have been many books and papers published since the First World War dealing with the subject of hypnoanalysis. It was Hadfield (1916) who first described the technique, he used the method of analysis, together with hypnosis, to relieve the psychological traumata of battle casualties. In those days there were few psychiatrists and little treatment, and 'shell-shock' was the common expression for what had become 'battle fatigue' by 1939–45.

The classical two-volume *Hypnoanalysis* by Wolberg (1946) is known to all who have studied this technique. Wolberg did a great deal to enlarge knowledge of the subject and to teach us how to use hypnosis; another great pioneer was Erickson (1952). These two men ensured that hypnoanalysis attained greater respectability in the hands of later workers such as Schneck (1955), Rosen (1960), Meares (1954), Raginsky (1961), and many others. Erickson and Wolberg were able to pinpoint a technique which was not only fascinating in its use but seemed to represent an acceleration of the deeper methods of analysis. In this respect it will be remembered that Freud (Jones 1953) discarded hypnosis (various reasons are given and have been given for why he did so) for psychoanalysis, which represented a very much broader and more complicated technique of exploration of the unconscious mind by so-called associative techniques. It was because Freud abandoned hypnosis as a therapy that hypnoanalysis exists at all! Freud wanted the patient to recall material (he described this material as 'psychic energy') and argued that forgotten or buried memories must be brought to the conscious mind for the patient finally to understand his conflicts. After this understanding, arising from continual searching for earlier memories, the psyche could re-evaluate and come to terms with past, infantile and childish problems.

The patient 'grew up' or became psychologically more mature. As J. A. Hadfield describes this in a personal communication of 10th September 1966: 'Hypnoanalysis was a term I invented in the First World War (see Crichton-Miller's *Functional Nerve Disorders*) to describe the method of using hypnosis as a means of reviving forgotten and repressed experiences, at that time mainly of amnesias in war shock cases, but also in earlier cases, as an alternative method to free association and dream interpretation, both of which, however, are of the greatest value.

'This process of recovering lost memories under hypnosis was of course previously used by Janet and later by Freud, so really it was only the name not the method which I invented. If, however, hypnoanalysis differs from their methods it was used after the lost memories were discovered and repressed emotions were released, and suggestion treatment was used as a means of *re-adjusting* the personality to the new material. In many cases the re-adjustment took place automatically when the patient realized where his symptoms came from: but in other cases, where you reverse the fear, or the rage, or the sex feelings of early life, the patient does not *automatically* adjust himself to it, for the emerging fear may persist as anger. In such cases suggestion may be given to find the patient's confidence and calmness of mind to help him to adjust. Suggestion was therefore usually included in hypnoanalysis.'

Hypnosis, as we have tried to show in this Handbook, is often an excellent method of exploring the unconscious mind and allowing old forgotten memories to flow back to consciousness. We have also stressed the re-educative value of hypnosis. During the hypnotic state a new appraisal becomes possible. We think that greater insight develops, and those individuals who require a more penetrating treatment and who can achieve a deep state of hypnosis should always be subjected to hypnoanalytical techniques.

Meares (1954) has described a technique of hypnography and hypnoanalysis which illustrates the benefit derived from deep states of hypnosis. One of us (G.A.) has used a far less directive method of hypnosis. In this respect hypnosis has been attacked for its directive uses. In apparently overpowering the patient and appearing to be complete master of the situation, the hypnotist might tend to forget the doctor–patient relationship. It is argued later in this chapter that for this very reason the hypnotist who intends to use deeper analytical methods should seek for himself a method of psychological enquiry into his own mind, preferably with a psychiatrist versed in analytical methods and who has had the benefit of a personal analysis himself. He will then, as has been stressed by

Wolberg and others, become better orientated to deal with the psyche of others.

As progress is made in the technique of hypnotherapy so we begin to understand only too well that there exists a deeper level of the mind, which hides the psychic material which must be eventually discharged to consciousness, if symptoms are to be combated by the patient. It is at this point that the hypnotist should adopt a most passive manner. It is not always necessary to insist upon a deep state of hypnosis from the first session. On the contrary, the patient learns from a process of conditioning how to deepen his own state of hypnosis as treatment continues. Perhaps it would be easier for the reader if an actual case was given and the history and treatment of the condition described.

> A man of 46 was seen complaining of difficulty of breathing and spasm of his chest. Apparently he had suffered the same symptoms as a child and could remember the doctor treating him for continual bronchitis up to the age of 7. After this he got better and had no further attacks until the age of 16. Now quite suddenly he had experienced the same symptoms and indeed had needed hospitalization on two occasions for an acute asthmatic attack. He was now taking corticosteroids. He said that he was alarmed over his last attack as he needed oxygen in the ambulance taking him to hospital. He felt that he would die if he had another attack like the last one.
>
> He was deeply hypnotized on his second visit and left for the entire treatment session of one hour in this state. Nothing was said to him except that he was asked if he was comfortable, warm, etc. To each question he would simply reply in the affirmative, saying that he was perfectly comfortable and felt very relaxed. For the first four sessions he made no comments except to introduce himself as he first came into the room, with such remarks as: 'Better weather lately', or 'Lots of rain, it will do the garden good'. He would then relax in a comfortable armchair and recite the words 'Dreamy, drowsy, heavy and sleepy', to himself. The doctor would simply count to ten and the treatment would commence. On the fifth occasion he quite suddenly and spontaneously said: 'It was when my parents came to live with us that all this started.' No comment was made by the analyst and nothing further was said by the patient until the seventh interview. He then elected to talk while in the hypnotic state about his childhood. His mother had always fussed a lot over his health and had 'worried herself sick' over his bronchitis. He was then regressed to the age of 5 (see p. 28) and told to experience what he felt when he suffered his bronchial attacks. He said he thought that they were really asthma attacks. At this point he was

Hypnoanalysis and Hypnosynthesis

told to relax and think of any dream which he could remember. He told the doctor that he had a recurring dream of swimming. He would be trying to get to dry land, but a big wave would drive him back and the more he tried to get out of the sea the more difficult it became to do so. No comment was made but the next session the patient admitted that he was feeling better and his breathing seemed easier. His head felt lighter. He was determined to cut down the number of tablets he was taking and had told his G.P., who had supported this suggestion.

The tenth session resulted in a continued lessening of tension and he began to recount certain fears that he suffered during his flying career in the Second World War. He was a navigator and had been given a high award for many hazardous flights over enemy territory. He was reassured at this point with direct hypnotic suggestion that anybody in danger would normally suffer fear. He saw clearly in the hypnotic state that this was a continuation of a pattern of fear induced in him during his first 7 years and when he first suffered illness. He could understand the psychosomatic nature of his complaint.

He was seen for a further seven sessions and simply left in a deep state of hypnosis. Certain sexual problems were discussed in the waking state, but were not considered serious. He was happily married. However, he was last seen when he told the doctor that he had bought a bungalow for his parents, near to his own home, and he felt that he would be fine now. He reported back one month later and had ceased taking any medication. He said that he felt very well. Two months after this he was again seen and reiterated that he was well and that he felt he would be able to carry on perfectly well without treatment. He promised to report back to the doctor at any sign of a relapse but he felt that this was a 'very remote possibility'. Very little explanation was given in this case and all the insight had been gained by the patient while in a deep hypnotic state. Regressive techniques had helped him to abreact certain traumatic situations and had given him the required insight into the psychodynamics of his illness.

The first session of this type of hypnoanalytical treatment should be used for assessment, explanation of the technique proposed and sometimes an attempt at hypnosis and the teaching of autohypnosis. Particularly the second interview should be used for teaching the patient how to enter the hypnotic state as he starts his analytical session. He should be encouraged to stay in the deep state of hypnosis throughout the session in the type of technique described above. Autohypnosis and post-hypnotic suggestions at the end of the session will sometimes be found of value, particularly where there is a psychosomatic problem. It will be found in practice that patients expect either to be quite silent during the session or to speak freely. They should be told from the outset that the choice is their own — how they feel within the deep state and what they wish to do or say is their own decision. It should be remembered that if the patient wishes to verbalize he will become less deeply hypnotized and will then enter a more superficial state of hypnosis. However, this can be countered, should the doctor think it necessary, by suitable suggestions for depth. It is also common to find a spontaneous deepening of hypnosis, probably as a form of resistance to deeper analysis. Occasionally it will be found that the patient will go to sleep in order to avoid fear and anxiety situations. Patience must be used at this point and gradually the resistance will either be worked through or, by gentle questioning, the reasons for the resistance can be analysed at a deeper level of hypnosis. At this point also may be seen a reluctance to terminate the hypnotic state, the patient wishing to remain in this peaceful and secure state of mind. The patient's conduct should then be explained to him and the reason for treatment repeated, i.e. the need for emotional maturity and his ultimate ability to face life as an adult. The doctor needs to interpret the conduct of his patient to himself. He must always try to understand what the patient is expecting from him. With experience it becomes more and more obvious how the patient will try to repeat the patterns of his childhood using the doctor as a parental figure.

The deeper state of hypnosis can obviously be used by the patient to avoid growing up. Hypnosis is said by some authorities to be simply a state of regression. The patient welcomes going back to babyhood and infantile fantasies. Be this as it may, any process of enquiring into the mind of another, using any technique to do so, demands regression. It is felt that the hypnotic state allows a greater chance of success for the patient to understand this regression and to face up to his responsibilities at an accelerated pace. It should be stressed that dream interpretation is of inestimable value for the doctor to gauge the resistance or otherwise of his patient. The author often uses dream interpretation together with deep hypnosis in order to keep abreast of the patient's unconscious. As Stekel (1943) said, it should be possible to train psychiatrists to analyse dreams just as one would and could read a book. Dreams difficult of interpretation in the waking state will yield up their conflicts and secrets in deep hypnosis. Patience is always advisable and it is often true that given time and sympathy and no panic or fear from the analyst himself, most resistance can be broken down and the patient enabled to cope with his anxiety, fears and conflicts.

A different type of technique exists where the analyst listens to the patient speaking his feelings during deep hypnosis. The same method is used as described above, but the patient now wants to speak. He is anxious to rid himself of emotions and, although often denying that he will remember anything, suddenly releases something that has been troubling him for years. This can be seen equally well in face-to-face analysis or free association, but during the hypnotic state the anxiety can be released with very strong emotion. The value of hypnosis, however, is that the patient is very much more aware of himself and greater control by the analyst is therefore possible. The hypnotic state in itself represents no danger for the patient, but the analyst, in the hypnoanalytical method, should learn to say very little and allow his patient to acquire insight slowly but surely. When treatment is first started it will be found beneficial to use the last 5 minutes of the session for suggestions. Gradually as the patient gains insight, he dispenses with the need for suggestion, realizing only too well that his problems can best be resolved by a greater maturity and a more sensible way of facing his difficulties. As he begins to 'grow up' he demands less and less that the analyst should act out the role of a parent. He is prepared to give up the need for guidance and overt sympathy for a more practical method of living his own life. The type of treatment outlined above is possibly more the choice where the patient presents for the cure of a habit such as excessive smoking.

It must be explained very early in the interview that a patient cannot be helped entirely by direct hypnotic suggestion. The author, for instance, has seldom found that it is smoking, or rather the inability to break the habit of excessive smoking, that is the real cause of a patient seeking psychiatric help; it is rather a search for a 'magic wand'. However, if an intelligent person is gently told that he may have other difficulties which he would possibly like to discuss, it will be found in practice that much time can be saved (indeed, patients are less likely to miss their next appointment and never be seen again) if the therapist is honest and explains that the difficulty of giving up any habit lies generally in a personality problem, and that the patient's inability to do so is due to various conflicts. Much energy has been expended in the past on the 'cure' of the tobacco habit, for example, and real permanency of 'cure' is doubtful if the case is followed up with any degree of accuracy. However, undoubtedly some people have been permanently relieved of an annoying habit by a deconditioning process over 6 to 8 sessions, but there is always a risk of relapse if the dynamisms of the problem are not understood by doctor or patient. It should be understood that an attempt must be made to enquire at some depth into a habit which overcomes a person to the extent of their seeking help. At least 20 to 30 sessions might be necessary to 'cure' certain of these problems. On the other hand patients have undoubtedly been helped to overcome this habit in a few treatments and have not relapsed. If the patient can be deeply hypnotized and allowed to verbalize his problems, much interesting material will be brought to the surface. In many cases no more reference is made to the habit of tobacco, but diverse problems are discussed which have been masked by the symptom which has brought the patient for treatment. Once the resistance is broken and the patient begins to understand that his problem is not just simply a habit, but more a complicated and deeper conflict, he will cease to 'tread water' and be prepared to swim to the shore on his own efforts.

With children the art of hypnoanalysis becomes easier of achievement. Children are easily hypnotized (possibly one of the really true statements seen in textbooks on this subject for other well-worn dogmas are often hardly as accurate) and are also sympathetic to any attempt to probe the unconscious. With children the art of keeping silent and allowing the child to verbalize is more easily appreciated than with an adult. In analytical work with children they are far happier if allowed to find their own level. They are immediately at home with a sympathetic listener and have an intuitive understanding of the various techniques used in hypnoanalysis.

The author has often found a technique of attempted recall in hypnoanalysis most useful with children, and the same technique can be used for adults. Later in this chapter the technique of hypnosynthesis, together with a case history, will be fully described. The child is placed comfortably in an armchair, preferably one which can be adjusted to a reclining position. The child is then deeply hypnotized and asked to think of the first initial letter which comes to mind following the tap of a pen or pencil upon a table nearby. The child has been told that this is a method of recalling a memory that has been forgotten. It will be found in practice that a number of letters from six to ten will be found satisfactory and these are written down by the doctor. They are then read back to the child who is told that he will now put the initial letter to a word which is the first word to come to mind after again tapping with the pencil. Six to ten words are asked for and these are written down. The state of hypnosis can now be deepened and the child told that certain associations will come to mind on his thinking of the words he has constructed. Often there is an immediate response and a memory will follow. At other times there is apparently no association possible. The analyst must be patient for at the next session the child may have remembered something that has come to consciousness since the last session. In other words, what appears at first simply to be a jumble of words masks a memory which if allowed to come to consciousness results in much alleviation of tension and subsequently leads to other memories. It is as well to remember at this point that every memory released guards, covers or acts as a screen to the next one. It is thus a necessity to bring to consciousness these old forgotten and repressed memories, so enabling the child to understand how he, or she, has failed in the past to make adequate adjustments to traumatic events, which has led to poor repression and subsequent ill-health in the form of symptoms.

On the surface this may appear to be a difficult feat with children for how would they understand such words as 'trauma', 'repression', 'symptoms', 'adequate adjustments', etc? Naturally the child is enabled to see these particular incidents, accidents and emotional crises in its life and the integration of conscious and unconscious then becomes possible.

With certain adults a deeper, longer and more penetrative technique can be used which will include several techniques described in other works on hypnoanalysis, such as mirror-gazing, use of a crystal ball, etc. (Wolberg 1946). Whatever technique is used the patient must be trained to enter a deep state of hypnosis. This is one of the great necessities of hypnoanalysis and hypnosynthesis. The patient must not only visualize but act out the problems and conflicts and thus gain insight. The reader must expect that as he becomes more proficient with the use of this method of psychological treatment, he will desire to know more about himself and nowadays it should be accepted that some form of personal analysis should be undertaken before delving into the deeper recesses of somebody else's mind.

It is not unusual that patients during hypnoanalysis will alter their depth of hypnosis. Hadfield's communication (page 123) specifically states: 'If, however, hypnoanalysis differs from their methods (Janet and Freud) it was used *after* [G.A.'s italics] the lost memories were discovered and repressed emotions were released, and suggestion treatment was used as a means of *re-adjusting* [Hadfield's italics] the personality to the new material.' Thus Hartland's (1967) 'ego-strengthening' becomes identical to Hadfield's 'hypnoanalysis'. This is why we use the term 'hypnosynthesis' to describe what might occur during the actual hypnotic session. If the patient is kept in a profound state of hypnosis it is suggested that recall of buried memories can take place.

The technique of hypnosynthesis is not difficult if the patient can visualize in the hypnotic state. Hypnosis is induced as follows. The usual neuromuscular relaxation is obtained by a simple relaxing technique which tells the patient to concentrate on his body-image: he will become conscious of the *space* he occupies. This suggestion can be conjoined with a positive attitude that he will mature emotionally in the future. The patient should be seated in a comfortable armchair: one that can be adjusted is ideal. Suggestion proceeds along the following lines: 'You will begin to relax all the muscles of your body and as you do so you will feel relaxed from the tip of your toes to the top of your head. You will become aware of the space that you occupy in the chair. This is known as the 'body-image' and is as unique to you as your finger-prints'. Emphasis is placed upon visualizing the body so that various techniques can be used later. As relaxation is deepened by control of breathing and suggestion, a state of hypnosis is induced by the use of four words — 'Dreamy, drowsy, heavy and sleepy' — repeated in a monotonous voice. When sufficient depth is obtained the patient is told that he is in a beautiful garden, one he seems to know and has always felt happy in — a 'garden of meditation'. He will now see all the colours of the rainbow. It is a beautiful day, the sun is shining and there is a blue sky. He sees a lily-pond with goldfish etc. Later the patient is taken out of hypnosis with the usual count-down from 5 or 10 and asked if he could see the garden, particularly the colours. This is said to be indicative that regression has occurred and the patient is making headway. In any case most people admit to seeing all the different subjective phenomena mentioned to them.

The next step is re-hypnotising into the garden of meditation and suggesting that the patient will 'come for a little walk in his mind's eye.' He is asked to see himself walking along a country road with a hedge on both sides. He cannot see over the hedge on the left but on the right he sees a panoramic view of the countryside. He walks further towards some crossroads. There is no traffic as he walks straight across the road and towards a level crossing. He can see a train is expected, for the gates are closed. As he waits for the train he sees a woman on his left-hand side. On his right is a butcher's boy leaning against his bicycle. He sees that the boy is working for B. Bloggs, Butcher, 1, Station Road, Basingstoke, Hants: it is written on his bicycle. The train comes past and the gates open. He crosses over the lines and now walks on alone until he comes to a cottage on his left. There are roses on the door and the front gate is open as is the front door. He enters the cottage, sees some stairs in front of him and climbs them. On his right are two bedrooms and on his left the same number. At this point the first bedroom on the right is number one, the other number two and so on. He is told that he will go to the door of number one bedroom and will find it open. He will see a bedroom, when he enters, which is vaguely familiar to him. There is a comfortable swivel chair in the room. In front of him is a window which he will call 'his window of the present' and on his left is another window known as 'his window of the past'. As he looks through either window he sees many things. Memories will come to his mind quite readily. The left window will allow the patient to regress, to take his mind back to the past. With a little practice (in the auto-hypnotic state) much repressed material can often be released. In the attempt at re-synthesis and de-synthesis, both windows will play their part.

Before outlining the case of a man treated by hypnosynthesis let us continue to discuss the technique which was first described by Hadfield during the First World War. From time immemorial suggestion has been used in the treatment of medical problems and 'positive suggestions' have been used by each and every Mesmerist. 'Ego-strengthening' is simply a valuable method of explaining what should take place following the release of forgotten memories. Naturally there is a danger that if *all* patients are simply treated by ego-strengthening then hypnosis is being used entirely at a superficial level, ignoring the necessity to rid the psyche of the conflicts and complexes first described by Freud. If Hartland uses the expression 'ego-strengthening' as Hadfield uses 'hypnoanalysis' there is no argument, but the author of 'Medical and Dental Hypnosis and its Clinical Applications', has been himself criticized for providing too little explanation of dynamic interpretation. One could accept this state of affairs ten years ago, but now, with many more psychiatrists and psychologists using hypnotherapeutic methods as part of their own psychotherapeutic work, it behoves us to be wary of too simple an approach, which encourages the inevitable search for 'magic'. It is a pity that the inability of many hospitals to cope with vast numbers of individuals demanding help for common neuroses has led to a belief in rapid methods of 'cure'. Would that a cure was so readily available. The use of tranquillizers has continued and will continue but it must lead to chronic conditions, particularly of the depressive and obsessional-compulsive type. The advent of so many 'schools' of therapy only adds to the patient's difficulty in seeking help in order to mature emotionally. Little thought is sometimes given to the goal-objective in modern day psychiatry. The following case is characteristic of the battle for the mind by both doctor and patient.

A young man was seen with a long history of emotional illness. He was fortunate in that his G.P. was a trained psychoanalyst, and had realised that his patient would best be helped by medication aimed at his severe anxiety symptoms. He supported his patient with counselling and was a tower of strength at this level, but was unable to keep him from trying to find a magic cure for all his ailments. These varied from gastric tension and headaches to sexual difficulties, lack of initiative, shyness, bad temper, inability to make friends, and gross feelings of inferiority. The young man had been forced to go from one therapist to another, always looking for a 'cure'.

The true picture slowly emerged with the use of dream-interpretation. As the patient needed a 'secret-weapon', as he termed it, he was taught hypnosis together with auto-hypnosis. Over the months his resistance became more and more obvious. It was established by painstaking analysis that he had had a most hazardous childhood and was also suffering a severe obsessional-compulsive illness, together with many fantasies and severe sexual parapathies.

It was considered that little hope existed for him in analytical treatment, for he had seen no less than 8 therapists ranging from Acupuncturists to Behaviourists via Sophrologists. The only person who had helped him was an analyst who followed the teachings of Jung; he had had treatment from him for some years. In the patient's words: 'He found me a bit of a handful'. He seemed dedicated to proving how resistant he could be, but insisted upon going on with supportive therapy. He was afraid of depression and lived all alone. Asked if he had told his analyst anything about himself in the many years he had been treated by him he said: 'As much as I thought good for him.' It was most noticeable that while he was in the hypnotic state, and directly after, he was a nicer person, much more rational and friendly. Slowly he began to use hypnosis as a further resistance, claiming that he had never been hypnotized. This is an extremely common defence against hypnotherapy. Nevertheless, hypnosis was persisted with in the form of hypnosynthesis (as described above). With this technique much material was released and the patient was able to talk about many things that he had previously denied to himself.

As a young child, before his teens, he would lure younger children, both male and female, to some woods and play with their genitals. He would always finish these games by hitting the children until they cried and ran away. He analysed this behaviour as an attempt to project his own guilt to the children and punish them for his 'sins'. Several times he had been reported for this behaviour, but he was protected by his family and was able to keep away from actual punishment. He had lived with his parents until his analyst suggested that he should try and 'get out into the world': he had left home in his late twenties. He still saw these relatives but bitterly described them as 'silly fools'. His mother in particular came in for abuse. The truth of the matter was that he was an only child, horribly spoilt and very hysterical. He admitted this but could do nothing about his behaviour. While in the hypnotic state, however, he would be near to tears and very contrite. Unfortunately, his 'paranoid' behaviour would slowly but surely return.

It was noticeable that he never used swear words and was amazed when the hypnotherapist used one. At this point he described his father as 'a swearing bully' and could remember being thrown across the room by him. As a teenager he sided with his mother against his father, whom he accused of always beating up his mother. This was not true. When describing these incidents and several sexual anomalies, he denied any guilt-feelings but gradually showed a much less psychopathic attitude, although his cruel behaviour was a noteworthy part of his illness. He would stroke cats, then suddenly hit them with the side of his hand. Afterwards, he would show remorse for his behaviour. He would visit shops and damage goods on display, again as a projection of his own guilt. He would go into hotels and turn off the power so that people would be in darkness and all the lifts would stop. He recited all these activities with laughter, but a few minutes later would be describing how ashamed he was. Naturally he had been afraid of telling others about his strange behaviour.

Gradually he began to display insight into his conduct but found grave difficulty in changing. It was only when he described more fully his sexual fantasies and behaviour that he began to take girls out, but he was still showing almost paranoid and childish behaviour. He had a boyfriend, however, who he claimed was a tower of strength to him. He was able to speak of homosexual feelings and realised that he was using his friend as another analyst.

As it became more and more obvious that the patient, although making slow progress, was excessively immature and dedicated to keeping his conflicts at fever-pitch, hypnosynthesis was witheld and a more active role was asked from him. In face-to-face therapy he was given tasks to accomplish and told to act more in keeping with his real desire to achieve emotional maturity. His compulsive behaviour persisted, albeit in a modified way. Each session proved him to be just as resistant to changing his behaviour. He supported this resistance by continual pleas for deeper hypnosis. At this time he could achieve a somnambulistic trance-like state. 'If only I could be deeply hypnotised I would be rapidly cured.' It is pertinent to ask whether a personality defect of this nature could be 'cured'. He persistently fought off any question of changing his own behaviour and always threatened to break off treatment; it demanded all the patience of the analyst not to ask him to do so. Against this, one could not discount the slow but steady improvement in his insight level and his obvious unhappiness with himself in his more rational moments. At no time did he show frank psychotic behaviour. He was in any case being prescribed various different tranquillizers as they came onto the market.

As he began to realise that the therapist represented his long departed father, on whom he was trying to get his own back, he was able to see that he was making progress. He was still trying to find another person to feed him magic, but agreed that each time he gave way to his childish impulses he was further traumatising his situation. True to earlier history, he found a way to escape having to grow up by breaking off treatment and finding another hypnotist.

It is hoped that from this chapter the hypnotherapist will be able to understand how hypnoanalysis should be used. As in any more elaborate technique in medicine or surgery, the doctor should acquaint himself with the psychiatry of the dynamisms underlying the condition he is treating. In practice it will be found beneficial if the analyst, before attempting to 'open all the doors of his patient's mind', has the opportunity of examining some of his own locked doors and finding the key to open his own mind to more profound horizons.

BIBLIOGRAPHY

AMBROSE, G. (1973) Hypnosynthesis. *Proc. 6th Int. Cong. Hypnosis, Uppsala: Sweden, 1*, 161.

AMBROSE, G. (1975) Technique of hypnosynthesis. *Proc. 3rd Cong. Int. College of psychosom. Med., Rome, 1*, 38.

ARLUCK, E. W. (1964) *Hypnoanalysis: A Case Study*. New York: Random House.

BRIGGS, G. J. F. (1977) Hypnotherapy versus society. *Proc. Br. Soc. med. dent. Hypnosis, 3*, 3.

CONN, J. H. (1956) Hypnosis as dynamic psychotherapy. *Sinai Hosp. J., 5*, 14.

CONN, J. H. (1960) The psychodynamics of recovery under hypnosis. *Int. J. clin. exp. Hypnosis, 8*, 3.

CONN, J. H. (1971) Hypnosynthesis. *Am. J. clin. Hypnosis, 13*, 3.

ERICKSON, M. H. (1952) Deep hypnosis and its induction. In: *Experimental Hypnosis*, ed. L. LeCron. New York: Macmillan.
KLEMPERER, E. (1972) *Ego Defense Mechanisms: Hypnoanalysis compared to Psychoanalysis*, p. 103. Proc. Hypnose und Psychosomatische Med. Stuttgart: Verlag.
KLINE, M. V. (1961) Hypnotic age regression. *Dis. nerv. Syst., 1*, 22.
KLINE, M. V. (1963) *Psychodynamics & Hypnosis*. Springfield, Ill.: Charles C. Thomas.
KOVEL, J. (1978) *A Complete Guide to Therapy*. Harmondsworth: Penguin.
LECRON, L. M. (1952) A study of age regression under hypnosis. In: *Experimental Hypnosis*. New York: Macmillan.
MARCUSE, F. L. (1970) *Hypnosis: Fact or Fiction*. Harmondsworth: Penguin.
MEARES, A. (1954) Hypnography – a technique in hypnoanalysis. *J. ment. Sci., 100*, 965.
RAGINSKY, H. (1960) The sensory use of plasticine in hypnoanalysis (sensory hypnoplasty). *Int. J. clin. exp. Hypnosis, 9*, 233.
ROSEN, H. (1960) Hypnosis applications and misapplications. *J. Am. med. Ass., 172*, 683.
SCHEERER, M. & REIFF, R. (1959) *Memory and Hypnotic Age Regression*. New York: International Universities Press.
SCHNECK, J. M. (Ed.) (1963) *Hypnosis in Modern Medicine*, 3rd ed., pp. 169–203. Springfield, Ill.: Charles C. Thomas.
SCHNECK, J. M. (1965) *Principles and Practice of Hypnoanalysis*. Springfield, Ill.: Charles C. Thomas.
STEKEL, W. (1943) *Interpretation of Dreams*. New York: Liveright.
STEKEL, W. (1953) *Patterns of Psychosexual Infantilism*. London: Nevill.
STORR, A. (1974) *Human Aggression*. Harmondsworth: Penguin.
TILLEARD-COLE, R. R. (1975) Parapsychiatric phenomena in relation to hypnosis. *Proc. Br. Soc. med. dent. Hypnosis, 1*, 6.
WATKINS, J. G. (ed.) (1963) *Psychodynamics of Hypnotic Induction and Termination*, 3rd ed., pp. 363–89. Springfield, Ill.: Charles C. Thomas.
WOLBERG, L. (1946) *Hypnoanalysis*. New York: Grune & Stratton.

CHAPTER 8

HYPNOSIS IN ANAESTHESIA

SURGERY

At first sight it would seem that there is little place for hypnosis as an anaesthetic agent in surgery. However, if the general practitioner knows that his patient can achieve a medium or deep state of hypnosis, analgesia by hypnosis is preferable to an anaesthetic for minor surgery or dental extractions. In children it should be considered a rule that some form of relaxation, with or without hypnotic suggestion, should be practised; the practitioner will often be astounded by the ease of inducing hypnosis in children. Over 60 per cent of them can reach deep hypnosis, and thus analgesia for such simple operations as lumbar puncture and incisions can be easily and rapidly obtained.

Hypnosis is theoretically the safest and best anaesthetic to use in minor surgery. Twenty-five per cent of people can in favourable circumstances enter a deep state of hypnosis on the very first induction, and therefore one person in four is a potential somnambule. Even in a medium state of hypnosis it is possible to obtain blunting of pin pricks and control of the fear and anxiety associated with a minor operation. In a series of experiments on the appreciation of ischaemic pain, Finer (1972) was able to show a significantly increased tolerance to pain while the subjects were under the influence of post-hypnotic suggestion.

It is well known that in the past hypnosis was resorted to as a means of relieving the pain of such major surgical operations as amputations. At the present time, although such procedures do not seem likely to be repeated, there is a real argument for more frequent use of hypnotism in ordinary hospital surgical practice. Apart from its role as an anaesthetic agent, the use of hypnosis in general surgery has been advocated because the calming effect of hypnosis makes the induction of general anaesthesia smoother

Hypnosis in Anaesthesia

and, consequently, the amount of any chemical or physical agent employed is likely to be less. Moreover, hypnotism can produce considerable muscular relaxation, which is particularly useful in, for example, abdominal surgery.

Goldie (1956) has described methods of using hypnosis in minor surgery in the casualty department of a hospital. The cases treated by Goldie were unselected patients. The aim of the work was to 'estimate the practcal value of hypnosis in the casualty department; to evaluate its function as an adjunct to, or substitute for, more conventional ways of producing anaesthesia; and to demonstrate a technique that is simple and effective with untrained subjects and based on principles that can be comprehended and used by patient and operator'.

Induction was very simple and is explained in some detail. There was little difficulty experienced in hypnotizing most of the patients and six cases are described. Goldie treated 28 consecutive orthopaedic cases in the month and failed to induce hypnosis sufficient for surgical reduction in only two of them. Earlier experimental work had suggested that only 30 per cent of hypnotized subjects were capable of reaching anaesthesia.

Goldie concludes that hypnosis can be used with advantage in the casualty department as an adjunct to the usual anaesthetic facilities. It may not only reduce the number of anaesthetics to be given but reduce the time for a meal to be digested so that the busy anaesthetist can save valuable time. He feels that the technique is effective with untrained subjects and asks for greater liaison between surgeons, psychiatrists and psychologists in setting up controlled experiments in hospitals.

No other worker in this field has been able to reach such a high rate of success in the induction of hypnosis with patients seen immediately on arrival in hospital. Esdaile (1846) used hypnosis extensively in major and minor surgery and even trained Indian ward orderlies to hypnotize for him, but he used a much more elaborate technique requiring about an hour before the patient was ready for operation (Esdaile 1852). Bramwell (1930) a master of hypnotic technique, actually stated that: 'The chief objection to hypnotic anaesthesia is the difficulty and uncertainty of the induction of the necessary degree of hypnosis . . . and generally hypnosis never becomes deep enough for operative purposes. Suggestive anaesthesia can only be induced in about 10 per cent of those hypnotized'. However, he gives thirteen excellent reasons why hypnosis, if it could be rapidly and successfully induced, should be used. Goldie makes hypnotic anaesthesia a practical procedure for the first time.

It is our custom to give patients achieving medium or deep hypnosis a small card, not unlike the cards carried by diabetics. Patients can then give these cards to their doctors or dental surgeons should they require hypnosis for minor surgery. With many patients it has been possible to give a post-hypnotic suggestion that they would, upon being asked by their doctor or dentist (and nobody else), suggest to themselves the counting of numbers up to five or ten. On reaching this number they would enter a light state of hypnosis, which the doctor or dental surgeon could deepen by pressing gently with his index finger on the patient's forehead. Hypnosis is terminated by counting to five slowly. In other words, both doctor and dentist have been placed *en rapport* with their patient, to their mutual benefit. As greater numbers of patients are hypnotized and can reach a medium or deep state, they can become recognized by the medical and dental profession by the card they carry. It is hoped that many patients will be conditioned to avoid pain and accept hypnosis as they would any anaesthetic, but with less fear, less risk of haemorrhage, quicker healing and a happier and more rested post-anaesthetic state.

DENTAL ANAESTHESIA

In dental surgery, hypnosis has a definite place as an anaesthetic agent. As long ago as 1837, Oudet described the extraction of teeth under what he called 'magnetic sleep'. Much research has been done by dental societies in America on the use of hypnosis, or 'psychosomatic sleep' as it has been labelled.

Deep hypnosis is not necessary for analgesia; pain can be abolished or reduced in many patients who are seemingly in a light state. No patient who has achieved hypnosis for psychiatric and other treatment should be subjected to dental anaesthesia before being tested for analgesia under hypnosis.

Under deep hypnosis it is possible to influence pain, salivation, muscular tension and so on. The hypnotic state can be induced rapidly and the patient then told to open his mouth wide and to keep it open without discomfort, pain or tiredness. The area of the individual tooth for which anaesthesia is needed can be tapped or touched and suggestions given for the abolition of pain. The following suggestions are given: 'The gum tissue will become numb, the bone around the tooth and the tooth itself will become numb. This will take a few seconds. Raise your index finger as soon as this takes place.' The patient will raise his finger and the work of the dental surgeon can proceed. Sometimes the patient will groan, but this is the same as the wincing or groaning observed during general anaesthesia, and there is amnesia afterwards for the whole incident.

Experience of such cases is necessary, but when it is gained induction and instruction are found to be simple and speedy. Suggestions for the well-being of the patient after dental surgery and post-hypnotic suggestions for lack of pain and haemorrhage should be given. The patient can be conditioned to further hypnosis in the usual way.

The advantages of using hypnosis are: (1) the facial muscles can be relaxed and held in position for long periods without pain or fatigue; (2) most dental operations can be performed under deep hypnosis without pain or discomfort, with the minimum shock and loss of blood and quick healing; (3) the frightened, panicky patient who is unable to face the thought of pain will be able to overcome excessive emotionalism and, by post-hypnotic suggestion, can be reassured for the next visit; (4) with the confidence gained by experience, it is a comparatively simple task to induce a depth of hypnosis sufficient to overcome a good deal of painful work that dentists must perform.

Wookey (1938) has stated: 'Whatever may be said to the contrary, anaesthesia, whether of the general or the local variety, is not a pleasant process, whereas hypnosis possesses no more discomfort than falling asleep and the awakening gives a very agreeable feeling of well-being.'

Becker has suggested to the author that children suffering dento-facial anomalies, caused by finger, thumb or lip-sucking, should always be subjected to suggestion at a hypnoidal level in an endeavour to break the habit before recourse is made to orthodontic appliances. He treats children from the age of six and his technique is to explain in detail, but in simple language, the ill effects that will ensue from continuing the habit. He glorifies the advantages in appearance of their teeth and faces (e.g. 'pretty like mummy') if they were to stop the habit. The children are made comfortable in the dental chair and told to close their eyes. Suggestions of sleepiness are given. Becker does not attempt any deepening of hypnosis and maintains that the light hypnoidal state is quite sufficient for his purpose. He has treated twenty children with this method. Eighteen of them ceased the habit after one treatment, two others needed to be seen twice to break the habit. He emphasizes the ease of inducing the hypnoidal state and mentions that he has been able to produce the condition in every child he has treated.

Many dental surgeons have emphasized the role which suggestive influences can play in rendering dental operations in children either difficult or easy to perform. One method which is much used by hypnodontists for inducing a trance state in young children consists of asking the patient to imagine his favourite T.V. programme and then making repetitive suggestions relating to this particular subject. As mentioned in the chapter dealing with paediatric hypnotherapy (p. 147), it is usually a comparatively easy matter to induce hypnosis in children. The main objective is to abolish the traditional fear of the dentist's chair, and many practitioners have reported that some of their young patients, when well trained, have even looked forward to the visit when they could 'dream' about their favourite pastime or summer holiday. It is usually advisable to have a separate room where the child can be relaxed in pleasing and comfortable surroundings before being led into the surgery.

Hypnodontics appears to be one of the fields in which the use of a tape-recorder is permissible, and indeed, at times, most valuable. Jacoby (1960) cites a number of cases where this technique for the initial induction was used in conjunction with a brief period of personal instruction by the dentist or his assistant. Since the object of hypnodontics is the limited one of facilitating dental operations there would seem to be little or no objection to the adoption of such aids as a more or less standard procedure for this particular purpose. If the dental practitioner is himself familiar with the phenomena of the hypnotic trance, and the 'relaxation' suggestions on the recording are made with care, he is not likely to meet with any untoward reactions on the part of his patients.

The majority of dental operations for which hypnosis is used alone consist of the preparation of cavities and fillings. Except for the removal of some deciduous teeth in young children, most extractions will probably also require an injection. However, as with all surgical operations, a calm and relaxed patient will greatly facilitate the administration, and possibly reduce the dose, of any local anaesthetic which might be required. Like all of his medical colleagues, the hypnodontist will need to ensure that when his patient leaves the surgery, he does so in an entirely normal frame of mind. If, for instance, dryness of the mouth has been suggested in order to reduce excessive salivation, care must be taken to countermand this suggestion so as to restore normal functioning of the salivary glands. Similarly, if the total abolition of pain had been achieved in a particular area of the mouth it would be unwise to discharge a patient until this effect had been removed or at least modified so that the anaesthesia persisted for only a limited time. Should the dental surgeon have any real cause to doubt the suitability of a patient for hypnotherapy he would be wise to seek the opinion of an experienced medical or psychiatric colleague. It is, however, most unlikely that this need will arise if he restricts the use of hypnosis to the promotion of relaxation and anaesthesia.

BIBLIOGRAPHY

AMENT, P. (1950) Illuminating facts in psychosomatic dentistry. *NW. Dent.*, *29*, 107.

BRAMWELL, J. M. (1930) *Hypnotism. Its History, Practice and Theory*, pp. 174-5. London: Rider.

BURGESS, T. O. (1951) Hypnodontia—hypnosis as applied to dentistry. *Cal. Mag.*, Chicago: Feb., March, April.

CHARLES, L. M. (1977) The psychology of pain. *Proc. Br. Soc. med. dent. Hypnosis*, *3*, 34.

COPPOLINO, C. A. (1965) *Practice of Hypnosis in Anaesthesiology.* New York: Grune & Stratton.

DYNES, J. B. (1932) An experimental study on hypnotic anaesthesia. *J. abnorm. soc. Psychol.*, *27*, 29.

ESDAILE, J. (1846) *Mesmerism in India, and its Practical Application in Surgery and Medicine.*

ESDAILE, J. (1852) *The Introduction of Mesmerism as an Anaesthetic and Curative Agent into the Hospitals of India.*

FAIRFULL SMITH, G. W. (1976) The modulation of fear, anxiety and pain with hypnosis. *Dig. Rep. Soc. Advmt Anaesth. Den.*, *3*, 76.

FAIRFULL SMITH, G. W. (1978) A case of dentalphobia combined with didaskaleinophobia (scholionophobia). *Proc. Br. Soc. med. den. Hypnosis*, *4*, 29.

FINER, B. (1967) Hypnosis as a psychosomatic weapon in the anaesthesiologist's armoury. In: *Hypnosis in Psychosomatic Medicine*, ed. J. Lassner, p. 104. New York: Julian Press.

FINER, B. (1972) The use of hypnosis in the clinical management of pain. In: *Pain: Basic Principles, Pharmacology. Therapy*, ed. J. P. Payne & R. A. P. Burt, pp. 168-170. Edinburgh: Churchill.

GOLDIE, L. (1956) Hypnosis in the casualty department. *Br. med. J.*, *2*, 1340-2.

HARTLAND, J. (1971) *Medical and Dental Hypnosis, 2nd ed.* London: Baillière Tindall & Cassell.

JACOBY, J. D. (1960) Statistical report on general practice hypnodontics: tape-recorder conditioning. *Int. J. clin. exp. Hypnosis*, *8*, 2.

LANGAN, D. & SPOERRI, T. (1968) *Hypnose und Schmerz die Hypnosuggestive Analgesie.* Basel: Harger.

LASSNER, J. (Ed.) (1962) *Hypnosis in Anaesthesiology: Proc. Int. Congress Anaesth.* Berlin: Springer.

MICHAEL, A. M. (1952) Hypnosis and pain. *Br. med. J.*, *1*, 734.

RAGINSKY, B. B. (1948) Mental suggestion as an aid in anaesthesia. *Anaesthesiology*, *9*, 472.

SCOTT, D. L. (1975) Hypnosis in pedicle graft surgery. *Proc. Br. Soc. med. dent. Hypnosis*, *1*, 10.

SCOTT, D. L. (1974) *Modern Hospital Hypnosis especially for Anaesthetists.* London: Lloyd-Luke.

SMITH, S. R. (1980) Hypnosis in dentistry – a critical survey. *Proc. R. Soc. Med.*, in the press.

TRAIGER, H. (1952) Children and hypnodontics. *Dent. Surv.*, Sept.

WIGGINS, S. L. & BROWN, C. W. (1968) Hypnosis with two pedicle graft cases. *Int. J. clin. exp. Hypnosis*, *16*, 215.

WOOKEY, E. E. (1938) Uses and limitations of hypnosis in dental treatment. *Br. dent. J.*, *65*, 562–8.

WOOKEY, E. E. (1975) The modern use of hypnosis in dentistry. *Proc. Br. Soc. med. dent. Hypnosis*, *1*, 10.

CHAPTER 9

HYPNOSIS IN PAEDIATRICS

It is now over 25 years since the author of this chapter was first asked to write an account of children treated by hypnotherapeutic methods.

In 1952 it was extremely difficult to find any references to the use of hypnosis in the treatment of children suffering from the effects of the neuroses or psychoneuroses. True, the word psychosomatic had appeared in the literature of the early 1920s, but only a few physicians were sympathetic to the broader concept of medicine embracing mind and body, with emphasis on the influence of the psyche over the soma. The idea that illness could be simply an attitude of mind only slowly gained acceptance in medical circles.

It seems obvious to the writer, as well as to many patients, that 'the dog must wag his tail, the tail must never wag the dog.' Yet how many patients do we see who are controlled by the 'negative' emotions ordained by their soma and overpowering their psyche? It is to the research of men like Dr. Hans Selye, working with a team in Canada, that we have to look for an understanding of stress in adult and childhood behaviour. Selye postulated states of Reaction, Resistance and Exhaustion following continued stress. He incorporated these three stages into his adaptation theory which showed that if a person has what Selye described as an adequate constitution and is subject to temporary stress, the body can cope, via the autonomic nervous system. The stage of Resistance is brought into effect. However, in those persons with an inadequate constitution, sustained stress produces Exhaustion and organic illness. A more detailed account of Selye's work is given in Chapter 5.

Fortunately in children the problem is less fundamental. Any psychosomatic illness is not yet so deeply conditioned as it is in the adult. The child is also more suggestible: he accepts suggestion with a less critical and more emotionally detached attitude than does the adult. Children seem more able to understand their 'psychosomatic selves'. D. L. Pedersen has told the author that he believes hypnotic phenomena may be a vital mental defense mechanism in children, from birth to 15 years of age. If this hypothesis is correct, it explains the understanding which children instinctively show in their need to ignore illness and get on with life.

The medical hypnotist must take advantage of this heightened suggestibility and realise the potential for conditioning the child to a more positive and healthier outlook. How then is this accomplished? How do we set about treating the child that is sent to us?

THE HISTORY OF THE COMPLAINT

It is not considered good practice to see the parents *after* speaking with the child. In the majority of cases children should be seen without the parents and preferably after the parents have been interviewed. First, both parents should be seen and careful notes taken of *their* complaints and *their* view of the child's problems. The doctor will ask himself 'What are these people telling me about *themselves*?'. So often it will be obvious to us that it is the *parents* and *their* interpersonal relationships that need analysis and help: the child is the barometer of the parents.

It would appear that the pattern of illness is ordained by two concepts: firstly, the role of the parents in the child's upbringing and secondly, the child's interpretation of the role indulged in by the parents. Hypnosis will be found to be of great value with those children incapable of defending themselves against the emotional machinations (often unconscious) of their parents.

It is possible to overcome a considerable amount of childhood neurosis by careful and sympathetic handling of the parents, particularly the mother. She is said to be the centre-piece of the family, the fount of love, happiness and security. She may have failed from the very beginning to match up to these ideals. During the history-taking questions should be asked about the actual birth of the child, whether the mother had difficulty during the confinement, whether she was looking forward to the birth of her child, and whether her general health was satisfactory during her pregnancy. She must be questioned about subsequent breast-feeding and potty-training. Careful note should be taken of the parents' insight into and understanding of their roles in the upbringing of the child and the mother's attitude to wet beds, constipation, periods, masturbation, religion and any other factors which, in the opinion of the medical hypnotist, may have had a deleterious affect upon the child. Much can be learned in the initial consultation about the personal relationships within the family constellation.

The author (G.A.) seldom treats hypnotically children under the age of six or seven. If the child is younger it will be found in practice that much can be achieved for the child by psychotherapy of one or both parents. This point will be elaborated further.

TREATMENT OF THE COMPLAINT

We are here concerned with the treatment of the psychosomatic aspect of the entire family constellation. It is not possible to separate the child from its parents in relation to any illness of this kind. However, it is one of the rewards the hypnotherapist reaps that, if it is at all possible to treat the child with a manoeuvre aimed entirely at the symptom, hypnosis can, in selected cases, be the method of choice.

TRANSFERENCE

To those readers more psychiatrically oriented, hypnosis will be found to be a useful tool in the enhancing of the transference so necessary in any manoeuvre involving the psyche. In our opinion, the transference is more easily handled with the use of hypnosis than it is in other schools of analysis.

Much has been written of the dangers of transference. It is true that experience in handling the rapport that exists between hypnotist and hypnotized is a necessity. Equally it is true that all psychotherapy produces a transference which must be understood if the patient is to derive most benefit from the treatment. The therapist must ask himself 'What is the patient trying to do to me? What is he seeing me as? Who is he seeing me as; am I his mother or father, and who am I in the various stages of treatment?' With experience it is not difficult to gauge the emotional need of the patient with respect to the therapist. In this connection, psychiatric accounts of transference should be studied and, where necessary, opportunity should be taken of discussing one's own emotional difficulties with a trained colleague.

THE ANXIOUS CHILD

There is much to commend the concept that illness, particularly of a psychosomatic nature, can be acquired even within the womb. Many years ago

Otto Rank propounded this 'pre-uterine' theory in his commendable book 'The Trauma of Birth'.

That anxiety can be environmental will surprise few of us. Anxiety is a prolonged state of fear and we have all met those anxious, fearful, fretful, mothers who bring us their anxious, fearful, fretful children. Often, they command us to help their ailing child. Anxiety in children is not difficult to diagnose but seems difficult to treat. A bottle of medicine or a tranquillizer does not answer the problem.

TECHNIQUES OF TREATMENT FOR ANXIETIES AND PHOBIAS

It will be found in practice that some knowledge of psychodynamic interpretation is particularly necessary with children. In the author's opinion (G.A.) it would be a mistake to give simple direct suggestion treatment to a child suffering an anxiety-phobic state without understanding the essential character of the phobia or anxiety state to be dealt with. After all, if we are treating a symptom of an underlying emotional conflict, we should endeavour to understand what the conflict means. The symptom is like a curtain behind which the underlying problem is hidden. Like his adult counterpart, the child uses symptoms as a defensive system. A neurosis indicates a need to keep the conflict from appearing in consciousness.

One could give a long list of symbols that may be encountered during the treatment of children at an analytical level, but a few examples will illustrate the sort of principles involved.

In those children suffering a fear of thunderstorms and floods, it might be tempting to expect a problem connected with God and religion. The voice of God could be heard as the thunder condemning the child for his 'sins'. Floods occur in the well-known biblical story of Noah: the wicked people were drowned for their sins. Religion foisted upon a child as a means of frightening him into being a 'good boy' is highly dangerous and can be the cause of much ill-health and misery. If a knowledge of religion is to be given to a child, fear must be avoided and God must be seen as a friend and a figure of love. Faith must be stressed and superstition avoided.

It is of course hardly necessary, in this day and age, to emphasize the chronic guilt and anxiety that can be projected onto a child over sexual matters. Sexual symbolism is only too common. Difficulty with writing, stealing — tape-recorders and radios are favourite targets — driving away cars, continually breaking things, damaging railway lines, throwing stones at trains, setting fire to haystacks and buildings, all these are only too common. Much delinquency is associated with the theft of bicycles,

Hypnosis in Paediatrics

cosmetics, handbags, perfumes, jewellery and other articles which symbolically represent repressed sexual fantasies. Both sexes illustrate their need to exploit the repressed emotions causing these conflicts and complexes (see Chapter 6).

In cases of anorexia and hysterical vomiting in childhood, the perplexing nature of the symptom can very often be better understood if the essential dynamism is fully realized. The child, nearly always a girl, is worried by tales of pregnancy. Several children treated by the author were attempting to rid themselves of a fantasy baby after being 'naughty' with their brothers or the next door neighbours' boy. They had never been told the true 'facts of life' and were guilty and ashamed of what they had done. It is much more satisfying to treat a child with the use of hypnosis if the treatment can be planned with some degree of hope that the fundamental roots of the problem can be pulled up and destroyed. Those readers eager to pursue the subject of symbols and symbolization are referred to the textbooks of psychiatry which deal with the subject.

TECHNIQUES OF HYPNOSIS WITH CHILDREN

It is true to say that almost 100% of children are easily hypnotized. If any difficulty is experienced, something may be wrong with the technique of the operator rather than with the child. Reassurance and patience will overcome most problems met with in the induction of the hypnotic state.

The child is made comfortable in a slightly darkened room. It is not necessary to keep to a rigid regimen for the induction of hypnosis. It is enough simply to ask the child to close his eyes. He is told to think of the words 'dreamy, drowsy, heavy and sleepy', and to think what these words mean to him. The hypnotist then counts to ten repeating the words thus:

'One for dreamy, two for drowsy, three for heavy, four for sleepy and five for dreamy, drowsy, heavy and sleepy; six for dreamy, seven for drowsy, eight for heavy, nine for sleepy and ten for ten times deeper.' Before counting to ten the suggestion is given that when the doctor reaches ten the child will feel himself going deeper and deeper 'asleep' until he 'sleeps deeply'.

Deepening techniques can be modified to suit each patient. Thus the child can be asked to visualize a thermometer tabulated between one and one hundred in figures. As he goes ten times deeper into the dreamy, drowsy, heavy and sleepy state he will see the thermometer rise ten degrees higher. Each time the child is told to go ten times deeper he receives the suggestion that he will see the thermometer rise ten degrees. This will also be found a useful test for visualization and for depth levels and can be incorporated into later methods of exploration for conflicts, catharsis and abreactive techniques.

Very often in practice it will be found beneficial to allow the child to express himself while in the actual hypnotic state. The value of hypnosis will be found in its ability to allow the child to feel his emotions: not only can he imagine situations but he can actually appreciate how he felt during certain traumatic occurrences. This method, entailing the acting out of emotions experienced previously, eliminates the need to spend time on purely intellectual understanding. The most spectacular affects of hypnosis are to be seen in the emotional realization of previously repressed traumatic experiences. Sometimes these are abreacted (acted out) with a good deal of feeling, sometimes the emotions are released gradually and gently with as much excitement as might be felt in a dream.

Other deepening techniques can easily be exploited in children. They are asked to concentrate on their breathing out (expirations) and as they do so to feel themselves relaxing deeper and deeper into the chair they occupy. This of course will be a physiological fact, but a useful suggestion none the less! Another situation that can be given to a child is to imagine himself in a large building. As he walks down each flight of stairs to descend to street or basement level, he will 'go ten times deeper' and he will see the 'ten times deeper' registered on the thermometer mentioned earlier.

An induction technique useful with younger children is to recite to the child his favourite television programme. The child is told to imagine a screen and to see the pictures emerging. It will be found in practice that as the hypnotist mentions the figures on the screen a story can be unfolded to the child. This can later be used in the uncovering of material from the unconscious. The child is told to think of his favourite programme and make up a story in his mind. The story will often give us the lead to problems at home or at school, with brothers or sisters, and so on.

TRAINING THE CHILD IN AUTO-HYPNOSIS

The importance of autohypnosis in the treatment of children cannot be overstressed. It is a very simple procedure but so often it is not insisted upon by hypnotherapists. It should be.

After using the technique for induction of hypnosis mentioned above, the child can be given a formula for attaining the 'dreamy, drowsy, heavy, sleepy' state. He is told that these words, together with the deepening techniques, can all be contained in a formula of two or three words. As he says these words to himself he will expect to go deeply into the hypnotic state, which most children call 'the sleepy feeling'. The words for induction can be, for instance, 'Right now' and then to bring the child out of hypnosis the words 'Out now' could be used. All this is told to the child while he is in the hypnotic state: it is therefore a post-hypnotic suggestion. Children will practice auto-hypnosis assiduously and use it two or three times daily. The child soon learns the best suggestions to give himself.

PSYCHOSOMATIC PROBLEMS

Every hypnotist starts his, or her, career with great success. He uses his 'magic' with deadly precision. However, there are, according to Wolberg, three stages in the hypnotist's life: (1) when he cures everybody and everything, (2) when he begins to find that he is not so successful and even loses his ability to hypnotize, and (3) when he uses his skill with understanding and imagination and chooses those cases for which hypnosis is the most effective method of treatment.

It is wise to choose the cases we are best suited to deal with and psychosomatic problems, as a general rule, fall within the realm of hypnosis.

Many psychosomatic difficulties cannot be divorced from an anxiety state. Many illnesses will have an overlay of fear, depression and anxiety. Hypnotherapy is commonly being used nowadays for conditions such as asthma, hay-fever and dermatoses, and for tension states such as migraine/tension headaches, stammering, enuresis, tics, habit-spasms and the like.

Rules for the treatment of psychosomatic states vary little from treatment for any conflict of the mind in child or adult. From the outset the therapist must assume a positive attitude: the child must be reassured that all will be well. Children are adept at accepting a positive attitude of mind towards any illness they may suffer, but often the parents find it hard to accept that the illness is organic and fundamental. They may well have been conditioned by years of contact with dogmatic, authoritarian doctors. A child seems to accept and will take for granted that his mind may be temporarily at fault and might be 'punishing' his body. Treatment must be aimed at this fact and built upon the essential positive factors that the child is only too willing to exploit, given the chance. The choice can become the patient's. It is, in practice, easier for the child to adopt a positive attitude than it is for the adult, hidebound by compulsive dogma. Hypnotherapy should be used to reinforce these sentiments and to defend the child against constant propaganda of an anxiety-provoking nature. Often parents must be helped themselves to a more adult attitude in their own concepts of right and wrong. Hypnotizing children makes their minds more receptive to the understanding and insight necessary to overcome the workings of their illness, which is, in many cases, directly attributable to the emotional immaturity of the parents.

ASTHMA

It is common in textbooks nowadays to read that asthma is the condition that is most likely to succumb to the efforts of the hypnotist. This is true for children, although, as we have pointed out, asthmatic children have been relieved by psychotherapy to one or other of the parents, more often the mother. However, it is not always possible to relieve the symptoms of asthma without giving some insight to the child. There is also a definite danger in attempting to abolish the symptoms in children receiving corticosteroids, but hypnosis is undoubtedly a powerful weapon in the hands of the understanding and careful practitioner.

EPILEPSY, STAMMERING, ENURESIS AND TENSION HEADACHES

Petit mal, stammering, bed-wetting and tension headaches are all susceptible to the same technique of treatment, namely an inquiry into the social and environmental problems of the patient. The child is forcibly telling us, through the symptom, that he is unhappy, or that school is too difficult, or home is unrestful, or life is more than he can abide.

Epileptics suffering from *petit mal* often prove susceptible to treatment by hypnosis. *Grand mal* sufferers present psychological difficulties best left to a psychiatrist, for often the chronic epileptic has repressed a great deal of trauma and much deep probing is necessary. We should be aware that in the child, just as in the adult, a psychosomatic illness may mask a psychotic condition. While treating the epileptic child thorough medication may be necessary while hypnotic suggestions are being given. Later, and particularly in the case of *petit mal*, recourse to drugs is not so important and the writer has treated cases where the mother has forgotten to insist on the medicine or tablets being taken, the child having shown such a marked improvement. It may gradually become possible for the child to use auto-hypnosis in lieu of medication. Auto-hypnosis should always be used when treating children.

Stammering is usually a problem of breast-feeding or potty-training: a child with a spasm at one end produces a spasm at the other. In other words, the alimentary tract commences at the mouth and ends at the anus. Constipation will often be admitted. Much therapy may be necessary before improvement can be seen in the child's speech and once again the fault will often be found to lie with the parents. We may find an aggressive, overpowering mother and a weak father who always gives in to his wife. All cases will be different and no two children can be treated the same way. One of us (G.A.) once treated a child for ten sessions with excellent results, using direct suggestions that the stammer would disappear within one year. However, his younger brother needed protracted treatment together with insight therapy to his mother before he was relieved of his stammer. It seemed that the mother had to have one son as a bed-wetter and transferred her attentions to her younger son when a cure was affected for the eldest boy. The mother was unhappy with her husband and had unconsciously transferred her love needs to her sons. When she understood the situation the younger boy got better. This case is illustrated in some detail by Schneck (1963).

It is not necessary to treat enuresis before the age of six, but if it is persisting after this age hypnosis can be of great help. However, it must be understood that treating the enuretic child calls for a careful assessment of the mother's role in the child's upbringing. The parents must be seen: much can be accomplished by simple explanation and family psychotherapy. Enuresis is a cry for help. Many bed-wetters recover spontaneously without treatment, often when they learn to cope with their emotional problems, but some proceed to more definite signs of neurosis. An interesting problem of this nature was successfully treated in a boy of 17. Treatment had to be hurried, as the boy was completing his education in the United States of America. Hypnotherapy was made easier by the subject's knowledge of psychology: he was entered for University as a student in psychology and was most interested in the clinical use of uncovering techniques combined with analytical psychological methods. He understood the implications of sexual frustration and the origins of fetishism.

The patient knew from the commencement of psychotherapy that he had to overcome his mother's morbid interest in his wet beds. During treatment the hypnotherapist was told by the father that he too was a bed-wetter when young and had told this to his son when the latter was 14 years old. The father was guilty that he had worsened the problem for his son. When the son began to realize that he was in rivalry with his father for his mother's affection, he ceased to wet the bed and was able to remove the rubber sheet, much to his mother's chagrin. Before leaving for America he revealed that he indulged in masochistic practices. He had a girlfriend considerably older than himself who liked spanking him. He would ask her to pull his hair during intercourse and tried to get her to cut his arm with a sharp instrument. He could remember that at the age of nine he had played at spanking games with two sisters who lived near him. He always wanted them to overpower him. He got into bed with them but was too young to do very much although he knew that the older sister (aged 12) wanted sex. Arrangements were made for him to continue analytical treatment in America.

CONCLUSION

It is hoped that the reader will be stimulated to use the methods of treatment by hypnotherapy laid down in this chapter. Hypnosis has been a fascinating technique for many years and children are possibly the most rewarding subjects. The same rules apply as in the adult: hypnosis should be used to achieve regression, revivification and progressive motivation to adulthood.

BIBLIOGRAPHY

AMBROSE, G. (1961) *Hypnotherapy with Children*, 2nd ed., p. 106. London: Staples.
AMBROSE, G. (1963) *Hypnotherapy for Children*, ed. J. M. Schneck, 3rd ed., pp. 204–28. Springfield, Ill.: Charles C. Thomas.
AMBROSE, G. (1977) Why, when and how does hypnosis fail? *Proc. Br. Soc. med. dent. Hypnosis, 3,* 10.
BARBER, T. X. (1963) The effects of 'hypnosis' on pain. *Psychosom. Med., 25,* 303.
BARRY, H., MACKINNON, D. W. & MURRAY, H. A. (1960) Hypnotizability in state hospitalised schizophrenics. *Psychiat. Q., 34,* 65.
BEECHER, H. K. (1956) Relationship of significance of wound to pain experienced. *J. Am. med. Ass., 161,* 1609.
BERNSTEIN, N. R. (1965) Observations on the use of hypnosis with burned children on a paediatric ward. *Int. J. clin. exp. Hypnosis, 131,* 10.
BURNS, C. L. C. & MORRISON-SMITH, J. E. (1960) Treatment of asthmatic children by hypnotic suggestion. *Br. J. Dis. Chest, 54,* 78.
CRASILNECK, H. B., McCRANIE, E. J. & JENKINS, M. T. (1956) Special indications for hypnosis as a method of anaesthesia. *J. Am. med. Ass., 162,* 1606.
DONALDSON, M. (1978) *Children's Minds.* London: Fontana/Collins.
EARL, C. J. C. (1941) A note on the validity of certain Rorschach symbols. *Rorschach Res. Exch., 5,* 51.
FALCK, F. J. (1964) Stuttering and hypnosis. *Int. J. clin. exp. Hypnosis, 12,* 67.

FREUD, A. (1973) *Normality and Pathology in Childhood.* Harmondsworth: Penguin.
FRIEDLANDER, J. W. & SARBIN, T. R. (1938) The depth of hypnosis. *J. abnorm. soc. Psychol., 33*, 453.
IKEMI, Y. (1959) Hypnotic experiments on the psychosomatic aspects of gastro-intestinal disorders in children. *Int. J. clin. exp. Hypnosis., 7,* 139.
LONDON, P. (1962) Hypnosis in children: an experimental approach. *Int. J. clin. exp. Hypnosis, 10,* 79.
MOORE, R. K. & LAUER, L. M. (1976) Hypnotic susceptibility in middle childhood. *Int. J. clin. Exp. Hypnosis, 60,* 167.
PIAGET, J. (1977) *The Origins of Intelligence in the Child.* Harmondsworth: Penguin.
RANK, O. (1957) *The Trauma of Birth.* New York: Brunner.
SCHNECK, J. M. (ed.) (1963) *Hypnosis in Modern Medicine*, 3rd ed., p. 218. Springfield, Ill.: Charles C. Thomas.
SMITH, F. G. W. (1979) The control of fear and pain in children with hypnosis. *Proc. Br. Soc. med. dent. Hypnosis, 4,* 3.
STERNLICHT, M. & WANDERER, Z. W. (1963) Hypnotic susceptibility and mental deficiency. *Int. J. clin. exp. Hypnosis, 10,* 104.
STONE, F. H. & KOUPERNIKE, C. (1974) *Child Psychiatry for Students.* Edinburgh: Churchill.
THORNDIKE, E. L. (1913) *The Psychology of Teaching.* Columbia: University Press.
VALENTINE, C. W. (1975) *The Normal Child.* Harmondsworth: Penguin.

CHAPTER 10

HYPNOSIS IN GYNAECOLOGY

Psychiatry excluded, it would be difficult to find in the entire field of medicine any area in which psychological factors play so important a role as in gynaecology. The emotions may be responsible for the occurrence of many well recognized gynaecological symptoms. Repressed unconscious material may also be the fundamental cause of a diversity of complaints ranging from disturbances of menstruation to various types of pelvic pain. In most of these cases, therefore, the primary requisite in treatment is not the surgeon's scalpel but the words of the physician. It is unfortunate that gynaecology is commonly regarded as a branch of surgery since the *person* may be lost sight of or regarded as of less importance than her vaginal bleeding or dysmenorrhoea. To a lesser extent this is probably true also of endocrinological factors although, of course, their function in the proper regulation of the female sexual physiology is a very important one.

Not for the first time in history, it is becoming apparent that emotional factors must nearly always be considered in gynaecological problems, and that a good gynaecologist must necessarily have more than a mere passing interest in psychology and psychiatry. This does not mean that he must adhere to the viewpoint of any one particular school of thought, although some acquaintance with psychoanalytic theory will often be found of value. Various methods of psychotherapy may be found useful in gynaecological practice, but one of the most beneficial is that which employs the hypnotic state either for direct symptom removal or else for deeper psychotherapy, including hypnoanalysis.

The general practitioner has always been faced with a considerable number of gynaecological complaints which range from the disturbances of puberty to the post-menopausal syndrome. The majority of these cases

Hypnosis in Gynaecology

are probably treated with sedatives or analgesics or sometimes with hormones, by the practitioner himself, while the remainder are referred to hospital for more specialized forms of treatment, including surgery. It is quite possible that in gynaecology the wrong line of treatment is adopted more often than is realized. If a woman complains of symptoms referable to her pelvic organis, treatment is focused upon this region of her body whereas the basic cause of the disorder may be in her mind. This has been demonstrated very clearly by Kroger (1953) working in Chicago. Psychotherapy, not hormones or surgery, is the chief requirement in these cases of psychogenic origin.

The incidence of psychosomatic disturbances among gynaecological patients has been variously estimated at between 30 and 70% of all patients. In this chapter those conditions having a wholly or partially psychogenic basis will be discussed and their treatment by hypnotherapy evaluated. In some of them it need be the only therapeutic measure employed while in others it is best used in conjunction with other methods in order that the most beneficial results may be obtained.

DISTURBANCE OF MENSTRUATION

Menstrual disorders are probably the most common of all gynaecological complaints and are frequently encountered in general practice. The offending symptoms may be some irregularity in the flow itself, e.g. in the amount of blood lost or the time of its appearance, or the flow may be regular and normal but associated with excessive pain. In all of these disorders psychic factors may be the fundamental cause of the symptoms.

Sometimes more than one symptom is present at the same time: the following conditions will be discussed.

(1) Functional uterine bleeding (menorrhagia and metrorrhagia).
(2) Amenorrhoea (including oligomenorrhoea).
(3) Pseudocyesis.
(4) Dysmenorrhoea.

FUNCTIONAL UTERINE BLEEDING

This may take the form of menorrhagia or metrorrhagia. Worry, shock and anxiety may all give rise to heavy bleeding from the uterus, and this symptom was common during the war years when large numbers of women were subjected to abnormal emotional stress. In a similar category are the stories of young brides who are startled and embarrassed by the unexpected appearance of their periods on their wedding nights. Some psychiatrists believe, however, that this bleeding acts as a kind of unconscious defence mechanism against the expected act of sexual intercourse. On the other hand, there is some evidence that menstruation may stimulate sexual excitement in the male, and a high incidence of rape and assault at this time has been alleged in support of this theory. Fear of pregnancy may be yet another aetiological factor in functional bleeding. It is also not uncommon for a broken engagement or a lovers' quarrel to be followed by vaginal haemorrhage. Whatever the unconscious motivation behind the appearance of this particular symptom, if there is a definite psychogenic factor involved the logical method of treatment is psychotherapy. Sometimes treatment on a superficial level may be sufficient to bring about a cure, but in many instances it will be necessary to probe considerably deeper. Whether therapy is directed to simple measures of explanation and reassurance, or to a search for unconscious motives, hypnosis will prove invaluable in many cases for enabling the physician to gain the best results from his endeavours. The following case illustrates the treatment of psychogenic bleeding by hypnotherapy.

> A married woman aged 32 developed irregular bleeding — often amounting to floodings — although previously her menses had occurred regularly every 28 days and had lasted about 4 or 5 days. She had married in her early twenties and had had two miscarriages and one child following a normal pregnancy. Her marriage, apparently, was in part an attempt to escape from the environment of her family but in spite of this inadequate motive was for several years reasonably successful. Before her marriage she had had several boy-friends. She had been greatly attached to one of them before the association had been broken up by his removal from the district. Nearly 3 years later she had married her present husband.
> Not long before the onset of the symptoms of which she complained, quarrels had arisen between her and her husband over the question of another woman with whom the patient believed her husband was having an affair. As a result the marital relationship became more and more discordant and not only did abnormal bleeding occur but she developed a marked aversion towards any attempt at coitus. Her general health also began to deteriorate and she suffered from insomnia and headaches. From her history it was fairly clear that the vaginal bleeding was probably an unconscious weapon used as a means of avoiding sexual contact with her husband.
> During the course of a few sessions the reason for her symptoms was explained to the patient and the whole situation 'worked

through' under hypnosis (for she was a good hypnotic subject). In the meantime the husband was seen and when the matter was discussed with him he became reasonable and promised that he would give his wife no further cause for suspicion. The patient was then reassured on this point and was given suggestions that the abnormal bleeding would now cease, as the cause had been removed, and that her general health would also begin to improve. After half a dozen sessions she was able to report that she was very much better. Her marital relations were now perfectly satisfactory and a normal menstrual cycle had been re-established.

Psychogenic bleeding will frequently clear up under the influence of direct suggestion alone. If a woman frequently responds in this manner to conditions involving emotional stress it is sometimes possible to fortify her neuro-endocrine system by suitable subliminal suggestion so that the symptom does not occur. As a rule, a fairly deep state of hypnosis — preferably somnambulsim — seems to bring about the best results.

Even if an underlying disorder of the uterus and adnexa is found, such as fibroids, emotional tension may be the decisive factor in precipitating or aggravating bleeding. The reason for this is presumably the increased vascularity which occurs due to psychic factors, in the same way that an embarrassing situation may cause blushing of the face and neck. However, before attributing any form of uterine haemorrhage to 'functional' causes an adequate physical examination of the pelvis must be carried out. Some cases may be partly 'organic' and partly 'functional'; a rational form of therapy would then be hypnotherapy combined with surgery or the administration of hormones, depending on the type of lesion present.

PSYCHOGENIC AMENORRHOEA

We shall now consider not only complete cessation of menstruation but also oligomenorrhoea, where the flow is much more scanty than usual. Both may be caused by psychic disturbances such as shock, worry, fear (commonly of pregnancy), a faulty attitude towards the sexual and reproductive functions, etc. It has also been suggested that complete deprivation of male society may also be responsible. It is said that some of the female inmates of the concentration camps during the Second World War who had many months, or even years, of amenorrhoea, were dramatically relieved of the symptom upon the appearance of the liberating troops. Change of environment is also well recognized as a cause of this type of amenorrhoea. Girls entering hospital to train as nurses may experience a sudden cessation of their periods soon after they leave home for new and unfamiliar surroundings.

When confronted with a case of this kind it is important for the physician to realize that sometimes no specific form of treatment may be needed at all. For example, a girl who leaves an environment where she is unhappy and goes back to her own home may find that her periods return to a perfectly normal cycle although there may have been no sign of them for several months. There are also cases on record of a long-standing amenorrhoea ending after a sympathetic talk with an understanding doctor.

If more powerful suggestive treatment is indicated then the hypnotic state provides an ideal medium in which this can be achieved. In some cases direct suggestion may be quite effective, while in others some degree of analysis may be preferable. In cases treated by direct suggestion it is sometimes remarkable how the menses can be made to occur at a specified date and time. A patient is told, for example 'You will have a normal period at 10 o'clock tomorrow morning' and the next day at the time stated or thereabouts she does indeed experience the onset of menstruation. Fortunately, in the majority of patients exhibiting this symptom, no deeply rooted unconscious conflicts are responsible for the amenorrhoea, and the gynaecologist or general practitioner who is acquainted with hypnotic techniques is usually well able to deal with the situation himself. Should deeper psychotherapy be necessary, however, the case should be referred to a specialist in psychiatry.

Psychiatric treatment is usually required for those women who develop amenorrhoea because they intensely resent menstruation owing to an inability to accept the feminine role. These patients wish they had been born male, since they feel that men have much greater opportunities in life than women. Some of them may adopt masculine habits and dress, or may appear as tomboys. Latent homosexuality is a possibility and if this is suspected skilled psychiatric advice should be sought. If the amenorrhoea is due to faulty sex education or to a belief that menstruation is 'unclean', re-education of the patient under hypnosis is usually within the scope of the general practitioner or gynaecologist.

PSEUDOCYESIS (PHANTOM PREGNANCY)

Amenorrhoea is one of the main symptoms of phantom pregnancy. Enlargement and pigmentation of the breasts, abdominal distension, heartburn and vomiting may also be present. The cause is undoubtedly psychogenic and the patient may show other evidence of a neurotic personality. Writers like Deutsch (1944 & 1945) and Dunbar (1938) consider that factors such as an intense, aggressive wish to be pregnant, or an ambivalent state of mind towards pregnancy, may be responsible for the condition. Sometimes it is amazing how persistent these symptoms can be, and it has been recorded that one patient believed she was pregnant for fourteen years! On occasions these patients will go to term and experience 'pseudo-labour' pains.

In the treatment of an individual with true pseudocyesis it is important to be sure that her personality will be able to accept the fact that no pregnancy exists. Hypnotherapy provides a valuable means of uncovering any unconscious motives which may be responsible for the symptoms, and for giving the patient any necessary insight into their nature. During the hypnotic state she is also re-educated and given positive suggestions that the symptoms will disappear.

FUNCTIONAL DYSMENORRHOEA

The type of dysmenorrhoea for which hypnotherapy is indicated is usually labelled 'functional'. Some cases of painful menstruation are due to 'organic' causes, such as a retroverted uterus or a small cervix with a 'pin-hole' os. These may include psychogenic factors in their aetiology, so that psychotherapy as well as other forms of treatment may be indicated. Before a diagnosis of 'functional dysmenorrhoea' is made it is, of course, essential that a thorough gynaecological examination be carried out. The condition is commonly regarded (Taylor 1949) as having an aetiology similar to such disorders as migraine, mucous colitis and asthma.

In a large number of women the belief exists that sickness and menstruation are, for all practical purposes, synonymous. As soon as their periods begin they are 'unwell'. In some cultures menstruating women are regarded as 'unclean' and society has surrounded them with a series of rigid taboos. In our own Western civilization generations of schoolgirls have learned to refer to their menses as 'the curse'. With such a background it need not surprise us to discover that numerous women suffer from dysmenorrhoea. The ground has already been prepared, as it were, by the customs and beliefs of society throughout the centuries. Any emotional stress may be sufficient to bring about the condition. Immediately precipitating factors may be guilt concerning masturbation, resentment of femininity or fears concerning marriage, sexual intercourse and pregnancy.

The usual treatment of functional dysmenorrhoea is by analgesics and sedatives in the milder cases, coupled sometimes with superficial psychotherapy such as attempts to reassure the patient. If this is not sufficient, surgery may be resorted to; this may range from dilatation and curettage to a pre-sacral sympathectomy. Before surgery the patient is sometimes given a course of endocrine therapy, e.g. progesterone or testosterone, a few days before the date of the expected period. This is usually repeated for several months.

With all of these methods of treatment successes have been claimed. If they fail, certain physicians have then been known to recommend marriage as a last desperate resort! It is probably for the same reason that unhappy and mismated couples have been advised to have children in order to restore marital harmony. There is no doubt that symptomatic cure, or at least considerable relief, has followed in many instances when the recognized medical or surgical measures have been instituted.

It is also true that hypnotherapy not only provides a rational approach to the problem of treatment but fully justifies its employment in cases of dysmenorrhoea of the 'functional' type. Many examples have been reported from various countries showing that suitable suggestion given during the hypnotic state may be completely effective in relieving symptoms. In a number of instances direct suggestion alone has been effective and treatment was not unduly prolonged. On an average one treatment weekly for a few weeks is sufficient, but it may sometimes be advisable to repeat the suggestion just before a period is due. If the dysmenorrhoea is related to considerable unconscious conflicts then it is nearly always best to give the patient insight into the basic cause, and to reintegrate her personality so that the symptom becomes unnecessary. This can be achieved most rapidly if the patient is a good hypnotic subject so that some degree of hypnoanalysis can be attempted.

Because of the widespread nature of this particular symptom, and because it is frequently the cause of considerable incapacity for the sufferer, the following case will be described showing the use of hypnotherapy in its treatment.

> A young woman aged 21 years was seen for severe dysmenorrhoea which had persisted ever since her first menstrual period at the age of 13 years. At first she had experienced some relief from analgesics and sedatives such as aspirin and the barbiturates and also, to a lesser extent, from injections of progesterone. Since she took up her present job 2 years ago the pain had become more severe so that for one or two days every month she was obliged to report sick and go to bed. Because of this interference with her working life she entered hospital for a dilatation and curettage, but this operation made no improvement.
>
> When the patient was first seen an attempt was made to induce hypnosis but this was only partly successful because of her nervous-

ness. A week or so later a second attempt was made and this time she entered a somnambulistic state. This was only 2 or 3 days before her next period was due. While under hypnosis she was given specific suggestions that this period would be quite painless and that she would be able to remain at work. She was also told that from then onwards she would never again be incapacitated by the occurrence of her periods, neither would she need any drugs. The suggestion was then repeated several times. On being 'awakened' she had complete amnesia and felt perfectly well. She was then given an appointment to attend two weeks later.

At the next interview she stated that she had been agreeably surprised to find that menstruation occurred with very little discomfort. She thought that the slight abdominal cramps which were experienced may have been due to anticipating a repetition of her former sensations. This time she remained at work. Although there was such a definite relief following the first real therapeutic session, it was decided to see her at monthly intervals for the next 4 months on days just before the expected arrival of her next period. This was done in order to reinforce the suggestions and to make reasonably certain that they would remain effective at the crucial dates, so that the patient could then be conditioned to *expecting* a painless menstrual cycle in the future. She was kept under observation for about 2 years and did not relapse: neither did she develop any other complaint as a replacement, in spite of the fact that only direct symptom removal was employed.

This particular patient was one of those whose normal menstrual cycle was almost an entirely regular one. She was therefore able to calculate with a high degree of certainly the date of the commencement of her next period. When faced with patients whose cycles are less regular it may be advisable to modify somewhat the therapeutic suggestions given under hypnosis, suggesting *not* a completely painless menstruation throughout the whole length of the period but a mild initial discomfort. The reason for this is largely a social one, for the sudden unexpected appearance of the menses could prove a source of embarrassment to the patient.

It is quite possible that a woman with a history of previous severe dysmenorrhoea would still experience some pain even if its total abolition were strongly suggested. This might suggest to her that hypnotherapy was ineffective, and the ensuing anxiety due to the anticipated failure of treatment might tend to nullify the beneficial results one would normally expect from this form of therapy. If the physician knows his patient well, and there is already a good doctor-patient relationship between them, possible failures from this cause may not arise. Every hypnotherapist must judge for himself, according to individual circumstances, the kind of suggestions best suited to the needs of the patients in his care.

CONTROL OF MENSTRUATION

In addition to the treatment of actual disorders of the menstrual cycle, hypnotherapy may be used to control the time of appearance of the flow. Some women, e.g. concert artistes and athletes, may find a distinct advantage in delaying the period for a few days so that it does not interfere with important activities they have to undertake. If hypnosis is used in this way its effect is similar to that which follows the administration of progestational hormones which are used clinically for this purpose.

It is also possible, in some patients, to change the rhythm of the menstrual cycle by suitable hypnotic suggestion. For instance, a three-week cycle may be converted into a standard four-week one. In the author's experience it is not easy to alter the rhythm in this way, especially if the cycle which it is sought to change appears to be 'normal' for the particular individual concerned. Furthermore, a deep state of hypnotic trance is necessary before any suggestions become really effective.

PREMENSTRUAL TENSION AND HEADACHE

Apart from a true dysmenorrhoea occurring at the time of menstruation many women suffer from a syndrome-complex for some days, usually a week or so, before the actual period begins. Feelings of general nervous irritability, tension and headache may occur. They feel 'on edge', sleep poorly and may find difficulty in concentrating on their normal daily duties. Whether the basic reason for the appearance of these symptoms is salt retention in the tissues or some other factor connected with the process of ovulation, the psychic and somatic components ultimately react upon each other. It is therefore reasonable to assume that hypnotherapy will provide a useful adjunct to other forms of treatment such as that aimed at the correction of any hormonal imbalance or the elimination of sodium chloride. The general calming and relaxing effect obtained through hypnosis can sometimes be of great value in helping to relieve the distressing symptoms of this condition.

PSYCHOGENIC LEUCORRHOEA

It is fairly common knowledge that a mucoid vaginal discharge may occur during periods of sexual excitement, even when coitus does not take place. The emotions which are aroused at this time appear to stimulate the glands in the vaginal walls to secrete and thus produce the leucorrhoea. Occasionally this type of discharge becomes very marked. This condition is apt to prove resistant to chemical methods of treatment.

A rational method of treatment in this condition is hypnotherapy, and a number of cases where it has been successfully used have now been reported in the literature. Bunnemann, for example, describes an interesting case where not only was long-standing leucorrhoea removed by hypnotic suggestion but it was brought back by the same means, thus proving its psychogenic origin. Another proof of the importance of mental and emotional factors in the aetiology of this type of discharge is the fact that it may occur during the course of erotic dreams.

Sometimes anxiety without the arousal of concomitant sexual emotions can give rise to a profuse vaginal discharge. This was demonstrated to the author (G. N.) by an overseas visitor who had been in the UK for about three months. Prior to coming to this country she had had a very slight occasional leucorrhoea which had not caused her any trouble. Just before leaving home she had mentioned it to a girl friend who said it might be due to disease. After her arrival in Britain the discharge became much worse, and her anxiety increased partly because of this and partly because of her inability to describe her worry adequately in English. When asked if she would rather talk in French, her native tongue, her relief was immediately apparent and she embarked upon a voluble description of her anxieties and symptoms.

During the course of the interview it became fairly clear that this leucorrhoea was largely, if not entirely, psychological in origin, and this was confirmed by negative gynaecological and bacteriological findings. The patient was strongly reassured that she had no disease whatsoever, and although hypnotherapy was considered in her case this proved to be unnecessary, for her symptoms largely disappeared following this initial reassurance. Catarrhal conditions of the genital tract may turn out to be psychosomatic problems, in much the same way as a 'cold' or an attack of 'bronchitis' may follow an emotional upheaval in susceptible individuals.

STERILITY

Since the Second World War the legal adoption of children by childless couples has become very widespread, not only in this country but elsewhere. One unexpected result has been that an increasing number of women who had previously regarded themselves as incapable of bearing children have within a few months of adopting a baby discovered that they were pregnant. It has also been noted that sometimes when patients have been told that pregnancy is impossible for them, the medical advisers have been proved wrong by the birth of children.

This sequence of events has now been observed often enough to warrant an explanation, and the most likely one is that the original 'sterility' was psychological in origin and was cured psychologically. It is now believed that an appreciable number of women fail to conceive for psychological reasons. Partly because of a faulty attitude to sexual matters in childhood and adolescence, many young married couples are extremely shy and uneasy concerning the physical act of copulation. They fear that it is 'dirty' and not for 'nice people'. This emotional outlook, allied to inexperience, leads to considerable difficulty and tension whenever sexual intercourse is attempted. A state of psychic tension leads to spasm of the Fallopian tubes so that the passage and union of sperm and ovum is prevented. If the condition is not relieved within a reasonable time and there is no sign of pregnancy after a few months in spite of fairly frequent coitus, a new source of anxiety arises — the fear that the wife will not be able to have children. A vicious circle is thus established and years of childlessness may ensue. If, however, such a woman decides to adopt a baby, her fears and anxieties are relieved and relaxation of the tubes during intercourse takes the place of the previous spasm. Similarly, if she becomes resigned to the idea that she is forever 'sterile', tension eases and a pregnancy may follow. This tubal spasm has been demonstrated experimentally by observing the progress of an injection of Lipiodol past an obstruction in the tube when the patient has been heavily sedated with drugs or given suggestions of relaxation under hypnosis.

Given the supposed aetiology of this kind of sterility, it is reasonable to use hypnotism in its treatment. Patients are given hypnotic suggestions of relaxation during coitus and also shown how to achieve mental and physical relaxation as part of their daily lives. This is coupled with reassurance of the patient and her husband.

As a rule it is not necessary for a deep state of hypnosis to be reached before therapeutic suggestions can become effective; the release of tension through adoption is obtained without any help from hypnotism at all. Nevertheless, in certain cases analysis under hypnosis may be the method of choice. Other neurotic traits may be exhibited by these patients, such as frigidity, narcissism, ambivalence, or the repudiation of femininity by the 'career woman'.

Finally, in addition to the type of sterility already described, it has been suggested that in some pre-menopausal patients hypnotic suggestions might be of value in temporarily stimulating ovulation, or perhaps postponing the menopause, in order to give a further opportunity for conception to occur. So far there is no evidence to support this idea but it might well merit some properly controlled experiments and clinical research.

FRIGIDITY

This condition has been termed 'the bane of married life' — often a just description. It is fairly widespread among women in our Western civilization and in most patients the symptom is characteristic of a psychosexual neurosis. Because of this, it is often stated that true frigidity is not merely a lack of clitoral or vaginal orgasm, but involves a complete lack of erotic response on the part of the female during intercourse and also during any attempts at 'love-making'. It is a disorder of the unconscious and is not likely to respond to local treatment of the pelvic organs although the condition is commonly included in the list of gynaecological complaints.

Although the majority of women who exhibit this symptom have some sexual response towards men, these are the ones who are usually most troubled by it. The completely frigid woman who is devoid of all sexual feelings may have no need of men and therefore no wish to marry; this is particularly true if the maternal instinct is also non-existent or very weak. If she does marry, discord is likely. Latent homosexuality should also be considered when assessing the needs and treatment of such patients.

In addition to frigidity a number of women complain of other symptoms as well, commonly dyspareunia, vaginismus, backache, headache and the various menstrual disturbances which have already been mentioned. Other patients, although more or less completely frigid with their husbands, may have satisfactory orgasms with other men. Prostitutes, on the other hand, are commonly frigid with all.

The treatment of frigidity may be relatively easy or exceedingly difficult. Should it be due to some initial physical obstacle or to inexperience in sexual matters, a cure may sometimes be effected rapidly. Any offending local condition, such as a tough hymen, is dealt with, and both husband and wife are reassured that their difficulties are not abnormal and can easily be overcome. However, true sexual frigidity is usually considered to be a manifestation of neurotic behaviour. Frigidity can be very resistant to any form of treatment and may require many sessions of painstaking endeavour during deep hypnotic states. Hypnoanalysis, by abreacting suppressed unconscious material, can be of considerable help in assisting the patient to live a more normal married life. Frequently it is found that her childhood upbringing was such that she regarded anything sexual as 'dirty' or 'nasty' and not fit to be discussed by 'clean-minded' people. In such cases much can be done by re-education under hypnosis until the patient accepts sexual experience as something perfectly normal and good among married persons, and not something about which she need feel ashamed. If there is reason to believe that the frigidity depends upon a homosexual orientation then it is much wiser for the patient to be referred to a psychiatrist for specialist treatment.

BLADDER DISTURBANCES

Symptoms which involve bladder function are commonly encountered in the practice of gynaecology. One of the most common is the so-called 'irritable bladder' where the patient has a frequent urge to pass urine. It is nearly always associated with a good deal of anxiety and can make life exceedingly uncomfortable for the sufferer. Hypnotherapy has been used with varying degrees of success, either through simple direct suggestion aimed at relieving anxiety and tension or else by some form of hypno-analysis so as to uncover and treat the psychodynamics underlying the condition. In a series of cases reported by Leckie (1964) suggestion alone was found to be effective.

Occasionally, very powerful unconscious motives may be at work in causing bladder dysfunction. One such case, treated by one of us (G.N.). was a girl of seventeen who was seen because of an acute urinary retention. At first she responded well to direct hypnotic suggestion but later she relapsed suddenly into an extremely refractory state which was only overcome by much patient psychotherapy without the aid of hypnosis, to which she had become resistant.

PRURITUS VULVAE

Although this condition is often associated with a vaginal discharge or less frequently with glycosuria or a local infection such as *pediculosis pubis*, it may be a manifestation of an emotional disturbance. Should this be so it is unlikely that it will be cured by physical or chemical methods. A considerable number of patients who develop psychogenic *pruritus vulvae* show a good deal of anxiety concerning masturbation, which many practise in order to obtain relief from sexual tension. In the treatment of this complaint by hypnotherapy it is usually necessary to give the patient insight into the causal factor involved; this may be done at a superficial level using a light stage of hypnosis but better results are sometimes obtainable if a state of somnambulism is reached so that a deeper analysis is possible.

THE MENOPAUSE

For many women the menopause, like the onset of menstruation, is approached with feelings of apprehension. The expectation of trouble at this time may be enhanced by reading advertisements which subtly suggest that the individual will feel unwell. In this respect the background to the menopause is similar to that of dysmenorrhoea, where the patient expects to be unwell. The 'change of life' is also anticipated with mixed feelings by many. Some may regret that the possibilities for childbearing are over, while others experience a sense of relief that the fear of pregnancy as a result of their sexual activities is ended. Again, others may be afraid of losing their physical attractiveness and, if they are married, of losing their husbands. Some may feel that they are about to be plunged into a premature old age and that their accustomed activities and interests will in many cases no longer be possible.

At this time there may be a diversity of symptoms, many of which are dependent upon psychological factors. They include hot flushes, various aches and pains in different parts of the body, especially headache and backache, arthritis and depression, which may lead to 'involutional melancholia'. Insomnia and emotional instability may also occur.

When undertaking the treatment of these cases the physician, like his patient, should remember that a considerable number of women go through the menopause with no unpleasant symptoms whatever. Some even say they never felt better in their lives. It is true that some of the symptoms can be relieved by the administration of oestrogen, but this does not invalidate the influence of emotional and suggestive factors in their aetiology. Few people would now dispute the existence of a close interrelationship between the endocrine system and the psyche, so that a disturbance of one is liable to influence the other. This makes it difficult at times to decide which is the primary agent.

The treatment of such symptoms as may be troublesome to the patient comprises drug sedation, hormonotherapy and suggestion, with or without the aid of hypnosis. Although the first two methods often prove effective, this chapter is concerned only with the third. There is of course no reason why a combination of two, or even all three, should not be tried.

Sometimes good results may be obtained from using suggestion at the most superficial level without hypnosis at all; it then usually takes the form of reassuring the patient about any anxieties she may have concerning the 'change' and emphasizing the fact that many women pass through this period quite comfortably and even gain a renewed and more vital interest in life. The patient is assured that there is no reason to think that she will become less attractive as a result; on the contrary, some women state that they never really enjoyed their sexual lives until the menopause was established. There is certainly no ground for the common belief that a failure of libido necessarily accompanies the end of menstruation: witness Ninon de l'Enclos, one of the mistresses of Louis XIV.

Suggestive therapy at a deeper level is carried out under hypnosis. As before, re-education and reassurance are the keystones of treatment, but in the deeper hypnotic states it is possible to bring greater influence to bear on the underlying psychic tension and emotional disturbances.

OTHER USES OF HYPNOSIS IN GYNAECOLOGY

There are three indications other than those already described for the use of hypnotism in gynaecological practice: in certain surgical operations, as an aid to diagnosis, and in the relief of some types of pelvic pain.

GYNAECOLOGICAL SURGERY

Minor operations, such as dilatation and curettage, can often be performed quite well under hypnotic anaesthesia. The patient need not necessarily reach a deep stage of hypnosis for anaesthesia to be adequate. Should she be a somnambule it would be possible to consider using hypnotism as the sole anaesthetic agent in operations of a more serious character, such as myomectomy, ovariectomy, or colporrhaphy. Many major surgical procedures have been carried out quite painlessly in this way (e.g. Esdaile's work in Calcutta) and it is still worth contemplating with suitable patients. Even if the state of somnambulism is not reached, hypnosis can help considerably in reducing the amount of anaesthetic required. An interesting case of removal of fibroids under hypnotic anaesthesia was reported by Rose (1953).

It is also possible for hypnosis to help an emotionally sick patient to face her operation better and thus increase the chances of complete and permanent cure. This use of hypnosis has been stressed by Harold Rosen (1953).

PELVIC EXAMINATION AND DIAGNOSIS

If it is impossible to make an accurate diagnosis with the patient in the normal conscious state, an examination under anaesthesia is now a recognized practice. The patient's nervousness and apprehension, which are usually responsible for the problems in making a proper examination, can also be allayed by hypnotic suggestion, so that the abdominal and perineal muscles relax sufficiently to enable an adequate exploration of the pelvis to take place. The differentiation between 'organic' and 'functional' illness may also be facilitated by hypnosis.

RELIEF OF PSYCHOGENIC PELVIC PAIN

Apart from that associated with dysmenorrhoea, some women may experience other types of local pain in the pelvic region (Taylor 1949). Commonly this is a more or less persistent dull ache which is felt over the lower lumbosacral area and for which no organic cause can be found. The medical practitioner must always be wary of labelling this symptom as 'functional' in origin, but if after a full and careful examination nothing abnormal is discovered it is legitimate for the patient to secure relief through hypnosis. Sometimes it is possible by hypnoanalysis to be certain that the pain is due to emotional disturbances and is founded upon a neurosis. In such cases the proper way of dealing with the symptom is by affording the patient insight into the aetiology of her complaint and then to follow up with re-education and assurances that the pain will vanish. If it is not possible to discover any motives, either at a conscious or an unconscious level, then direct symptom removal may be resorted to. If this is done some patients will develop other symptoms in its place but it is true nevertheless that the judicious use of direct suggestion still has a place in hypnotherapy. Bramwell (1930) quotes many cases from British and European sources where this was the only method adopted by the medical hypnotist, and where the patient was cured of her complaint and did not relapse or develop any other symptom of the 'conversion' type met with in hysteria. As in all treatment of gynaecological cases by suggestion, the physician needs to assess the personality needs of each individual patient separately and to vary his method of approach accordingly.

BIBLIOGRAPHY

AUGUST, R. V. (1960) Hypnosis: an additional tool in the study of infertility. *Fert. Steril., 11*, 118.

BAIRD, G. M. (1971) The treatment of certain psycho-sexual disorders with hypnosis and drugs. A critical evaluation. *Br. J. clin. Hypnosis, 2*, 73.

BANCROFT, J. & COLES, L. (1976) Sexual dysfunction in general practice. *Jl. R. Coll. gen. Pract., 26*, 514.

BRAMWELL, J. M. (1930) *Hypnotism, its History, Practice and Theory,* 3rd ed. London: Rider.

BUNNEMANN, O. (1921) quoted by DUNBAR. Ueber psychogenen fluor albus. *Ther. d. Gegenw., 62,* 132.

CARNEY, A., BANCROFT, J. & Mathews, A. (1978) Combination of hormonal and psychological treatment for female unresponsiveness. A comparative study. *Br. J. Psychiat., 132,* 339.

CRASILNECK, H. B. (1979) The use of hypnosis in the treatment of psychogenic impotence. In: *Proc. 8th int. Cong. Hypnosis psychosom. Med.* Amsterdam: Elsevier/North Holland.

DEUTSCH, H. (1944-5) *Psychology of Women* (2 vols). New York: Grune and Stratton.

DICKS, H. V. (1967) *Marital Tensions.* London: Routledge & Kegan Paul.

DUDDLE, M. (1979) Provision of facilities for treatment of sexual dysfunction. *Br. J. sex. Med., 6,* 42.

DUNBAR, F. (1938) *Emotions and Bodily Changes.* New York: Columbia University Press.

FREUD, S. (1932) Female sexuality. *Int. J. Psycho-Analysis, 13,* 281.

FRIED, P. H., RAKOFF, A. E., SCHOBACH, R. R. & KAPLAN, A. J. (1951) Pseudocyesis: A psychosomatic study in gynaecology. *J. Am. med. Ass., 145,* 1329.

GARDNER, K. (1979) Premenstrual tension. *Br. J. sex. Med., 6,* 42.

KAPLAN, H. S. (1974) *The New Sex Therapy.* London: Baillière Tindall.

KROGER, W. S. (1953) Hypnosis in obstetrics and gynecology. In: *Hypnosis in Modern Medicine,* ed. J. M. Schneck, pp. 128-37. Springfield, Ill.: Charles C. Thomas.

LECKIE, F. HAMILTON (1964) Hypnosis in gynaecology. *Int. J. clin. exp. Hypnosis, 12,* 3.

NEWBOLD, George (1953) *Medical Hypnosis,* Ch. 8. London: Gollancz.

NOVAK, J. & HARNIK, N. (1929) Psychogenic origins of dysmenorrhoea. *Medsche Klin., 25,* 251.

ROSE, A. G. (1953) The use of hypnosis as an anaesthetic, analgesic amnesic agent in gynaecology. *Br. J. med. Hypnot., 5,* 1, 17.

ROSEN, H. (1953) Hypnosis in surgery. In: *Hypnosis in Modern Medicine,* ed. J. M. Schneck, pp. 61-86. Springfield, Ill.: Charles C. Thomas.

TAYLOR, H. C. (1949) Vascular congestion and hyperemia. *Am. J. Obstet. Gynec., 57,* 637.

CHAPTER 11

PSYCHODYNAMICS OF PREGNANCY AND LABOUR

Increasing attention is being focused today on the psychosomatic aspects of childbirth. The use of hypnosis, in some form or other, has much to commend it for relieving some of the more distressing symptoms which may accompany pregnancy and also as a means of making the actual confinement easier for the mother and safer for the baby. Whatever method of psychoprophylaxis is practised as a technique for rendering the process of childbirth more tolerable, it is the hypnotic state which is largely responsible for the success of the method. This even applies to those techniques which are usually grouped under the heading of 'Natural Childbirth' and which make use of various exercises designed to induce muscular relaxation. Such exercises, which often involve the control of breathing, are calculated in many cases to induce varying degrees of hypnosis in the patient. If the expectant mother is a member of a class or group under the supervision of a midwife, physiotherapist, or doctor, the effect is often enhanced by the suggestive element present in such a group, as well as by the soothing words of the one in charge. Although the induction of hypnosis is not a conscious part of such techniques — and its occurrence is often denied by those who practise them — it is probable that it does sometimes occur unrecognised.

When hypnosis is deliberately employed, the emphasis is generally upon mental and physical relaxation. The hypnotic state is induced primarily to help achieve this objective more readily. Other suggestions aimed directly at the relief of certain specific symptoms may also be given. The principal use of hypnosis in obstetrics is to influence the course of labour: some practical ways of doing this are described below.

INDICATIONS FOR HYPNOTHERAPY DURING PREGNANCY

Hypnosis and appropriate suggestive therapy may be of value from the earliest days of pregnancy. It is universally acknowledged that pregnancy may be productive of many psychosomatic disorders which respond more readily to psychotherapy than to other methods of treatment. The work of Dunbar (1938), Deutsch (1944-5) and Kroger (Kroger & Freed 1951) has given considerable prominence to the importance of psychological factors in the problems of pregnancy and childbirth. Many of these factors are believed to be buried in the depths of the 'subconscious' or 'unconscious' mind, and hypnosis – especially if combined with some form of analysis – may be instrumental in bringing about complete cessation of the offending symptoms. Some of the disturbances occurring during the antenatal period in the treatment of which hypnotherapy has proved effective are heartburn, nausea, backache, pruritus, insomnia, malpresentation of the fetus and hypertension.

HEARTBURN AND FLATULENCE

Certain cases of heartburn occurring during the early weeks of pregnancy are believed to be caused by a neuromuscular imbalance which gives rise to spasm of the sphincter at the junction of the oesophagus and cardiac end of the stomach. In an appreciable number of such cases the direct cause of the imbalance is an emotional one – mental tension, anxiety or anger. For the complete relief of symptoms in these patients psychotherapy and relaxation under hypnosis may prove of great value. Sometimes this should be combined with small doses of drugs such as atropine in order to obtain the best results.

NAUSEA AND VOMITING

This is one of the commonest disorders to be met with in the early weeks of pregnancy and psychogenic factors may play a prominent part in its aetiology. The remedies which have been tried are legion and because most of them have had some measure of success certain obstetricians have come to the conclusion that the essential element in the cure of all of them has been suggestion. With regard to the psychodynamics of the situation, many authorities believe that vomiting may indicate an unconscious wish to get rid of the developing embryo. Some case histories obtained by the process of hypnoanalysis have tended to confirm this opinion. Among the more common factors responsible for the psychogenic component of the disorder are illegitimacy, frigidity (with a refusal of the patient to accept the maternal role), lack of love and affection for the husband and fears connected with bearing and rearing a child. In addition, some women seem to develop nausea and vomiting – 'morning sickness' – because they expect to do so as a result of their own sexual education and upbringing. It is noteworthy that in some cultures and among some races, e.g. Africans and Eskimos, hyperemesis gravidarum rarely occurs. The 'facts of life' seem to be accepted more naturally by primitive peoples, so that disorders of function resulting from psychosexual disturbances occur much less commonly than they do in our Western civilization.

It is not surprising that hypnosis has frequently been remarkably effective in bringing about a cure of hyperemesis. Platanov and his colleagues (1950) reported that of almost 600 cases of hyperemesis gravidarum treated with hypnosis more than 84% were completely relieved of their symptoms.

The degree of vomiting may vary from slight to severe, even involving complications such as dehydration and jaundice. In all types hypnotic suggestion may be used with good effect, although obviously in many instances other forms of treatment are indicated at the same time to correct any concomitant nutritional and metabolic disturbances.

THREATENED ABORTION AND PREMATURE LABOUR

It is well known that psychic shock may be responsible for the termination of a pregnancy at almost any stage of its development, although the precise mechanisms involved are still unclear. Cases of miscarriage and premature labour have frequently been reported as the result of emotional trauma caused by shelling and bombing during war, the witnessing of unpleasant scenes or the hearing of unpleasant news. We might expect that hypnotic suggestion would prove of value in preventing a wastage of fetal life from such causes and enabling the gravida to go to term. At the time of writing a number of obstetricians have reported cases that seem to confirm this expectation. Although the numbers involved are small, there have been cases of patients showing signs of threatening abortion who, when placed in a deep hypnotic 'sleep' for several hours, lost all their symptoms, such as abdominal cramps, and carried on normally until term. Accounts have also been published of women who have never been able to give birth to a viable fetus, in spite of several pregnancies, but who have been enabled to do so with the help of appropriate hypnotherapy. In all the cases so far reported, however, somnambulism is necessary if this method of treatment is to have any chance of success. Patients who tend to abort for emotional reasons do not as a rule require any other therapeutic measures apart from psychotherapy. If they are not capable of reaching a deep stage of hypnosis for this purpose sedatives may be necessary in order that appropriate psychotherapy may be carried out.

An interesting case involving the possible effect of hypnotic suggestion upon the postponement of labour concerned a gravida with an unsuspected twin pregnancy. The patient was given repeated strong suggestions during the ante-natal period that after her baby was born she would recover rapidly and breast feed the baby herself. In the minds of the patient, her family, the doctor and the hypnotist, there was no doubt at all that a single fetus only was present.

Following delivery, however, the existence of a second child was confirmed. Contrary to expectation, uterine contractions did not return within a reasonable time and ten days elapsed before the second twin was eventually born. The interesting point was then raised as to whether the pre-natal hypnotic training could have been responsible in any way for this delay in the return of labour. A definite answer is impossible in the present state of knowledge.

BACKACHE

Many women complain of backache during the latter months of pregnancy. Occasionally it may be relieved by a properly fitting maternity corset, but frequently the response to the usual conventional methods of treatment is unsatisfactory. In an appreciable number of these cases the symptoms appear to depend on neuromuscular tension: yet another psychosomatic disorder. Such patients often respond well to hypnotherapy. It is noteworthy that women who are systematically trained in the technique of hypnorelaxation during pregnancy rarely develop this symptom. Before attributing the backache to psychological factors, however, other causes such as pyelitis, or even the unexpected onset of labour, should be excluded.

PRURITUS AND PARAESTHESIAE

These are distressing symptoms which may occur at any time during pregnancy. The aetiology of the condition has been variously attributed to toxic factors, nutritional and endocrine disorders and psychological disturbances. Whatever the fundamental cause, satisfactory treatment is frequently difficult and usually consists of sedatives plus antipruritic ointments.

Psychodynamics of Pregnancy and Labour

Now it is common knowledge that most people have at some time experienced itching of the skin purely as the result of suggestion. If a number of persons are gathered together in a room or a railway carriage, for example, it is surprising how many will follow suit if one of the company starts to scratch himself. Many people also begin to itch if they see an insect crawling on the hand of another person who is oblivious to its presence. Such subjective skin sensations are closely linked with psychological suggestion and can, therefore, be expected to respond well to counter-suggestion under hypnosis. An equally good response can also quite often be obtained when the symptoms occur during pregnancy and have no such demonstrable cause. As a rule, direct hypnotic suggestion is sufficient to bring about a regression of the symptoms.

INSOMNIA

A large number of women complain, at some time or other during pregnancy, that they have great difficulty in falling asleep, or in remaining asleep thereafter. Foetal movements are not always responsible for the insomnia, which may be so marked that considerable distress is caused to the patient.

Sleeplessness in pregnant women, and in many other persons, is a definite indication for hypnotherapy, and as such is often best dealt with by training the patient in autohypnosis (see pp. 187-9). Furthermore, a good deal of insomnia may be *prevented* if, at each prenatal hypnotic session, the hypnotist lays emphasis on the fact that the patient will enjoy sound and healthy sleep.

MALPRESENTATION OF FETUS

If a malpresentation such as a transverse lie or a breech is discovered on antenatal examination, an attempt is usually made to correct it by performing an external cephalic version. In the majority of cases this is done fairly easily but sometimes, owing to rigidity of the abdominal muscles, considerable difficulty may be experienced. Hitherto it has been the custom for many obstetricians, when confronted with this type of patient, to administer either a sedative drug or a general anaesthetic in order to produce a greater degree of muscular relaxation. Hypnorelaxation, on the other hand, will enable the patient to relax just as completely as when an anaesthetic is used, but at less risk. Moreover the hypnotised patient remains fully co-operative so that the version can be even more easily performed.

HYPERTENSION OF PREGNANCY

During pregnancy there is an increase in blood pressure which, if untreated, may lead to eclampsia. According to Dieckmann (1941) and others working in the USA it is distinct from essential hypertension, in the aetiology of which psychogenic factors play little or no part. Rest and sedation find a prominent place in the treatment of both essential and pre-eclamptic hypertension, and it has been established that suggestion under hypnosis is capable of causing vascular dilatation and a definite fall in the blood pressure in the treatment of essential hypertension. It therefore seems that hypnotherapy may be of some use in treating the hypertension associated with pre-eclampsia. In this particular disease, however, there is little doubt that other therapeutic measures will also be required to redress nutritional and metabolic disturbances. The diet may have to be supplemented with vitamin B and the biochemistry of the salt-water balance of the body will require attention. In the treatment of pre-eclamptic toxaemia, hypnosis is best regarded as a useful ally rather than a specific remedy.

CERTAIN MEDICAL DISORDERS COMPLICATING PREGNANCY

Heart disease

Hypnotherapy is indicated if the patient suffers from heart disease, such as mitral stenosis, and is allowed to proceed to term. One of the primary objectives in training such patients in hypnorelaxation is to ensure that labour becomes less of an ordeal and less strain on the cardiac muscle. If, as an additional precaution during delivery, a prophylactic forceps extraction is carried out, this operation will be much easier because of the relaxed condition of the muscles forming the birth canal.

Thyrotoxicosis

In a condition such as thyrotoxicosis a course of prenatal hypnotherapy can be of value in reducing nervous and emotional tension and hopefully in preventing a thyrotoxic crisis or any aggravation of the disease. The frequency with which this condition has been found to have a psychogenic basis is well known, and any form of treatment which reduces mental stress and anxiety is likely to prove beneficial. If hypnosis is used, and the patient is a reasonably good subject, heavy drug sedation can usually be avoided, or at least the dose can be appreciably reduced.

In addition to the two conditions mentioned above, hypnotherapy may be employed during pregnancy if the patient suffers from any other complaint for which this particular method of treatment is recommended.

Anxiety states

Emotional states involving anxiety and tension are, without any doubt, responsible for a good deal of trouble during pregnancy, confinement and the puerperium. Some of the symptoms dependent upon such emotions have already been listed; it is possible that other conditions, less clearly defined, may similarly be traced to psychogenic causes. Whether or not actual symptoms are present, it is generally conceded that a mind at peace and free from unnecessary strain can do nothing but good to its fortunate possessor. Nowhere is this more evident than in the practice of midwifery. If the mind of the gravida is filled with ideas of a dignified and relaxing nature, she is likely to be well-equipped for the process of childbearing. For those patients who are not naturally gifted with a placid personality, skilled and sympathetic suggestion given by an experienced physician or obstetrician can do much to help them at this momentous period of their lives: 'Pleasant words are as an honeycomb, sweet to the soul, and health to the bones' (*Proverbs 16 v. 24*).

A satisfactory state of mental relaxation with hypnosis does not generally require a deep state of trance although the treatment of certain specified disorders does require somnambulism for the best results. If women are introduced early in pregnancy to training in hypnorelaxation, it is possible to prevent many undesirable conditions from occurring.

Provided that the indications for using hypnosis are legitimate, there are very few disadvantages in its application to the problems of pregnancy and childbirth. It should not, of course, be employed in cases where the patient is suspected of being actually or potentially psychotic and a minority of persons may be found to be not sufficiently susceptible to warrant its use. It has frequently been noticed, however, that during pregnancy the degree of susceptibility is increased, and some obstetricians have reported large numbers of successful cases without a single failure. Furthermore, the percentage of obstetric patients able to reach a deep stage of hypnosis can be expected to be higher than the average, since only the younger age groups will be involved. This means that the number of potential somnambulists is probably nearer 30% than the 25% in the general population.

INDICATIONS FOR HYPNOTHERAPY DURING LABOUR

Labour, although an event itself, is probably best regarded as a continuation of the state of pregnancy, especially if one proposes to conduct it with the help of hypnotism. This means that the best way of ensuring a successful delivery with the minimum discomfort is to make certain that the patient is properly prepared during the antenatal period. Sometimes good results may be possible if the first attempt to induce hypnosis is made during labour but adequate prenatal training *must* remain the basis of all our efforts to secure an easier labour. The same rule applies to the puerperium: the correct time to start hypnosis is during pregnancy, although the suggestions may need reinforcing at any time 'post-partum'.

Nowadays it is generally accepted that the obstetrician should take into account his patient's own attitude of mind towards childbirth when faced with the problems of parturition. Every obstetrician should, therefore, be concerned with the psychodynamics of labour. Ideally, women in labour should not be forced to conform to the routine acceptance of drugs. If they are asked, a surprising number of patients say that they would prefer to do without drugs or anaesthetics, if possible, when they have their babies. To meet this need is one of the major aims of the obstetrician who is versed in hypnotic techniques. He is in a very favourable position to conduct the process of labour so that it corresponds with the gravida's own wishes and her personality requirements. In this way labour can be considered more 'natural' than if the usual stereotyped methods are used. Kroger and Freed (1951): '... good obstetric practice must concern itself more with preparation of the woman's mind and less with the administration of noxious drugs ... suggestions given under hypnosis can equal or exceed the effects of analgesic and anaesthetic drugs in many properly prepared patients.' The author (G. N.) has also had numerous cases where this has been proved to be true.

For convenience, the indications for the use of hypnotism during labour can be most easily considered in relation to (1) the health and safety of the mother, and (2) the health and safety of the child. When one considers the many advantages which this particular method of delivery has over most of the others in current use, it would seem to be no exaggeration to state that almost every labour is an indication for hypnotherapy. In fact it is a common clinical experience that some women appear to enter automatically a mild form of hypnosis during labour, especially during the second stage. This appears to be one of nature's own ways of mitigating the pangs of what would otherwise be a painful confinement.

HEALTH AND SAFETY OF THE MOTHER

One of the cardinal principles in the conduct of any labour is to ensure that the mother suffers the very minimum amount of injury (to body and

Increased mental and physical relaxation

This has already been stressed in connection with pregnancy; it is equally important during labour. The part played by fear and tension as factors in the production of pain has become widely recognized since the earlier work of Janet and, more recently, of Dick Read (1944) and others. In many instances the cycle ' fear — mental tension — muscular tension — pain ' develops into a vicious circle which must be broken if a satisfactory delivery is to take place.

Up to now the most common method of breaking this circle has been either by blocking the painful impulses somewhere along the pathways of the sensory nerves by local and spinal anaesthesia or by using analgesic drugs and general anaesthetics which effect a physiological change in the brain cells themselves. An alternative approach is to reduce the anxiety which so often acts as the starting point of the process. The increased mental relaxation obtainable through hypnosis leads in most cases to a corresponding relaxation of the muscles concerned in parturition and therefore to an easier labour. As a direct result of this, perineal tears and the need for sutures are reduced.

Dick Read's method of 'natural childbirth' relies upon the use of certain physical exercises in order, it is claimed, to enhance muscular relaxation and render parturition thereby less painful. There is no doubt that his pioneering work did much to pave the way for the present widespread adoption of psychoprophylactic methods of 'painless' childbirth. However, it is now becoming apparent that in many instances any system of muscular exercises is little more than a smokescreen for the induction of the hypnotic state in susceptible subjects. This seems to apply especially to those women who derive most benefit from such a course. When Dick Read began his work, the word 'hypnosis' undoubtedly conveyed a suggestion of something sinister in the minds of many and until it became more respectable it would probably have met with little response as a form of treatment, particularly in the practice of midwifery. Today the pattern has changed, and there seems little reason to deny the fact that hypnotism has been used unwittingly under other names in the past in the successful conduct of many labours. It has also been the experience of some obstetricians and physiotherapists who have carried out so-called 'relaxation classes' that patients frequently appear to be in a trance-like condition and occasionally react as automatons, just as if they were in a state of hypnotic somnambulism. This is not surprising when we consider that the production of certain trance phenomena in yoga is often linked with exercises involving the control of breathing and muscular activity.

If the patient is able to reach one of the deeper hypnotic states she can be further helped by direct suggestions of analgesia.

Analgesia and anaesthesia through direct suggestion

Direct suggestion is a means of producing analgesia or anaesthesia in any desired area of the body. This will prove most useful for rendering insensitive the perineal region during the second stage of labour; it will also permit minor operations such as episiotomy or the repair of tears to be carried out quite painlessly. If reliance is placed on muscular relaxation alone it is found in a proportion of cases that acute pain is felt just at the moment when the head is being crowned, at the time when the distension of the vulva is at its maximum. In order to lessen the intensity of pain at this moment direct suggestion may be tried. The patient is told, under hypnosis, that when the baby appears at the vulva the entire area involved will become numb and insensitive and that the only sensations present will be those of something coming through the outlet of the birth canal.

Should the patient prove to be a somnambulist, labour can be rendered entirely painless. Not only will direct suggestion of anaesthesia be very effective but good use can be made of post-hypnotic suggestion. The gravida is told, for example, that at a prearranged signal she will enter a state of hypnosis and from then onwards her labour will proceed comfortably and without pain. This does not necessarily mean that she will be unaware of the events of the actual birth. Many mothers, if given the opportunity, will choose to stay 'awake' when their babies are born. Somnambulists can be assured that although perfectly conscious of what is taking place they will feel no discomfort but will experience only the pleasurable and satisfying emotions of motherhood.

Shortened duration of labour

According to Abramson and Heron (1950) the length of the first stage of labour can be decreased by an average of about two hours for all patients. For primigravidae alone, the results are even better; for them the duration of labour may be shortened by as much as 3¼ hours. These figures are derived from the results of a controlled experiment carried out on a fairly large scale. The experience of other obstetricians tends to confirm them.

Diminished shock

The reduction in the length of the first stage of labour observed during hypnotic deliveries is often accompanied by a decrease in the degree of obstetric shock. This is partly due to the less exhausted condition of the mother because of an easier first stage, but hypnosis also increases the resistance of the patient to fatigue. Yet another contributory factor is the decreased blood loss that commonly occurs during the hypnotic state. This phenomenon can easily be demonstrated by pricking the finger of a hypnotized subject with a pin or needle and noting the almost complete absence of any bleeding. The reason for this may be a localized vasoconstriction – for this has been shown to occur experimentally – but whatever the fundamental cause there is reliable clinical evidence that bleeding is reduced to a minimum during hypnotic deliveries. Moreover, as a result of the conservation of the patient's physical strength, the risks of infection and sepsis are also considerably diminished.

Rapid recovery

One of the things which patients usually notice after a hypnotic confinement is that they feel perfectly fit and well as soon as the labour is over. In the great majority of cases the delivery is spontaneous (except for the occasional 'prophylactic' low forceps extraction) and the third stage is completed without any difficulty or complication. In fact many obstetricians who use hypnotism maintain that the incidence of complications during labour tends generally to be lowered, as one would expect if the whole process is made easier for the patient. Certainly rapid and uneventful recovery is the rule and there is no danger of pulmonary complications, such as collapse of the lung or pneumonia, which may on occasion follow the administration of a general anaesthetic. Post-operative vomiting is similarly avoided.

Another advantage of hypnosis is that patients are able to move about easily after labour is over. They can therefore adequately exercise the muscles of the legs and pelvic regions and thereby reduce the risk of venous thrombosis and pulmonary emboli.

Decreased need for drugs

A decreased need for drugs is one of the most important benefits which can be obtained from using hypnosis for the relief of pain in childbirth. The late J. B. De Lee, formerly Professor of Obstetrics and Gynaecology at Chicago, writing about the use of hypnosis in obstetrics, declared

'... the only anaesthetic that is without danger is hypnotism' (De Lee & Greenhill 1939). There is no record of any death having been attributed to this method of anaesthesia; De Lee's own experience of its use has been amply confirmed by others.

In many instances drugs can be dispensed with altogether. Should they be required the dose is usually much reduced. They should not, of course, be deliberately withheld if there are obvious indications for their use, or if the patient herself demands them. It is sometimes reassuring to patients if they know that such drugs are available should they want them. The point to be stressed is that such supplementary methods of analgesia should rather remain unobtrusively in the background for use only if necessary. For the best subjects, hypnosis fulfils the generally accepted requirements for the 'ideal' obstetric analgesic. Moreover, its action, unlike that of drugs, is easily controlled and can readily be removed at any time by means of counter-suggestion.

Normal mechanism of labour unaltered

With hypnotic anaesthesia there is no depressant action on the contractile powers of the uterine muscles and the normal mechanism of labour remains undisturbed. This contrasts favourably with the effects of heavy drug sedation.

The importance of securing good uterine contractions in conditions such as multiple pregnancy and hydramnios is well recognized. Should the contractions be poor the risk of a post-partum haemorrhage is increased. This is particularly true if there is a large placental area, as may occur with twins. It is therefore important to avoid, if possible, the use of any drug which might tend to diminish the force of the contractions, and to conserve the patient's strength and prevent her from becoming exhausted. Hypnosis, in certain of the best subjects, actually increases the strength of the uterine contractions by means of direct suggestion. There is as yet no definite experimental confirmation of this, and the evidence rests largely upon clinical impressions. However, we do know from numerous experiments that hypnotic suggestions can influence the force and rate of the heart beat and that the muscle of the myometrium, like that of the heart, will respond to psychogenic stimuli; one has only to think of women who have gone into premature labour as a result of receiving a psychic shock.

Co-operation of patient secured

One of the great advantages of using hypnotism during labour is that the gravida remains much more co-operative than she would be if sedative drugs or a general anaesthetic were employed. If she is placed in a deep state of hypnosis it is amazing how easily she is able to co-operate with the doctor or midwife, even when her contractions are strong and recur at frequent intervals. She will carry out any of the natural functions, such as eating, drinking or defaecation, quite normally and without any difficulty. She will also be well able to assist delivery by making use of her expulsive muscles at the right time and by relaxing to the fullest extent possible when asked to do so. Even in the lighter stages of hypnosis the patient's co-operation is more easily obtained than it would be if she were under the influence of drugs.

HEALTH AND SAFETY OF THE CHILD

Decreased risk of fetal anoxia

If any of the drugs commonly employed for the purpose of obstetric analgesia and anaesthesia are to be given in effective doses there is a risk that the fetus may suffer from some degree of anoxaemia. Even a mild or transient anoxia may, as Barcroft (1934) has shown, affect the delicate cells of the central nervous system, which are more sensitive to oxygen lack than those of any other tissue. The cells of the fetal brain are particularly susceptible to damage; convulsions have been produced experimentally in pups whose mothers received an inadequate supply of oxygen during labour. Such animal experiments have led some physicians to wonder if interference with the oxygenation of the brain during intra-uterine life might be a factor in the causation of diseases such as idiopathic epilepsy. Certainly anoxia may give rise to difficulties in the establishment of satisfactory respiration following delivery. This is presumably due to a depression of the fetal respiratory centre. In the most severe cases, there may be a complete failure of respiration and pulmonary complications such as pneumonia or atelectasis may ensue.

As a method of analgesia which is entirely free from this risk, hypno-relaxation should commend itself to all obstetricians. There is no anaesthetic depression of the respiratory centre and it is the rule for babies born under hypnosis to cry lustily and breathe normally as soon as they are separated from their mothers.

Reduction in toxins affecting fetus

The tragedies of congenital abnormalities due to thalidomide are now well known. It is possible that other drugs may give rise to similar toxic effects in certain cases, especially if given during the early weeks of pregnancy, in much the same manner as certain strains of the rubella virus. The developing embryo seems to be most sensitive to any deleterious influence by chemical agencies such as drugs and physical ones like irradiation from about the 18th to the 38th days following implantation. A good case can therefore be made out for restricting the prescription of drugs or exposure to radiation when the patient is a woman of reproductive age. If there is any suspicion of pregnancy it is better to rely upon some form of psychotherapy, such as hypnosis, if possible.

Decreased risk of fetal injury

Damage to the fetal brain may be caused by anoxia or by trauma received during labour. In many cases of cerebral haemorrhage both factors are found to be involved. Hypnotism may be of considerable value in reducing the risk of intracranial injury, by producing a high degree of muscular relaxation in the mother. For the same reason one would expect a lowered incidence of other injuries such as fractured limbs, and if the baby is delivered as a breech the increase in relaxation of the muscles forming the birth canal should facilitate such procedures as bringing down an arm or the extraction of the head.

In numerous instances forceps deliveries have been made easier by hypnosis, and it is possible that, by its use, more pregnancies would end in vaginal deliveries rather than Caesarian sections.

Sometimes, in spite of adequate relaxation and good contractions, the presenting part of the foetus may make rather slow progress in its emergence from the vulval outlet. In many of these cases the perineal tissues are especially thick and harm may result to the baby should it remain for too long on the perineum. If the labour is being conducted under hypnosis it is usually quite a simple matter to make a small, and painless, episiotomy in order to expedite delivery.

BREAST FEEDING ENCOURAGED

Satisfactory breast feeding still possesses definite advantages over artificial feeding. The breast-fed baby, for example, may have increased resistance to certain infections — especially those affecting the gastro-intestinal tract — and is less likely to suffer from other digestive disturbances or from skin rashes like the very familiar ammonia dermatitis which is frequently found in the napkin area of bottle-fed babies.

One of the main reasons why numerous mothers are unable to feed their babies satisfactorily themselves is because lactation is disturbed by psychological factors such as anxiety. In these particular cases suitable hypnotic suggestion may prove invaluable in stimulating a good flow of milk and enabling normal breast feeding to take place. Cases are on record of mothers with failing lactation who, after suggestive treatment during the hypnotic state, soon experienced milk flowing in their breasts, sometimes to such an extent that they became engorged and tender.

IDEAL FOR PREMATURE BABIES

One special indication for the use of hypnosis during labour is when a premature baby is expected. This is because in these cases the risk of damage from asphyxia and trauma is greater than in those babies who go to term, and also because of the greater need of premature babies for human breast milk.

DISADVANTAGES OF HYPNOSIS IN LABOUR

Disadvantages are few in number and mainly concern the relatively small number of patients who do not respond satisfactorily to hypnosis or have pre-psychotic personalities that make hypnosis unwise because of the danger of precipitating the onset of a psychosis such as schizophrenia. There may also be the occasional problem with a patient who has been trained in hypnorelaxation but is then left in a disturbing environment and loses her self-control so that the effectiveness of her antenatal preparation is destroyed.

At first sight it may seem that if hypnosis were used as a standard method of analgesia in midwifery the time devoted to securing an effective level of analgesia or anaesthesia would need to be considerably increased. However, if hypnosis is employed intelligently and with the right patients (i.e. in a majority of maternity cases) the time may often be markedly reduced. This is largely achieved by the use of group therapy for the routine induction of hypnosis, with individual treatment only when necessary.

ANTENATAL TRAINING IN HYPNORELAXATION

OFFICE EQUIPMENT AND ENVIRONMENT

The equipment of the hypnotist's office need only be simple; usually a comfortable armchair and a couch is sufficient. The environment should be quiet and peaceful so that the general atmosphere is one of a restful hypnotic centre rather than that of an ordinary antenatal clinic. If the patient is attending hospital it is preferable for the training in hypnorelaxation to be carried out in a department set aside for this particular purpose, away from the busy surroundings of the hospital out-patients department. First impressions can be very important in helping the patient to achieve a satisfactory state of mental and physical relaxation. It may be an advantage if the room is decorated in a soothing colour scheme; Bordeaux (1950) recommends a combination of dark purple and lilac.

FREQUENCY AND NUMBER OF CONSULTATIONS

It is usually advisable for the patient's first visit to take place as soon as possible after the pregnancy is confirmed. There are several reasons for this. The patient can be early accusomed to the atmosphere of the clinic and a friendly relationship established with the medical and nursing staff. The medical hypnotist is able to discover in plenty of time the most suitable method of approach to his patient so that the best results are obtainable. Any disturbances of pregnancy — such as nausea and vomiting — can be prevented by appropriate routine suggestion under hypnosis.

With the average patient about half a dozen attendances during the antenatal period are usually sufficient. The first two or three can be at fortnightly intervals and the remainder at monthly ones. Towards the end of the pregnancy it may be desirable to see some patients more frequently.

THE APPROACH TO THE PATIENT

The first visit is largely devoted to making the expectant mother feel at ease and in assessing her personality with regard to hypnosis and the maternal role. In a number of patients some degree of hypnosis will be obtained at this first session. Somnambulism may even be achieved with a few. These may be placed in a separate category, for the subsequent visits of such patients will tend to be infrequent.

The subject who is not a somnambulist should attend regularly for training in hypnorelaxation. The emphasis in such cases should be on training and relaxation. Experience shows that after a few sessions patients improve and are finally able to reach quite a satisfactory state of mental and physical relaxation while in a light or moderate hypnotic condition. The degree of relaxation attained through hypnosis (or 'suggestive relaxation', as it is sometimes termed) is usually considerably greater than that achieved by other methods. In any case, many antenatal relaxation exercises merely act as a 'smoke-screen' masking a mild hypnotic state which is the factor really responsible for the production of 'psychological analgesia'. While in the trance the patient may be given direct suggestions of anaesthesia to certain localized areas of the body. If these suggestions meet with a satisfactory response it can then be explained that this anaesthesia can be transferred to any other desired region should it become necessary during the course of labour.

One important type of suggestion which is given as a routine at each visit is to tell the patient that, when in labour, she will experience each uterine contraction but will interpret it as a reasonably pleasant sensation; during the second stage of labour she will feel that she is undertaking a task requiring muscular effort and her experiences will roughly resemble those accompanying any physical exertion. Care must be taken not to suggest that all sensation will be abolished, otherwise the onset of labour may occur unknown to the patient. Indeed, cases have been reported where this has happened so that no proper arrangements were made to deliver the baby. It is probably wise to suggest that some discomfort will be present when labour begins.

Another routine suggestion is that the patient will have a sense of general physical and mental well-being throughout her pregnancy. This is given at the termination of each hypnotic session. Even if she is not a somnambulist, and does not experience amnesia of events during hypnosis, such post-hypnotic suggestions are not without effect. She is further told that on each subsequent occasion she will improve still more in her ability to achieve a high degree of relaxation, so that her confinement becomes easy and natural.

AUTOHYPNOSIS

At every session the aim should be to enable the patient to obtain 'a greater control over her own organism' (to quote the words of the late Milne Bramwell). In many cases it is possible, by proper antenatal training and skill on the part of the hypnotist, to arrive at the stage where satisfactory self-hypnosis can be induced. In order to bring this about the same type of suggestions are given at each session. These may be linked up with certain physiological procedures such as rhythmic breathing. As the patient breathes quietly and regularly, suggestions are given to the patient of increasing mental and physical relaxation with each inspiration. The effect of the suggestions is often heightened by this process and the patient may be so conditioned that on subsequent occasions when she repeats the performance of regular breathing and at the same time gives *herself* suggestions of relaxation, the required phenomena follow automatically. In the USA this method is becoming increasingly popular with medical hypnotists and interesting cases demonstrating its efficacy have been reported by Schneck (1951), Kroger and Freed (1951) and Newbold (1953).

There are two ways in which hypnosis can be self-induced during labour. The gravida may be able to enter a satisfactory state of hypnosis right at the onset of labour and maintain it more or less continuously for some considerable time. Alternatively, she may induce successive hypnotic states of short duration each time she feels the beginning of a contraction. With each method there is an increase in muscular relaxation. As an example of the second method, a case is reported by Schneck who quotes the patient's own personal experiences of her confinement. As a rule the depth of hypnosis reached by auto-suggestion is not very deep but if the environment is favourable it is quite sufficient, as the following case illustrates.

A primigravida aged 22 was first seen when about two months pregnant. At this visit the question of hypnosis during labour was discussed with her and her husband, since both of them had expressed a wish that this method of analgesia should be used for the confinement. It was explained that the essentials of the method were (1) to aim at the greatest possible degree of mental and physical relaxation so that labour and delivery would be much easier and (2) to help her gain increased control over the functioning of her own body by establishing a positive and healthy attitude of mind. The mechanism of labour was also explained to her in simple terms.

After the ground had been thus prepared a simple suggestibility test was performed so that some idea could be obtained of the patient's possible response to hypnosis. Since this proved satisfactory she was seated comfortably in an armchair and told to commence regular breathing; at the same time suggestions of increasing relaxation were given. After 10 minutes or so it was noticed that she was appreciably more relaxed and seemed rather drowsy. She was then given suggestions that as she continued to breathe quietly the relaxation would increase and that she would be able to relax in a similar manner during the birth of her baby. It was also suggested that she would keep perfectly fit and well throughout the whole of her pregnancy. At the end of half an hour the session was terminated by telling her to awaken slowly after a count of three; this was followed by an assurance that she would feel perfectly normal and that any feeling of drowsiness or lethargy would rapidly disappear.

The patient was then seen at approximately monthly intervals until the sixth month, and then fortnightly during the seventh and eighth months. There was a definite increase in the depth of relaxation with growing practice and by the time the fourth session was reached good analgesia to a pin-prick was also obtained. This patient was not a somnambulist and remembered most of what was said to her during the hypnotic state. By the sixth interview she was able to induce a moderate depth of hypnosis herself by following the same technique.

During the course of this prenatal training the following suggestions were given to her frequently:
(1) that she would continue to keep fit and well
(2) that everything was perfectly normal (as indeed it was)
(3) that she would experience the contractions of her womb during labour as reasonably pleasant sensations
(4) that she would be able to bring about great muscular relaxation herself, so that her womb and the birth passages dilated to the fullest extent and thus made plenty of room for the baby to pass through easily
(5) that she would be able to breast feed her baby satisfactorily as a good supply of milk would be available for this purpose.

This particular patient was booked for hospital confinement, since she was a primigravida, and it was impressed upon her not to delay in going to the hospital once she was in labour. She was also given the suggestion that she would have some initial discomfort from the early contractions so that she would have sufficient warning of the onset of labour; as soon as their significance was appreciated she would be able to induce a satisfactory condition of hypnosis and from then onwards experience the contractions as pleasant.

Twelve days after the estimated date of delivery she went into labour and the result of her antenatal preparation was most gratifying. She suffered no distress during the first stage and if she had not been specially warned might easily have not realized that she was in labour. During this period, when contractions were occurring every 3 minutes or so, the discomfort was so slight that she later stated '... I felt quite unconcerned, and almost wondered if the baby really was on the way'. Throughout the second stage she relaxed extremely well and co-operated fully and without difficulty with the midwife. The only time when she experienced any definite pain was at the moment of the crowning and delivery of the head, when the vulval outlet was stretched to its greatest extent. The baby, which weighed 7 lb 11 oz, was delivered in good condition and the third stage was perfectly normal. In all, labour lasted between 9 and 10 hours and at no time were any drugs administered. The puerperium was uneventful and on discharge the baby was purely breast fed. Later, the patient declared that she felt perfectly fit the moment the baby was born and expressed herself as most satisfied with her experience.

THE SOMNAMBULISTIC PATIENT

Antenatal training need be less prolonged if the patient is a somnambule and labour is likely to be *entirely* painless. Greater use may be made of post-hypnotic suggestion and of direct suggestion during labour: the more profound the state of hypnosis the more effective will such suggestions be. Anaesthesia can frequently be induced very quickly indeed: more rapidly than with drugs. If the subject has been specially conditioned prenatally and given the appropriate post-hypnotic suggestions, anaesthesia may be induced during labour at any prearranged signal; it has even been initiated by instructions given over the telephone.

CONDUCT OF LABOUR UNDER HYPNOSIS

The medical hypnotist may choose to make no attempt at suggestion or hypnosis during the actual course of labour. Instead, reliance is placed entirely upon self-hypnosis by the patient and the antenatal training which she has received. This training, of course, includes the frequently repeated suggestions of analgesia which are given to her at each hypnotic session. In most instances self-hypnosis will prove quite satisfactory, but on occasion it may be an advantage if the hypnotist is present at the confinement in case any 'reinforcement' of the hypnosis is desirable. This may be especially valuable at the time when the baby's head is being crowned.

The conduct of a labour which utilizes hypnorelaxation as the analgesic agent differs somewhat from that conducted with the aid of drugs. Firstly, no drugs or anaesthetics should be given as a routine measure; they should only be administered if there is a definite indication for their use. Secondly, the patient should not be spoken to unnecessarily. This applies particularly to those patients who are in a fairly deep state of hypnosis. In every case the emphasis should be on quietness. Special care should be taken to ensure that the patient is not placed in close proximity to other patients who might be a source of disturbance or annoyance. Lastly, the medical and nursing staff should be particularly careful not to make any inadvertent remarks of an alarming nature within the hearing of the patient.

Should the hypnotic state not be maintained by means of auto-suggestion it will be necessary for the patient to be placed *en rapport* with another individual. This may be the hypnotist, obstetrician, midwife or even the husband. The depth of hypnosis involved varies from a medium one, in which such phenomena as surface analgesia may be elicited, to the condition of somnambulism. If the rapport is to be transferred from the hypnotist to another person one of the deeper stages provides the best results.

A gravida in a deep state of hypnosis can carry out all the natural functions such as defaecation, micturition and eating perfectly normally and calmly if she is given clear instructions what to do.

If the patient is a somnambulist she should be asked before labour begins whether or not she would like to be 'awake' when her baby is actually born. A surprising number of mothers, if given the opportunity, will declare that they do not wish to be deprived of this experience which they consider to be an essential part of motherhood; they look forward to hearing their babies cry for the first time. Should they be unconscious from the effects of a general anaesthetic this particular experience is denied them, but if hypnosis is employed the emotional content can be preserved and at the same time made more pleasurable. Under hypnosis the patient may be quite conscious and yet feel no pain if suitable suggestions are given.

Before being 'awakened' from the hypnotic state the patient should be given routine suggestions of fitness and well-being and told that she will make a rapid recovery. If any suggestions of anaesthesia have been given they should be removed by counter-suggestion. If she wishes, as most mothers do, to breast feed her baby, it should be stressed that a good supply of milk will be available for this purpose.

After the baby has been born and the placenta expelled it is usually quite easy to insert stitches while the patient is still under the influence of hypnosis. As a rule no local anaesthesia is required. Practically all patients who have had a hypnotic delivery feel well directly afterwards, for there are no 'after effects' of analgesic drugs or anaesthetics to be reckoned with.

HYPNOSIS AND DOMICILIARY CONFINEMENTS

One decided advantage of using hypnoanalgesia is that if the patient has responded well to hypnotic suggestion it makes things considerably easier for the obstetrician who is obliged to conduct a delivery single-handed. Rural general practitioner obstetricians are often engaged in domiciliary midwifery and might otherwise have to bear responsibility for the administration of an anaesthetic as well as for the delivery of the baby.

Apart from hypnotism (and here the results of 'relaxation exercises' are included) the only methods of relieving pain open to the rural practitioner are general anaesthesia, spinal block and local or regional anaesthesia. Spinal anaesthesia is usually contra-indicated in the home environment owing to the difficulty of securing efficient sterilization. Even if local anaesthesia is resorted to there are some authorities who believe that healing of the tissues may be delayed or impaired because of the action of the injected fluid: in this case, hypnoanalgesia has yet another advantage over other methods of relieving pain. In addition to the complete absence of any devitalizing action there is also a certain amount of evidence for supposing that the process of healing may be accelerated in some subjects by means of subconscious suggestion. In surgery, too, cases have been reported which have tended to show that healing by first intention may be encouraged by the operation of psychic factors.

Hypnosis is not necessarily contra-indicated if the patient is delivered at home by a midwife in the absence of a doctor. If self-hypnosis is the method chosen then obviously the gravida herself is largely responsible for the control of her sensations during labour. In other properly selected cases the midwife or a trusted member of the patient's own family can be placed *en rapport* with her. The only necessary stipulation is that the midwife, like the doctor, should herself be familiar with the relevant phenomena of the hypnotic state and should know how to manage a confinement under these circumstances.

PATIENT EN RAPPORT WITH HER HUSBAND

A multipara who had been told following her third confinement that any further childbearing would be dangerous for her because of some obscure lesion of the spinal vertebrae decided nevertheless that she would like to have another baby with the aid of hypnosis. She was particularly keen on having her husband present at the birth and it was arranged that he should be placed *en rapport* with his wife.

The patient proved to be a good hypnotic subject and attained a medium-deep state of hypnosis. Although she appeared to be in deep hypnosis she seemed somewhat doubtful about analgesia for, when tested to pin-prick, she said there was definite 'blunting' but she still felt a 'pricking'. She was seen on several occasions and taught how to relax. During this time post-hypnotic suggestions were made that she would accept the instructions of her husband, her midwife and the obstetrician. The original medical hypnotist was not to be present and the husband was going to give all necessary instructions during the labour. These instructions would be given by the obstetrician and passed on to the patient by her husband. It was thought worthwhile to place both midwife and surgeon *en rapport* with the patient in case the husband could not be present at the delivery. This was accomplished by suggestions to the patient while in hypnosis. It was further suggested that she would go to 'sleep' when her husband counted to five.

Psychodynamics of Pregnancy and Labour

The training of the husband took place after the tenth interview with his wife. He was brought into the room and was told to count slowly to five; as he said 'five' his wife would become very relaxed, her eyes would close and she would go to sleep. This occurred and was repeated several times in the first session to give him confidence that he would be able to accomplish the same effect if the hypnotist was not present. After two interviews the husband showed a good response to his duties, and he was seen twice more before the expected date of delivery for final instructions.

Three weeks before this date the couple left the country on business and the patient went into labour before she could return. A doctor who had never seen her before was hurriedly summoned. Meanwhile the husband had put his wife into the hypnotic state, since he felt that it would be valuable in counteracting the excitement and shock of the sudden onset of labour in a strange environment. When the doctor arrived he found his patient so peaceful that he was somewhat astonished and, as she made no attempt to speak to him or to open her eyes, he anxiously enquired if everything was well with her. The husband then stated that he had put his wife into hypnosis whereupon there was a somewhat strained silence. However, labour proceeded smoothly enough and after 5 hours the practitioner applied forceps although the patient was still quite peaceful.

The husband, meanwhile, had attempted to contact the medical hypnotist for instructions, but a storm had broken down telephone wires and no contact could be made. However, he went on with his task, telling his wife what he felt was necessary and translating to her the instructions of the physician. Part of her experience at this time was written down in a letter after her labour. She stated: 'I was in labour for five hours and up to a few days ago I was under the impression that I was under sedation for at least four hours of that time, when in fact it was just a few minutes. I cannot help feeling that they might have waited a bit longer as I was not in a hurry and could have gone on for another three or four hours easily. Now I would like another... I think hypnotism is really wonderful and have recommended it to several mothers-to-be, but they all look at me as if I'm half mental. They are quite convinced that they must suffer. If only they knew!'

This case is interesting from the point of view of technique. The idea of putting the husband *en rapport* with his wife is not new. It is apparently gaining ground in countries like the United States where a good deal of research is being undertaken into the phenomena of hypnosis. This approach has considerable value if the wife is timid and the husband is desirous of witnessing and helping in his wife's confinement. Provided the husband is a well-balanced and responsible individual there are no contra-indications and no danger arises from this technique.

MULTIPLE PREGNANCY WITH TOXAEMIA

This patient, aged 30 years, was in her second pregnancy, the first having terminated in a miscarriage about 18 months previously. At the thirty-third week she developed a mild hypertension of 140/88 and was told to get extra rest. There were no other findings and she had no symptoms at all. Two weeks later there was a further slight increase in the blood pressure to 150/90 and she had slight hydramnios, but no oedema or albuminuria. In view of the twin pregnancy, however, it was decided to institute more or less complete rest in bed while the hypertension persisted.

Towards the end of the thirty-seventh week the blood pressure increased to 164/98 and the patient developed a slight albuminuria. She still had no symptoms except for some restlessness due to abdominal distension and foetal movements, but in order to help her to rest more fully she was given sedatives. Two days later she developed irregular painful uterine contractions and backache. This caused considerable distress and lasted for just over one day. Her blood pressure then varied around 166–170/96–100 and there was still some albuminuria. Fetal movements continued strong and the condition of the babies appeared satisfactory.

At this point, instead of using further sedative and analgesic drugs, it was decided to try the effect of hypnotic suggestion as a means of affording her relief from pain and discomfort. This patient had never been hypnotized before but a fairly satisfactory response was obtained at the first attempt although this did not seem sufficient should very painful contractions occur. Later the same day, therefore, another attempt was made and this time a much greater depth of hypnosis was obtained and the patient became considerably more relaxed. The procedure was repeated the following day.

The next day her contractions recurred and it soon became apparent that she was in labour. Her blood pressure and urine still remained about the same. She was rehypnotized and given repeated suggestions of mental and physical relaxation which were combined with ones of comfort and analgesia. After 20 minutes or so she was sleeping quite soundly and continued to do so for several hours, although now and then there were some slight signs of restlessness. When the patient awoke the first stage was well advanced, the cervix being about three-quarters dilated, and she was given some nourishment. Hypnorelaxation was again induced and she remained comfortable and relaxed until the second stage. Her blood pressure, meanwhile, had fallen a few points to 166/88. During the second stage she was able to co-operate well and both babies were delivered in good condition. In all, this stage lasted between 2 and 3 hours, and the third stage was completed satisfactorily and with minimum loss of blood. Afterwards the patient said that she felt fine, and that for a good part of her labour the only sensations she could remember were vague ones of 'floating in space'. Sometimes she felt as if she 'were another person' and that her mind had become separated from her body. The remainder of the puerperium was uneventful and both babies were breast-fed on discharge.

This case illustrates one way in which hypnotism may help to solve the dilemma of the best way of treating cases of pre-eclamptic toxaemia near term, especially when the condition is likely to be associated with a premature birth. In this particular instance the foetal maturity was about 38 weeks. Rest and relaxation for the mother was obviously indicated, but the possibility of damage to the babies from the use of drugs had also to be considered. Here the problem was resolved by using hypnotism as the patient was a good subject. If she had not been, the method would probably have failed in this particular case, since there had been no systematic antenatal training in hypnorelaxation except for the three occasions shortly before the onset of labour. The possibility of failure to induce hypnosis during labour in untrained patients should, therefore, serve once again to focus attention on the necessity for adequate prenatal preparation.

BIBLIOGRAPHY

ABRAMSON, M. & HERON, W. T. (1950) An objective evaluation of hypnosis in obstetrics. *Am. J. Obstet. Gynec., 59*, 1069.

AUGUST, R. V. (1961) *Hypnosis in Obstetrics.* New York: McGraw-Hill.

BARCROFT, J. (1934) *Features in the Architecture of Physiological Function.* Cambridge University Press.

BORDEAUX, J. (1950) Hypnotic experiments with light and colour. *Br. J. med. Hypnot., 1:4*, 7.

CHERTOK, L. (1957) *Les Méthodes Psychosomatiques d'accouchement sans Douleur.* Paris: L'Expansion Scientifique Francaise.

DAVIDSON, J. A. (1962) An assessment of the value of hypnosis in pregnancy and labour. *Br. med. J., 2*, 95.

DE LEE, J. B. & GREENHILL, J. P. (1939) *Year Book of Obstetrics and Gynecology*, p. 164. Chicago: Year Book Pub. Co.

DEUTSCH, H. (1944-5) *Psychology of Women* (2 Vols). New York: Grune & Stratton.

DIECKMANN, W. J. (1941) *Toxaemias of Pregnancy*. St. Louis: C. V. Mosby.

DUNBAR, F. (1938) *Emotions and Bodily Changes*. New York: Columbia University Press.

GOODING, H. K. (1973) Obstetric hypnosis in general practice. *Br. J. med. clin. Hypnosis*, 4, 42.

KELLY, J. V. (1962) Effect of hypnotically induced anxiety on uterine muscle. *Am. J. Obstet. Gynec.*, 83, 582.

KROGER, W. S. & FREED, S. C. (1951) *Psychosomatic Gynecology*. Philadelphia: W. B. Saunders.

LOGAN, W. G. (1963) Delay of premature labour by hypnosis. *Am. J. clin. Hypnosis*, 5, 209.

NEWBOLD, G. (1953) Hypnosis and home confinements. *Br. J. med. Hypnot.*, 5:1, 3.

NEWBOLD, G. (1965) Suggestions in health and sickness. *Nursing Mirror*, 2nd July, 326-7.

PERCHARD, S. D. (1956) Suggestion and hypnosis in obstetrics. In: *Modern Trends in Psychosomatic Medicine*, ed. Desmond O'Neill. London: Butterworth.

PHILLIPP, E. E., BARNES, J. & NEWTON, M. (1977) *Scientific Foundations of Obstetrics and Gynaecology*, 2nd ed. London: Heinemann.

PLATANOV, M. V. (1950) quoted by F. A. VOLGYESI in: The recent neuropsychiatric and bio-morphologic justifications of hypnotherapeutic empiricism. *Br. J. med. Hypnot.*, 2:1, 6.

READ, G. D. (1944) *Childbirth without Fear*. London.

SCHNECK, J. M. (1951) Self-hypnosis in obstetrics. *Proc. Soc. clin. exp. Hypnosis*. (May 1951).

SCHWARTZ, M. M. (1963) Cessation of labour using hypnotic techniques. *Am. J. clin. Hypnosis*, 5, 211.

SHAW, H. L. (1977) *Hypnosis in Practice*. London: Baillière Tindall.

STONE, P. & BURROWS, D. G. (1980) Hypnosis and obstetrics. In: *Handbook of Hypnosis and Psychosomatic Medicine*, ed. Burrows & Dennerstein. Amsterdam: Elsevier/North Holland.

TRUE, R. M. (1954) Obstetrical hypnoanalgesia. *Am. J. Obstet. Gynec.*, 67, 2, 373.

CHAPTER 12

HYPNOSIS IN DERMATOLOGY

According to McDowell (1953) the following skin conditions have been treated effectively by hypnosis:

alopecia areata	neurodermatitis
arsphenamine dermatitis	pemphigus vulgaris
dermatitis artefacta	pruritus
eczema	psoriasis
erythrodermia	rosacea
herpes simplex	spontaneous haemorrhage
hyperidrosis	urticaria
lichen planus	verrucae

The general practitioner viewing this list will agree that the majority of these conditions are seen in general practice almost daily.

In the study of dermatology we are dealing not only with the pathology of the skin, but also with emotional factors likely to cause a somatic reaction (MacCormac et al. 1946; Wisch 1935).

A man of 52 died suddenly from hypertension and coronary thrombosis. Although the doctor and the hospital physicians had warned him that he must be careful, he had not let his family know about his serious condition, for he did not want to upset them. His wife was seen 14 days after his death, showing symptoms of anxiety and panic. She also had an irritating rash over the legs and upper thighs. Her sister, who had been called to the husband as he lay dead, complained of headaches and tiredness. A younger daughter of 16 was seen one month after the father's death complaining of a wet irritating rash where her suspender had rubbed her thigh. She also had a rash on the wrist corresponding to a watch strap which was metal. Her brassière had two small tabs on each side, which had produced a rash on her breasts. In addition to the shock of her father's death, she had recently begun a new job which involved a great deal of responsibility.

When one bears in mind that both the central nervous system and the skin are of ectodermal origin, it is not difficult to understand in some measure the underlying cause for all three of these somatic reactions. The skin often mirrors the mind and acts as a defensive weapon in times of stress. At two large hospitals in the London area psychiatrists and dermatologists are working as a team. In the future it will be necessary for the dermatologist to embrace psychiatry in his speciality, and the reverse procedure might also be of value. The general practitioner sees the skin manifestation in the acute phase, i.e. before the somatic reaction becomes conditioned, and he should be capable of preventing the illness from becoming chronic.

A psychosomatic reaction of the skin has been produced experimentally by instilling an artificial conflict in the subconscious mind of a patient under hypnosis. Just as it is possible to abreact a psychic trauma, we can create an artifical trauma which will produce a tissue reaction and change in cellular structure and function.

It is important in skin cases to be certain that adequate analysis has been accomplished, for occasionally the skin rash clears and another symptom of a psychosomatic reaction takes its place. Use should always be made of direct suggestions of well-being, happiness, positive behaviour in the future and a constant feeling of relaxation and security, but only as an adjunct to superficial analysis.

The analysis in these cases is usually simple. Patients suffering from a skin rash can pin-point fairly accurately the date when they first contracted the rash, and usually recall any stress experienced at the time. If the patient should find it difficult to remember these facts, they will be quickly elicited with the aid of light hypnosis. The patient is relaxed and told that he will remember any incidents which caused stress, shock or fear at the time his skin complaint first worried him, and that if he cannot remember while relaxed, the reason will come to him before he sees the doctor again. It is extraordinary how the patient will successfully recall certain data, while on the hypnotic couch or on his next visit, which will enable the therapist to work out the psychogenic picture with a fair degree of accuracy.

To be successful at overcoming irritating dermatoses is not difficult and is most rewarding. Patients who are resistant to hypnotherapy will be resistant to most other forms of treatment and if conditions such as asthma, migraine, hay-fever, etc., take the place of the skin rash, no other form of treatment, short of deep psychoanalysis over some years, will achieve any better result. In any case the substitution of another psychosomatic symptom for the rash is rare and will be found only in cases of hysteria and anxiety-hysteria. These cases should best be dealt with by psychiatrists, for they need protracted treatment. Enthusiastic hypnotists with great experience of hypnotic technique but little knowledge of psychiatry have been guilty of mistreating cases of hysteria presenting with a skin symptom. If proper analysis and re-education of these cases is not accomplished, not only is the patient made worse but he may be resistant to further hypnosis. An interesting case of this description occurred in general practice.

A young married woman complained of an irritating rash covering her arms, breasts and shoulders. The condition had been variously described for over 5 years as dermatitis, eczema, urticaria, seborrhoeic eczema and non-occupational dermatitis. The case was sent to another specialist, for the patient had changed her doctor and the latter wanted a diagnosis from a trusted colleague. This specialist described it as seborrhoeic eczema and suggested injections of liver extract for 6 weeks, two injections weekly. She felt better for 14 days after the injections were terminated, and then relapsed. The situation was considered desperate by patient and doctor. She had been unable to wash or bath for over 5 years. It was decided to use hypnosis, on the assumption that the condition could not be made worse.

Analysis of the case using deep hypnosis, was particularly straightforward. She revealed a deep guilt reaction associated with her mother, who had suffered from asthma and who had told her that the complaint had started on the day the daughter was born. The mother had eventually been found dead in bed beside the girl. The doctor gave the cause of death as 'asthma'.

Suggestions, once weekly for 6 weeks, were given at the conscious level and under deep hypnosis (she became a somnambule), causing a rapid improvement in the condition. This improvement ceased after 3 months. Analysis of the relapse revealed that she had had a sudden urge to place flowers on her mother's grave. This impulse had been stifled, as she could not manage the time to visit the cemetery. A further four treatments helped her to overcome this setback and she remained well for 4 months. During this time she was bathing and washing with soap and water. Later she relapsed again and this time she was sent to St. Thomas's Hospital, where she received Methedrine abreaction. The improvement was never as great as under hypnosis. About 6 months after treatment had ceased, she developed an acute attack of asthma. Unfortunately the patient was then lost sight of and further history was unobtainable.

This patient was not made resistant to hypnosis but her attitude to the psychiatric treatment of her illness was one of doubt. She did not really believe that she could be cured and the improvement in the skin reaction was accepted by her as a miracle. She found it difficult to understand that her mother's asthma could cause a skin reaction in herself. The length of time the woman suffered from her illness was of grave import. After it had proved resistant to excessive treatment by the usual means, a chronic reaction had been produced which continually sapped the patient's confidence.

The beginner should confine his therapy to dermatological cases showing an acute rather than a chronic reaction. For example, cases of psoriasis would appear to offer scope for hypnotherapy but in practice they are often resistant to treatment. If, however, an early case of psoriasis in a child is subjected to psychotherapy before the parents have become obsessed by the illness, gratifying results can be expected. Too often the sufferer has been subjected to many different treatments.

Certain cases can be found where the skin rash serves an emotional or sexual purpose.

> An attractive girl of 15 was seen, together with her father. The child's mother had run away with another man 5 years previously. The psoriasis had first been noticed after the mother disappeared. The child became acutely ill with the skin complaint. Several unctions were ordered and the father adopted the ritual of bathing his daughter every evening and applying the ointment to all parts of her body. The father said in the course of conversation that his daughter closely resembled his good-looking young wife.
>
> The child became a somnambule and there was a rapid improvement of the skin. Notwithstanding, the father continued his ministrations and refused treatment from the psychiatrist, who felt that he was more in need of psychotherapy than his daughter. After a few months the skin became just as bad as when first seen.

It must be remembered that most skin conditions are associated with anxiety and tension. Patients often agree that they have been terrified by the thought that they might be contagious to others. The fear that accompanies every skin rash must be adequately dealt with by reassurance. So often the victim is treated for years with various changes of medicaments with little benefit to the skin. Cohen has described her treatment of over one hundred chronic hospital patients suffering various skin conditions. Subjected to hypnosis (only superficial psychotherapy seems to have been required) nearly 70% of them recovered. That hypnotherapy can change the picture for many chronic dermatological cases is well known by the physician using the method in hospital and general practice. Kennedy (1957), Fry (1957) and Stewart (1957) have described cases in general practice treated by superficial psychotherapy using hypnosis.

Suggestion, with or without hypnosis, has been used since time immemorial for the treatment of warts. The 'charming' of warts presents no real difficulty with suggestible patients and of course when using hypnosis the effect of suggestions will be magnified. Block (1927), Zwich (1932) and McDowell (1949) have described the successful treatment of warts by hypnotism. Large warts which require treatment by surgery may also be found amenable to treatment by suggestion. Both patient and doctor may be greatly surprised by the rapid and beneficial results sometimes possible. Cases have been described of large warts of the thumb which appeared to require amputation, with resultant uselessness of the hand. Following deep hypnotic suggestion, the warts eventually disappeared entirely.

Cases of hyperhidrosis have also been helped considerably by hypnotherapy. In these cases excessive sweating is due to the increased release of acetylcholine at the post-ganglionic nerve-endings, and this release is probably due to increased central nervous system activity. Hypnosis would seem to combat this nervous activity, as the following case illustrates.

> A boy aged 13 was seen with a history of excessive sweating of the hands and feet. The condition had appeared suddenly. If the patient wiped his hands, drops of sweat appeared immediately and fell freely from the fingers. All manner of treatments had been tried without result. The condition first started when he was evacuated during the war; he was then 8 years of age. He remembered that his hands were quite dry before he left home.
>
> Under deep hypnosis he was regressed to the age of 8 and was able to remember incidents on his first day at the new school. On the way to school he was attacked by a gang of boys, who shouted anti-Semitic slogans at him; eventually the gang set on him and beat him up. He became acutely tense while reciting these incidents. On being awakened he remembered the fighting, and stated that he had felt he would have liked to 'murder all of them' but was too terrified to hit back because there had been too many against him. He said he thought they were going to murder him. He was abreacted on three more occasions. After being seen at six sessions he was no

longer hyper-conscious of his hands and feet; he could do his school work without the sweat pouring over his books, and remained well, without relapse.

In general practice, the doctor is in a more personal relationship with his patient than the dermatologist who is at a disadvantage as far as rapport is concerned. This being so, the general practitioner should always attempt hypnotherapy in acute cases: the more acute the condition the better the chance of quick response. Where the condition has become chronic the battle may have to be long and tedious. A method of reaching the deeper recesses of the mind and thus helping the autonomic nervous system to cushion tension and shock might very well be used.

Hypnotherapy should be attempted particularly in cases of chronic pruritus and in certain cases of chronic eczema. Often a great deal of treatment has been given to these patients and in order to break the conditioning and pessimistic viewpoint of their long, painful and itchy careers, a treatment must be found which displays an attitude of positive expectancy rather than a negative acceptance of their state. So often patients go from doctor to doctor with a change of ointment and little encouragement for their well-being. In certain of these cases much can be accomplished by a change of attitude and if combined with psychotherapy results are sometimes dramatic.

A middle-aged woman complained to her GP that she was suffering from an itchy scaly rash of her elbows and lower back, particularly in the sacral region. Her face would also show skin blemishes. In addition, she could not understand why she was still suffering headaches and 'hot flushes' despite oestrin therapy. She was sent to a dermatologist who wrote 'I spend more time trying to overcome this lady's aggression than her skin complaint . . . but I suppose we are getting somewhere for after she has had a real row with me she says she feels much better, her headaches improve and her skin is less itchy.' Eventually she found her way to a medical hypnotist who established that she had planned to divorce her husband after she had been analysed. She felt that she would never be well until she could gain her freedom. All attempts at explaining her symptoms as being unconscious aggression against one or other parent and the substitution of her husband as her rationalised somatic manifestation was fruitless. The patient refused to believe that she would ever be rid of her skin troubles while she continued to live with her passive, egocentric husband. It was later revealed that she suffered from chronic dental disorders and undoubtedly her psychosomatic illness was a problem that existed long before her marriage. Hypnosis, if used, might have allowed this unhappy person to face the possibility that her husband and her marital problems were not entirely responsible for her skin complaints. She did finally divorce him, but later reports stated that she was still indulging in too much alcohol, was still needing oestrins and her skin was as worrying to her as it had been several years before.

This lady has been subjected to much psychotherapy in the course of the later decades of her life. It is tempting to suggest that hypnotherapy used several years before might have saved a situation which became progressively more complicated and involved more of her family as time went on.

A case of this description illustrates only too clearly the value of planned psychotherapy. For too long hypnotherapists have been fooling themselves into believing that producing the hypnotic state is tantamount to curing a patient once and for all. Many hypnotists are reluctant to explain what they mean by 'cure' and in fact this is a word which should not be used. We cure nothing. What we can do is to establish rapport and treat the entire person. It is still necessary to ask 'What am I, who am I, why am I? The question 'Why am I? can best be answered by a trained, deeply hypnotised person. Freud must have understood only too well that patients were not symptoms but people. Gradually doctors are becoming more and more understanding of the psychological problems of their patients. They are beginning to concern themselves with the emotional immaturity of their patients, rather than being preoccupied with symptoms or obsessed by skin rashes. It is now well-known that the soma works only because the psyche allows it to do so; the emphasis has now shifted — finally, we hope — to the body, spirit and soul as the modern rationale of medicine and particularly of dermatology.

BIBLIOGRAPHY

AMBROSE, G. (1952) Nervous control of sweating. *Lancet, 1*, 926.

BETTLEY, R. (1970) *An Introduction to the Biology of the Skin.* Oxford: Blackwell.

BLOCK, B. (1927) Ueber die Heiling der Warzen durch Suggestion. *Klin. Wschr., 6*, 2271–2320.

BROD, J. (1970) *Advances in Psychosomatic Medicine.* London: Butterworth.

CHALMERS, T. M. & KEELE, C. A. (1952) The nervous and chemical control of sweating. *Br. J. Derm., 64*, 43.

DAVIS, D. B. & BICK, J. W. (1946) Skin reactions observed under wartime stress. *J. nerve. ment. Dis., 5*, 503.

ERICKSON, M. H. (1944) The method employed to formulate a complex story for the induction of an experimental neurosis in a hypnotic subject. *J. gen. Psychol.*, *31*, 67.

FRY, A. (1957) The scope for hypnosis in general practice. *Br. med. J.*, *1*, 1302.

GLENN, T. J. (1976) The stabilizing effect of hypnosis on the autonomic nervous system's control of skin temperature. *Proc. 7th int. Cong. Hypnosis psychosom. Med.*, *1*, 274.

KAYWIN, L. (1947) Emotional factors in urticaria. *Psychosom. Med.*, *9*, 131.

KELSEY, D. & BARRON, J. N. (1958) Maintenance of posture by hypnotic suggestion in a patient undergoing plastic surgery. *Br. med. J.*, *1*, 756.

KENNEDY, A. (1957) The medical use of hypnotism. *Br. med. J.*, *1*, 1317.

LABORIT, H. (1959) *Stress and Cellular Function.* New York: Lippincott.

MacCORMAC, H., SONDIFER, P. H. & JELLIFFE, A. M. (1946) The itchy patient. *Br. med. J.*, *2*, 48.

McDOWELL, M. (1949) Juvenile warts removed with the use of hypnotic suggestion. *Bull. Menninger Clin.*, *13*, 4.

McDOWELL, M. (Ed.) (1953) *Hypnosis in Modern Medicine.* pp. 101–12, Springfield, Ill.: Charles C. Thomas.

OBERMAYER, M. E. (1955) *Psychocutaneous Medicine.* Springfield, Ill.: Charles C. Thomas.

PATTIE, F. A. (1947) The production of blisters by hypnotic suggestion: a review. *J. abnorm. soc. Psychol.*, *36*, 62.

ROTHMAN, S. (1945) The role of the autonomic nervous system in cutaneous disorders. *Psychosom. Med.*, *7*, 90.

SCHNECK, J. M. (1954) Ichthyosis simplex treated with hypnosis. *Dis. nerv. Syst.*, *15*, 211.

SCOTT, M. J. (1960) *Hypnosis in Skin and Allergic Diseases.* Springfield, Ill.: Charles C. Thomas.

SCOTT, M. J. (1963) Hypnosis in dermatology. In: *Hypnosis in Modern Medicine*, ed. Schneck, 3rd ed. Springfield, Ill.: Charles C. Thomas.

STEWART, H. (1957) Some uses of hypnosis in general practice. *Br. med. J.*, *1*, 1323.

STOKES, J. H., KULCHER, G. V. & PILLSBURY, D. M. (1935) Effect on the skin of emotions and nerves; aetiologic background of urticaria with special reference to psycho-neurogenous factors. *Arch. Derm. Syph.*, *31*, 470.

STOKES, J. H. & BERMAN, H. (1940) Psychosomatic correlation in allergic conditions. *Psychosom. Med.*, *2*, 438.

ULLMAN, M. (1946) Herpes simplex and second degree burns induced under hypnosis. *Am. J. Psychol., 103*, 830.

WISCH, J. M. (1935) Hypnosis in psoriasis. *Derm. Wschr., 100*, 234.

WOOLEY-HART, A. (1972) Some physical and physiological aspects of the passage of an electric current through the skin. *Br. J. clin. Hypnosis, 3*, 129.

ZINNITZ, F. (1954) Hypnose für psychogenische Hautleiden. *Medsche Mschr., Stuttg., 8*, 743.

ZWICH, K. G. (1932) Hygiogenesis of warts disappearing without topical medication. *Archs Derm. Syph., 25*, 508.

INDEX

abortion, threatened, 173
abreaction, 29, 106
acid–base balance, 32
adaptation to stress, 60, 97, 143
adoption, effect on 'sterility' 163
age regression, 28–30
amenorrhoea, psychogenic, 157
amnesia in somnambulism, 28
anaesthesia, hypnosis in, 136–42
   in gynaecology, 168
analgesia in labour, 180
animal magnetism, 2, 3, 22
   Elliotson's work on, 5
anorexia, 64
   in children, 147
anoxia, fetal, 183
antenatal training
   in autohypnosis, 187
   in hypnorelaxation, 185
antibacterial activity of blood, 34
anxiety, 98
   in children, 145
   of hysteria, 108
   in multiple sclerosis, 88
   during pregnancy, 177
   symptoms, 98
   treatment, 101
asthma, 62
   in children, 150
autogenic training, 50
autohypnosis, 50
   in antenatal training, 187

autohypnosis (*continued*)
   in children, 148
   in labour, 188
   for migraine, 71
Azam, Dr, 7, 8

backache of pregnancy, 174
baquets (of Mesmer), 3
Becker, on children's dento-facial habits, 139
behaviour of patient during deep hypnosis, 126
belle indifférence, la, 109, 110
Bennet's physiological theory, 23
Bernheim, Professor, 8
bile secretion, 34
birth impressions, 29
blackmail, of hypnotherapist, 13
bladder disturbances, 166
blindness, hysterical, 2
blister formation, 32
blood loss during labour, 181
blood pressure, 85
blood sugar level, 33
BMA Report on Hypnotism (1892), 9, 14
body-image, 130
Bompard–Eyraud case, 14
Braid, James, work with mesmerism, 6–8
Braidism, 7, 43

Index

brain, *see* anoxia, fetal
Bramwell, J. Milne, 9
  on anaesthesia, 137
breast feeding, 184
Brown, William, 10

calcium, blood levels, 34
cancer, emotional aetiology, 34
cardiovascular stimulation, emotional, 33, 86
catalepsy, 27
catarrh, genital, 163
Charcot, Jean Marie, 9
childbirth, *see* labour
children, 136, 143–53
  dento-facial habits, 139
  hypnoanalysis, 128
  techniques of hypnosis for, 147
chronic patients, 96
common cold, link with depression, 113
company for the depressive, 115
compulsion, 116
confidentiality, 11
conflict, artificially induced, 61
confusional technique of induction, 46
contractions, labour, 182
convulsions, 55
co-operation of patient in labour, 182
coprophagia, 114–15
corticosteroids for asthma, 150
counter-transference, 82
counting method of induction, 45
crime, 13
  commission under hypnosis, 15
  detection by hypnosis, 18

dangers of hypnosis, 54
deep hypnosis, 124
  in hypnoanalysis, 129
  self-inquiry of the practitioner, 123
delinquency, 146

dental anaesthesia, 138
depression
  of the hypnotist, 116
  mild psychogenic, 111–16
  types, 111
depth of hypnosis
  assessment, 42
  in children, 147
  in depression, 116
  technique for increasing, 48
dermatology, 197–205
diabetes mellitus, 84–5
diminished personal responsibility, 15
direct suggestion of symptom removal, 56, 77
  for amenorrhoea, 158
  for functional dysmenorrhoea, 160
  in labour, 180
  opponents of, 82
  physiological effects, 32
displacement of affect, 117
doctor–patient relationship, 11, 26, 36–8, 101
  antenatal, 186
  see also rapport
domiciliary confinement, 191
dream interpretation, 126
druidic sleep, 1
dysmenorrhoea, functional, 159
dyspepsia, chronic, 66

eclampsia, 176
eczema, 202
ego-strengthening, 129, 131
electro-encephalogram, 34
electronic induction, 48
Elliotson, John, 4–5
emotions
  effect of suggestion, 24
  recall, of Rosen, 119
  physiological effects of stimulation, 33
endocrine system, relation to psyche, 167

Index

enuresis, 151
environment
   as cause of amenorrhoea, 157
   for hypnosis, 38, 185-6
   in hysteria, 108
epilepsy, in children, 150
Erickson, work on hypnoanalysis, 122
Esdaile, James, work with mesmerism, 6, 43
   on surgery, 137
ethics, 11
expectation, role in susceptibility, 25
experimentally induced skin reaction, 198

Fairfield, Letitia, on diminished personal responsibility, 15
falling test, 44
Fallopian tubes, spasm of, 164
false pretences, 16
family treatment of neurotic child, 145
fear
   as basis of anxiety, 98
   in dermatology, 200
   of the obsessive, 117
fear-tension syndrome, 179
feminine role, rejection of, 158, 165
fibroids, uterine, 157
flatulence, 172
flexibilitas cerea, 27
fetus, injury during labour, 184
fractional induction, 49
frequency of consultations
   antenatal hypnorelaxation, 186
   obsessive states, 115-19
   see also repeated attempts
Freud, Sigmund, 9
   abandonment of hypnosis, 122
   and treatment of hysteria, 111
   technique of hypnotherapy, 104
frigidity, 165
functional uterine bleeding, 155-7

gastro-intestinal secretion, 32, 33
genital catarrh, 163
Goldie, on anaesthesia, 137
Guillotin, Dr, 3
guilt feelings
   in functional dysmenorrhoea, 159
   of the anxious, 105
gynaecology, 154-70

Hadfield, J.A., 10
   on depth of hypnosis, 129
   on hypnoanalysis, 123
hallucinations, 30
hay fever, 62
headache
   premenstrual, 162
   tension, 69
healing by first intention, 192
heart disease complicating pregnancy, 176
heartburn, 172
heat sensation, 32
Heidenhain's physiological theory, 23
Hodgkin's disease, psychosomatic aspect, 91
home confinement, 191
homosexuality, 20, 114
   latent in women, 158, 165
honeymoon period of analysis, 116
husband's rapport with wife in confinement, 192
hyperemesis gravidarum, 172
hyperhidrosis, 201
hypertension, essential, 85
   pregnancy, 176
hypnoanalysis, 122-9
hypnoidal stage, 26
hypnosis, first use of the term, 7
hypnosynthesis, 129-34
Hypnotism Act (1952), 20
hypnotist, personal properties, 35
   see also doctor-patient relationship
hysteria, 108-9

imagination, role in susceptibility, 25
induction, 42–57
   in children, 147
   confusional technique, 46
   counting method, 45
   electronic methods, 48
   for hypnosynthesis, 130
   fractional methods, 49
   hazards, 35–8
   indirect methods, 47
   use of music, 42
   physical methods, 43
   physiological effects, 31
   psychological methods, 43
   role of hearing, 43
   variations of technique, 42
   yo-yo method, 49
infectious disease, 34
insomnia, 100
   in pregnancy, 175
integrity of hypnotherapist, 13
International Society of Hypnosis Conference, Glasgow (1983), 60
international work in hypnosis, 59-60
interrogation under hypnosis, 18

Janet, Pierre, 9, 24

Kelsey, work on age regression, 29

labour
   conduct under hypnosis, 190
   disadvantages of hypnosis, 185
   domiciliary, 191
   drugs, decreased need for, 181
   indications for hypnotherapy, 177
   postponement, 174
   psychodynamics, 171–96
   psychoprophylaxis, of Read, 179
   safety of baby, 183, 184

labour (*continued*)
   shortening of duration, 180
   woman's attitude to, 178
lactation, 184
law and the hypnotist, 11–21
leucorrhoea, psychogenic, 162
libido, at the menopause, 168
Liébeault, A.A., 8

magnet, healing powers, 2
magnetism of metals, 5
malign influence, 14
malpresentation of fetus, 175
masturbation, 114, 166
Meares, Ainslie, 28
Medical practitioner as hypnotherapist, 12–13
meditation technique, 113
menopause, 112, 167
   postponement, 164
menorrhagia, 155
menstruation, 155
   control of, 162
   cultural influences, 159
   control of cycle length, 162
   effect of stress, 156, 157
mental damage, risk of, 15
mental defectives, 25
Mesmer, Franz Anton, 2–3
mesmerism, 1
   Elliotson's practice of, 5
   in India, 6
   in the USA, 6
metabolic activity, 32
metals, 'magnetic', 5
metrorrhagia, 155
migraine, 69
   personality, 72
mind–body relationship, role of stress, 60
monoideism, 7, 22
morals, strengthening by hypnosis, 15
morning sickness, 172
mother, health and safety in labour, 178
   role in child neuroses, 144

Index

multiple sclerosis, 87
muscle spasm, role in arthritis, 90
music in induction, 42

Nancy school of hypnotism, 8, 24
nature of hypnosis, 22–6
nausea of pregnancy, 172
negligence, legal aspects, 12
neuroses, 96–121
   in children, 143–9
   in the normal person, 119
   of sterility, 164
normality, role in susceptibility, 25
number of consultations
   in treatment of obsession, 117
   see also repeated attempts

obesity, 85
object of hypnotherapy, 82
obsession, 116
obsessional-compulsive patient, the 115–19
odour-suggestion test, 44
oligomenorrhoea, 157
oxygenation of fetal brain in labour, 183

paediatrics, see children
pain
   hypnosis during, 90
   tolerance to, 136
paraesthesiae, 174
parents, role in paediatric hypnosis, 144
Pavlov, physiological theory, 23
   work on stress, 60
'Pearlies', the, 79
pelvis
   examination of, 168
   psychogenic pain, 169
peptic ulcer, 68
   research, 83
personality
   hypertensive, 86
   hypnotic, 26

personality (*continued*)
   influence in pregnancy, 177
   migraine, 72
   obsessive, 116–17
   role in relinquishing of habits, 127
phenomena of hypnosis, 26–31
phobias, 105
   in children, 146
physiology, psychological influences, 61
physiological theories of hypnosis, 23, 31
pictographic recall, 28
Planetarum Influxu, de (Mesmer), 2
pleasurable experience of hypnosis, 42
post-hypnotic suggestion, 31
   hazards, 56
   in dentistry, 140
   in labour, 180, 187
pregnancy
   indications for hypnotherapy, 172
   medical complications, 176
   multiple, with toxaemia, 194
   phantom (pseudocyesis), 158
   psychodynamics, 171–96
prematurity, 185
premenstrual tension (headache), 162
pretence, defensive, 53
pre-uterine theory of anxiety, 146
prolonged hypnosis, 87
protein dynamics, 33
pruritus, 166, 202
   during pregnancy, 174
pseudocyesis, 158
psoriasis, 200
psychic dysfunction, physiological effects, 61
psychodynamic interpretation in paediatrics, 146
psychological theories of hypnosis, 24–6
psychosomatic illness, 59–95
   in children, 149

Index

psychosomatic illness (*continued*)
    in gynaecology, 155
psychotherapy, 13
    following drug treatment for depression, 113
    'supermarket', 97
psychotic patients, 55
puerperium, 178
    avoidance of complications, 181
pulmonary ventilation, 32

rapport, 30, 82
    in labour, 190, 192
    see also doctor–patient relationship
rash, substitution by other conditions, 199
Read, Dick, on natural childbirth, 179
reassurance during induction, 42
    in depression, 113–15
recall of buried memories, 28
    in children, 128
re-educative value of hypnosis, 123
regression, age 28–30
    hypnosis as, 126
relaxation
    in antenatal training, 185
    for hypnosynthesis, 130
    in labour, 179
    suggestive, 186
    in treatment of organic disease, 61
religion
    as defence against wrongful suggestion, 54
    rites, 1
    role in childhood phobias, 146
renal function, 32
repeated attempts at induction, 42
    see also frequency of consultations
research, 83–91
resistance to hypnotherapy, 52, 104, 166
respiration rate, 32
restlessness, defensive, 52
revivification, 106
rheumatoid arthritis, 90
Rorschach inkblot test, 44
Rosen's emotional recall technique, 119

Salpêtrière School, 9
scotoma, 82
sedative, pre-hypnotic, 38
seduction, sexual, under hypnosis, 17
self-enquiry, of the practitioner, 123, 129, 134
self-hypnosis, *see* autohypnosis
Selye, stress adaptation syndrome, 60, 97, 143
sensory changes, 27
sensory stimulation in induction, 43
sexual
    assault during menstruation, 156
    inhibitions as cause of sterility, 164
    symbolism in children, 146
shock, diminution of obstetric, 181
sight, in induction, 43
simulation, defensive, 53
skin as mirror to the mind, 198
skin conditions, *see* dermatology
sleep
    defensive, 54
    druidic, 1
    of the anxious, 100
sleep-walking, *see* somnambulism
smoking, 78, 127
Society for Psychical Research, 9
somnambulism, 4, 27
    in labour, 190, 191
spasm illness, 90
speech, of hypnotherapist, 12
stages in the hypnotist's career, 149
stages of hypnosis, 26–31
stammering, 150
sterility, 163
stethoscope, introduction into England, 4

stress
    adaptation syndrome of Selye, 60, 97, 143
    causing diabetes mellitus, 84-5
    effect on menstruation, 156, 157
    reaction to, 60
subliminal consciousness, 24
subsequent hypnosis, hazards, 56
subservience, risk of, 15
suggestibility, 24-6
    in children, 144
    test of, 44
suicide, in depressives, 112, 115
surgery, 136
    dental, 138
    gynaecological, 168
susceptibility and age regression, 30
    in pregnancy, 177
sweating, excessive, 201

talking, defensive, 53
tape-recording hypnotic proceedings, 14
    in hypnodontics, 140
television, role in child hypnosis, 148
tension headache, 69
tension as cause of pain, 179
termination of hypnosis, 50
third party at hypnosis, 14, 38, 47
thumb-sucking, 139
thyrotoxicosis, 176
time sense in post-hypnotic suggestion, 31

touch in induction, 43
toxaemia, with multiple pregnancy, 194
toxins, fetal, 183
transference, 57, 82
    in children, 145
    in hysteria, 111

ulcerative colitis, 73
uterine disorder, functional, 155-7

vaginal discharge, psychogenic, 162
Van Pelt, S.J., 10
verbal induction, 43
Völgyesi, physiological theory, 23
vomiting
    hysterical, in children, 147
    of pregnancy, 172

waking hypnosis, 52
Wakley, Thomas, on magnetism, 5
war casualties, hypnotherapy, 10
warts, 201
witness, see third party
Wolberg, work on hypnoanalysis, 122
Wyke, B.D., physiological theory, 23

yoga, 180
    relation to self-hypnosis, 51
yo-yo induction, 49